Unlocking Potential

Based on **UNLOCKING POTENTIAL**
by Barbara Scheiber and Jeanne Talpers

Unlocking Potential

College and Other Choices for People with LD and AD/HD

Edited by Juliana M. Taymans, Ph.D.
and Lynda L. West, Ph.D.,
with Madeline Sullivan, M.A.

Woodbine House ◆ 2000

First Woodbine House edition
Based on *Unlocking Potential* by Barbara Scheiber and Jeanne Talpers

Library of Congress Cataloging-in-Publication Data

Unlocking potential : college and other choices for people with LD and AD/HD / edited by Juliana M. Taymans and Lynda L. West with Madeline Sullivan.—1st Woodbine House ed.
    p.   cm.
  Rev. ed. of: Unlocking potential / Barbara Scheiber, Jeanne Talpers. 1987.
  Includes bibliographical references and index.
  ISBN 0-933149-94-8 (pbk.)
   1.Learning disabled youth—Education (Higher)—United States. 2. Attention-deficit-disordered youth—Education (Higher)—United States. 3. College student orientation—United States. I. Taymans, Juliana M. II. West, Lynda L. III. Sullivan, Madeline. IV. Scheiber, Barbara. Unlocking potential.

LC4818.5 .U54 2000
371.9—dc21   00-034945

Table of Contents

Chapter 12 .... **319**
After School, What Next?

Michelle Sarkees Wircenski, Jerry Wircenski, & Lynda West

Businesses, Organizations, and Government Offices

ACKNOWLEDGEMENTS

Our thanks go to: Jeanne Talpers and Barbara Scheiber for their guidance and loyalty through the revision process.

Susan Stokes, who is a kind and gentle editor.

The network of colleagues and friends we have developed through our work in the Transition Special Education Program at The George Washington University. We have gained great personal and professional insights from our work together.

FOREWORD

Barbara Scheiber and Jeanne Talpers

When we sat down to write the first edition of *Unlocking Potential* more than 15 years ago, we never dreamed there would be a second edition.

We worked on that first edition during an exciting era. Change was in the air. Though time can easily cast a mythic glow on distant periods, it is not an exaggeration to describe the atmosphere in that period as exhilarating, filled with unprecedented promise.

During the decade following passage of Section 504 of the Rehabilitation Act of 1973, doors began to open that brought sizeable numbers of students with disabilities onto American campuses for the first time in history. Legal words requiring such things as "modifications," "accommodations," and "auxiliary aids" were resulting in flesh-and-blood differences in people's lives.

As parents of children with learning disabilities, we were painfully aware of the need for these changes. We knew how limited the choices beyond high school had always been for people with learning disabilities. We were thrilled by the hope inherent in the new wave of opportunities—the hope that our children and millions of others could get the education and training they needed to lead successful adult lives.

For that hope to become a reality, we needed to know the nuts and bolts of making it happen. We needed to turn to the people who were doing the work—not only on college campuses, but in vocational classrooms, vocational rehabilitation programs, independent living centers, apprenticeship and job training programs, and other non-academic settings.

We interviewed teachers, students, parents, counselors, administrators, and vocational instructors, all of whom were creating and advocating new ways to unlock potential. And so the book was created out of the shared wisdom and experience of these pioneers.

Underlying all of our research was the conviction that no matter what the level of ability, each person's strengths, skills, and learning styles should be assessed so that appropriate choices could be made for post-secondary planning. We believe then and believe today that the purpose of diagnosis and assessment is not to mark individuals with labels or scores—but to identify strengths and to create environments in which those strengths can flourish.

Since our book was published in 1985, much has happened. Advances have taken place on all levels of education. Knowledge has grown. Transition programs, which did not exist in our children's day, are preparing students with disabilities for life choices after high school. The use of technology— just beginning when we started our research—has exploded. A disability not even named at that time— Attention Deficit/Hyperactivity Disorder (AD/HD)—is now better understood, and effective ways to work with people with AD/HD are being developed. The Americans with Disabilities Act, passed in 1990, opened even more opportunities.

A new day has dawned; a new book was needed. We are deeply grateful to Juliana Taymans and Lynda West of The George Washington University for carrying out this undertaking with so much grace and hard work and to Susan Stokes of Woodbine House for her wonderful support of the enterprise. It is our fervent wish that new generations of young people will use this wealth of information to raise their hopes, to believe in their strengths, and to unlock their potential for happiness and fulfillment.

1 NTRODUCTION

Juliana M. Taymans, Ph.D., Lynda L. West, Ph.D.,
& Madeline Sullivan, M.A.

We are pleased to be able to update this groundbreaking guide to postsecondary options for individuals with learning disabilities (LD), originally written by Barbara Scheiber and Jeanne Talpers. In the 15 years since the publication of the first edition of **Unlocking Potential,** there have been significant developments in our understanding of how to prepare students and their families for the transition from high school to the world of postsecondary education and employment. In addition, attention deficit/hyperactivity disorder (AD/HD) has become well-recognized as another hidden condition that affects children and adults. In many ways, AD/HD poses challenges similar to LD for individuals with the condition, their families, teachers, friends, and employers. We have therefore expanded the guide to address transition planning, employment, and the postsecondary education needs of individuals with AD/HD.

Legislative strides have also been made since the first edition was published. The Americans with Disabilities Act of 1990 has greatly enhanced the rights of individuals with disabilities in postsecondary education and employment. Amendments to the Rehabilitation Act of 1973 and the Individuals with Disabilities Education Act have mandated collaboration between schools and adult services to support young people as they leave secondary school and prepare for productive adult lives. Transition from secondary schools to postsecondary education and jobs has become a field of its own. Thus, in addition to updating legislative information, we have added a chapter on self-determination and transition.

Our information base on LD, AD/HD, and postsecondary options and services has exploded in the past ten years. We have devoted a section at the end of each chapter to print and electronic resources that may be of interest to a wide range of readers. In addition, the final section of the book lists organizations that have been referenced in the text or that can be valuable sources of information on particular topics.

Why This Book Is Needed

The transition to adulthood should be a time of positive self-discovery, in which young people learn from stressful situations but also celebrate successes. For many individuals with LD and AD/HD, however, this transition takes much trial and error, and goals and successes can be elusive.

In addition, the hidden nature of LD and AD/HD can pose a challenge. Unfortunately, some employers and teachers do not understand that these are real disabilities. This makes it very important for young people with LD and/or AD/HD to understand their own strengths and needs.

This guide to transition planning and postsecondary options for individuals with LD and/or AD/HD is meant to take some of the bumps out of the journey to self-understanding and adulthood. Ultimately, we hope the book will help young people with LD and AD/HD find their own niches in the adult world by discovering ways to structure learning and work to fit their strengths and interests.

Unlocking Potential has been designed to address the information needs of all readers with LD or AD/HD, no matter how mild or severe their disabilities, including:

- adolescents and young adults diagnosed when they were young who have benefited from special services in school;

- people who were not diagnosed until adulthood;

- individuals who see traditional education (college, technical school) as the best way to prepare for their careers;

- people who are planning to make their own way without formal postsecondary education.

In addition, the book includes information and advice helpful for family members and the secondary education and postsecondary professionals who work with them.

In deciding what information to include in this book, we were guided by the knowledge that there are several important principles by which successful adults with disabilities live. These principles were first identified by Paul Gerber and Henry Reiff, through their research on adults with LD:

1. **Self-determination.** Successful adults with LD set goals that build on strengths and downplay areas of need.

2. **Persistence.** When needed, they work harder and longer but do not give up.

3. **The right match.** They find working and learning situations that lead to success.

4. **Problem solving.** They develop skills to find ways to use strengths.

5. **Social support.** They find people who understand and can help. Also, they find ways to support others.

These success principles can work for any adult, but have special meaning for adults with LD and/or AD/HD. By including information that we think will help readers make these principles their own, we hope we have written a guide that will allow young people with LD and/or AD/HD to know themselves and to take charge of their lives to reach realistic and positive goals.

We are pleased to include the knowledge and experience-base of the network of transition-focused professionals whom we know through our work in the Transition Special Education Program (TSE) at The George Washington University. TSE has a 20-year history preparing special education and rehabilitation professionals to work with young people and adults in ways that connect education with employment and careers.

We are especially grateful to Barbara Scheiber and Jeanne Talpers for offering us the opportunity to revise their original guide, which has served as a resource for so many individuals.

1

LEARNING DISABILITIES
What Are They?

IN THIS CHAPTER:

- Overview
- Defining Learning Disabilities
- What Is It Like to Have a Learning Disability?
- Causes, Theories, and Concepts
- Specific Learning Disabilities and Associated Perceptual Problems
- Fallout
- What We Know about Successful Adults with Learning Disabilities

Virginia Salus & Denise Bello

Overview

We all learn differently. We all gather and express information in our own special ways. Some of us learn more readily by reading or by seeing; some by listening. Some of us use our sense of touch to diagnose illness, to find the beauty in clay or wood, or to make machinery work smoothly. Some of us function efficiently and productively, with occasional lapses and mistakes; but some of us find academic or work tasks difficult and confusing.

A striking example of learning differences comes from the life of Albert Einstein. Despite his phenomenal gifts, Einstein had great difficulties with academic learning. He said of himself, "writing is difficult, and I communicate this way [by speaking] very badly. . . . I very rarely think in words at all."

Einstein was unable to learn in traditional ways. His genius was rare, but his difficulties with school work were similar to those of many students with learning disabilities. Like Einstein, people with learning disabilities often acquire and express information in different ways. They have many kinds of abilities, but often feel defeated by the differences that may stand out in the classroom and in interactions with peers.

Researchers tell us that 5 to 10 percent of Americans have learning disabilities (LD). So, even though people with LD may feel isolated and as if they are the only one with their difficulties, they actually are in good company. Of course, no two people with LD are exactly the same, but many do share certain characteristics. This chapter looks at some of those common characteristics to help you better understand what LD is and how it can affect you.

Defining Learning Disabilities

Since the early 1960s, professionals and professional organizations have attempted to define *learning disabilities.* There are currently many "official" definitions in use in the United States. The difficulty in formulating one definition that everyone can agree upon is that learning disabilities result in different learning and working profiles, depending on age, settings, strengths, and needs of each individual.

TABLE 1.1—NJCLD DEFINITION OF A LEARNING DISABILITY

Learning disabilities is a general term that refers to a heterogeneous group of disorders manifested by significant difficulties in the acquisition and use of listening, speaking, reading, writing, reasoning, or mathematical abilities. These disorders are intrinsic to the individual, presumed to be due to central nervous system dysfunction, and may occur across the life span. Problems in self-regulatory behaviors, social perception, and social interaction may exist with learning disabilities but do not by themselves constitute a learning disability. Although learning disabilities may occur concomitantly with other handicapping conditions (for example, sensory impairment, mental retardation, serious emotional disturbance) or with extrinsic influences such as cultural difference, insufficient or inappropriate instruction), they are not the result of those conditions or influences.

School systems use the Individuals with Disabilities Education Act (IDEA) definition that focuses on the profile of *children* with learning disabilities. Rehabilitation services use a slightly different definition that focuses on needs of *adult learners and workers.* And postsecondary educational settings combine the definitions of the Americans with Disabilities Act with the language in Section 504 of the Rehabilitation Act. These laws are discussed in Chapter 3.

We have chosen to use the definition developed by the National Joint Committee on Learning Disabilities (NJCLD) because it is supported by many different groups from the LD community. *(See Table 1.1 on previous page.)*

Let's take this definition part by part to explore the complex nature of defining what learning disabilities are and are not.

TABLE 1.2—UNDERSTANDING THE DEFINITION

NJCLD Definition	What It Means
Learning disabilities is a general term that refers to a heterogeneous group of disorders	There is not one type of LD. Each person with LD has his own profile of learning strengths and weaknesses. There are many different patterns of LD. For example, one person may be a good reader but a poor speller. Another person may struggle with reading but be excellent in math.
manifested by significant difficulties	Individuals with LD will have serious problems that will affect how they function in school, home, or at work.
in the acquisition and use of listening, speaking, reading, writing, reasoning, or mathematical abilities.	Learning disabilities are specific in nature. They affect one or more ability areas such as writing or listening. For example, a student may have a large vocabulary but may have difficulty recalling keys words when answering a question orally.
These disorders are intrinsic to the individual,	Learning disabilities don t go away. Areas of difficulty can be strengthened but they will remain areas of relative weakness.
presumed to be due to central nervous system dysfunction,	Researchers think that LD is caused by some differences or difficulties in how the brain works.
and may occur across the life span.	Learning disabilities may become obvious at many different stages in a person s life, and the symptoms may change over time. For example, a person s reading difficulties may look different in elementary school than in college.

(Continued on next page.)

TABLE 1.2—Understanding the Definition *(Continued)*

NJCLD Definition	What It Means
Problems in self-regulatory behaviors, social perception, and social interaction may exist with learning disabilities	Some individuals with LD have difficulty with self-control or understanding social situations, and communicating with others. For example, a person may interrupt others during conversations or have difficulty reading others body language.
but do not themselves constitute a learning disability.	Problems with self-control, understanding social situations, and communicating with others can occur with individuals who do not have LD. There can be many other reasons for these types of difficulties.
Although learning disabilities may occur concomitantly with other handicapping conditions (for example, sensory impairment, mental retardation, serious emotional disturbance)	LD may be present with other disabilities but these should not be the cause of the LD. For example, a student who is legally blind could also be considered to have a learning disability, but only if that learning disability is not caused by the visual impairment.
or with extrinsic influences (such as cultural differences, insufficient or inappropriate instruction), they are not the result of those conditions or influences.	Learning disabilities are not the result of external conditions that can result in lack of stimulating or challenging school, family, and community experiences. LD is not caused by attending a school with low academic standards or watching too much TV.

Adapted from Bridges to Practice: A Research Guide for Literacy Practitioners Serving Adults with Learning Disabilities, Guidebook 1: Preparing to Serve Adults with Learning Disabilities. *Published by the National Center of Adult Literacy and Learning Disabilities and the National Institute for Literacy.*

What Is It Like to Have a Learning Disability?

There is no typical profile of a person with a learning disability. One person is poorly coordinated; another is an outstanding athlete. One person is socially awkward and immature; another has excellent social skills. One highly intelligent student reads slowly and unsurely. Another reads well but struggles to recall facts, proper names, or correct spelling. Another person, adept at mechanics, has difficulty orienting his body in space and frequently drops equipment and bumps into machinery. His boss is afraid his clumsiness will cause an accident, and his job is in jeopardy.

For Dale S. Brown, an author and well-known advocate for people with LD, difficulty with social skills is a major problem. She writes:

> Many people with learning disabilities have. . . difficulty right in their own homes. Some are unsure of where their bodies are in space. They do not have a secure sense of the floor beneath their feet. . . . It is extremely difficult for [them] to pick up the social customs many of their peers take for granted: small talk, entering a circle of people, introducing themselves to strangers. Learning disabled people are in culture shock in their own culture. . . . Learning disabled adults receive inaccurate information through their senses and/or have trouble processing that information. Like static on the radio or a bad TV picture, the information becomes garbled as it travels from the eye, ear, or skin to the brain.

Other individuals with LD experience their disability differently. Below are some experiences of people who told their stories in the book *Succeeding with LD* by Jill Lauren (Free Spirit, 1997):

> Anitra Simpson is fifteen years old. She remembers school being difficult from the very first day of first grade. Her learning disability makes it difficult for her to understand and use language. She has trouble remembering and pronouncing words, as well as understanding what she has read. Anitra had to repeat first grade and was placed in special education classes.
>
> Despite early setbacks, Anitra is finding the route to success. She loves art and draws pictures to help her study. She has worked hard to gradually reduce the amount of time she attends special education classes. In high school she is in mostly general education classes and is earning A's and B's. She is beginning to see college in her future.
>
> Megan Wilson's LD affects her math, memorization, and spelling. In spite of these difficulties, she was known as a bright student and placed in advanced classes. In high school, her learning disabilities caught up with her. Advanced algebra was a huge struggle, and the memorization needed for other subjects put her on overload. She studied much

more than her friends but received lower grades. Her grades also suffered due to her poor spelling and punctuation.

One of Megan's teachers suggested that she be tested for learning disabilities. Once she was diagnosed, life changed for the better. Her grades improved and counseling helped her strengthen her self-esteem. She went to a college that was reported to have a learning specialist for students with LD. When she arrived at college there was no learning specialist and no plan to hire one. She organized a two-year campaign that resulted in the hiring of a learning specialist.

Megan knows what she needs to do to be successful. She gets books on tape, has someone proofread her papers, uses note-taking services, has mastered a multisensory approach to memorization, and uses the latest computer technology. She enjoys speaking to high school students about what it is like to have a learning disability.

Paul Orfalea failed second grade because he didn't know the alphabet. In third grade the only word he could read was *the.* He would keep up with his reading group by following from one *the* to the next. He graduated from high school with a 1.2 grade point average.

Paul's family and family friends owned their own businesses. Paul went on to college with the desire to have his own business. During college he thought there was a market for reasonably priced school supplies, so he rented a garage and sold supplies like pens and notebooks. He hired student workers and relied on their reading and mechanical skills. This was the beginning of Kinko's office supply, named after Paul's kinky hair. Paul reports his business controls more than 800 stores across the world. Paul still finds reading difficult but loves listening to his wife read to him.

Causes, Theories, and Concepts

So, what causes learning disabilities? Are they inherited? Did something go wrong during pregnancy or at birth? Are they a result of an injury or illness? There is no *one* answer and the answers that do exist are complex and incomplete. Not only are scientists seeking explanations for the origins of learning disabilities, but they are also trying to analyze how thinking processes work. The closer researchers come to understanding learning disabilities, the closer we will come to understanding how we all learn.

All learning occurs in the brain and is facilitated by the central nervous system. Theories about how the brain works, intelligence, and the ways intelligence is measured help us understand learning disabilities. The following three theories provide a perspective on learning disabilities. While only brief descriptions are provided here, further references on each of these topics are included at the end of the chapter.

Information Processing Theory

Using a computer analogy, we can focus on what and how information is learned and what happens when the learning process is interrupted. Processing information requires:

- taking in information (*input*),

- integrating the information (*processing*),

- and expressing the information (*output*).

Input is how our senses (seeing, hearing, touching, smelling, or tasting) take in information. If perceptions from the *input* channel are not functioning well, information can become *mis*information. For example, visual material may be scrambled or reconfigured; auditory material, garbled and confused; and physical sensations, misinterpreted.

Processing is how we convert information into meaning based on our experiences, knowledge, and understanding. Processing involves:

- *sequencing* (organizing what is seen or heard in a logical order),

- *remembering* (storing information), and

- *abstracting* (seeing relationships of parts to the whole or deriving meaning from a specific word or symbol.

If the processing channel is not working well, an individual can lose, misfile, mismatch, or simply confuse the information that has been taken in.

Output is the way we show what we know. This can be through spoken or written words, music, graphics, or body language (gestures and facial expressions). In a school setting, output often involves writing papers, taking tests, giving oral presentations, participating in class discussions, etc. If an output channel is affected, then the act of speaking, writing, or physically responding can be challenging.

In people who have learning disabilities, certain situations can overburden one or more of the information-processing functions. By using the information-processing theory, we can analyze where the breakdown in learning might be occurring and then outline appropriate support strategies.

Brain Function Theory

Brain researchers are searching for the answer to the question, "What causes learning disabilities?" Subtle disturbances in brain structures and functions may begin before birth. Pregnancy and delivery problems, or maternal use of drugs, alcohol, smoking, and toxins may affect brain development. Since learning disabilities tend to run in families, there may also be a genetic link.

When scientists compare brains of individuals with and without learning disabilities, they see differences in the structure of the brain. For example, there is a language-related area on both sides of the brain called the planum temporale. In people with reading disabilities, the right and left planum temporale are the same size. In people *without* reading disabilities, the left side of this area of the brain is larger.

The goal of brain research is to learn *how* differences in brain structures and processes affect learning. Then we may be able to prevent some learning disabilities and develop more precise interventions.

Multiple Intelligence Theory

The Multiple Intelligence (MI) theory was developed by Howard Gardner, a neurologist at Harvard University. Gardner observed that intelligence is made up of many different types of abilities rather than one general intelligence. Originally, Gardner identified seven intelligences, but has added an eighth (see Table 1.3, page 9) and is researching two more:

1. **Logical/Mathematical Intelligences:** reasoning logically, sequentially, and mathematically; recognizing patterns; enjoying experiments and puzzles

2. **Verbal/Linguistic Intelligences:** strengths in using language, such as in reading, telling stories, debating, telling jokes, learning vocabulary and foreign languages

TABLE 1.3—MULTIPLE INTELLIGENCES

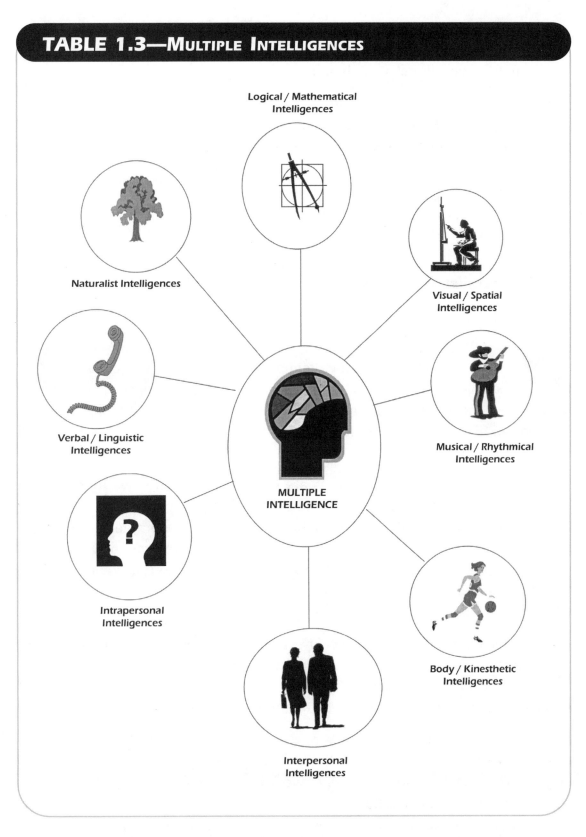

3. Visual/Spatial Intelligences: thinking in pictures; understanding the relationship of objects in space to each other

4. **Musical/Rhythmical Intelligences:** strengths in appreciating and creating music, remembering sounds and rhythmic patterns, mimicking others' speech patterns

5. **Bodily/Kinesthetic Intelligences:** the ability to use one's body with skill and grace—making things with the hands, playing sports, dancing, communicating through body language

6. **Interpersonal Intelligences:** understanding others and working well in groups

7. **Intrapersonal Intelligences:** understanding one's inner feelings and desires

8. **Naturalist Intelligences:** the ability to identify plants and animals in the environment

Unfortunately, schools usually emphasize logical/mathematical and verbal/linguistic intelligences the most, and many tests only tap these two types of intelligence. Fortunately, more and more teachers are using the MI approach to observe and appreciate the different ways individuals learn, and to work with each student's strengths.

With the MI approach, students are given a variety of ways to learn new information and to show what they know. For example, someone with strength in verbal-linguistic intelligence may be encouraged to complete a research project by listening to and reporting into a tape recorder. Someone with strong visual-spatial intelligence may prefer to report using video recording and photography. Someone with bodily-kinesthetic intelligence may use drama to show what was learned.

The learning strengths and weaknesses of someone with LD may add up to a MI profile with dramatic differences among some of the intelligences. For some learners, being able to describe their learning strengths and needs in terms of multiple intelligences may help teachers understand them better.

The three theories described above provide evidence that the learning process can be scientifically observed, tracked, and measured. Translating this knowledge into practical and useful ways to work with people who have learning disabilities depends on accurate diagnostic evaluations (see Chapter 4) and individualized interventions and adaptations (see Chapters 9 and 11).

Specific Learning Disabilities and Associated Perceptual Problems

Learning disabilities and academic difficulties go hand in hand. As mentioned previously, learning disabilities can cause difficulties in a variety of areas, including reading, written language, oral communication, and mathematics. Terms commonly used to describe specific difficulties include dyslexia, dysgraphia, and dyscalculia.

Dyslexia. Dyslexia is a language-based learning disability. People with dyslexia have difficulty understanding, remembering, and working with letter sounds (phonological awareness), in isolation and/or within words, sentences, or paragraphs. Dyslexia not only affects reading, but also spelling, writing, and listening.

Dysgraphia. Dysgraphia is a learning disability that affects the written formation of letters or words. People with dysgraphia have difficulty with printing and/or cursive handwriting and with drawing and copying.

Dyscalculia. Dyscalculia is a learning disability related to arithmetic operations and mathematical calculations. People with dyscalculia can have difficulty with both simple and complex math functions and problem solving.

Usually, specific academic difficulties are linked to problems with certain learning processes. Learning processes that are often connected to specific learning disabilities include:

- visual perception,
- auditory perception,
- spatial perception,
- motor skills,
- memory, sequencing, and organization.

Visual Perception

People with visual perception problems may have perfect eyesight but fail to see the difference between some letters, numbers, words, or even whole paragraphs, and confuse letters or numbers that look alike, such as **b** and **d, g** and **q,** or **6** and **9.** When reading, they may omit ends of words, reverse words, or misperceive the spacing between words and sentences. Visual perception difficulties may also make it harder to understand social cues such as facial expressions or body language. This can lead to embarrassment or problems in working with others.

Auditory Perception

Auditory perception problems interfere with the accurate interpretation of information received through the ears. Despite normal hearing, people may have difficulty telling the difference between similar sounds (e.g., "crashed the car" for "washed the car" or "ninety minutes" for "nineteen minutes"). When trying to focus on a specific task, they may also have trouble screening out background noises such as traffic, other people's conversations, or music.

Auditory perception problems also have implications in social settings. For example, an individual may have difficulty paying attention to vocal intonations or may simply miss something that is said. This can lead to misunderstandings in social and work settings.

Spatial Perception

Someone with spatial perception problems may have difficulty telling the difference between right and left, following directions when traveling, or judging distances. Someone who has these problems may misjudge where his body is in space, get misdirected, or become lost, even in familiar territory. Some educational theorists believe that these perceptual difficulties may impair one's ability to perform academic tasks. For example, handwriting may be labored due to problems with right and left, reading may be hampered due to letter or word reversals, and math skills such as geometry and graphing may be challenging due to difficulties with spatial configurations.

Motor Skills

People with learning disabilities can have difficulty with either fine or gross motor skills. Gross motor skills are those that involve large muscles, such as those in the legs, arms, and trunk. Fine motor skills involve smaller muscles, such as those in the fingers and face. People with gross motor difficulties may have trouble throwing and catching, skipping and running, and with more complex motor tasks such as swimming or riding a bicycle. Individuals with fine motor difficulties may have problems with drawing, copying, writing, or other activities requiring dexterity.

Memory, Sequencing, and Organizing

Many individuals with learning disabilities have problems with short- and/or long-term memory, sequencing, and organization. These problems can lead to forgetting assignments and appointments, not completing tasks, and poor planning and time management. Some strategies that individuals with learning disabilities can use to address these issues are discussed in Chapter 11.

The processing difficulties outlined above are not always easy to diagnose. Moreover, the connection between these processing deficits and specific learning problems such as dyslexia or dyscalculia is often unclear. What we do know is that training individuals in their specific area(s) of perceptual difficulties does not help them improve their academic skills. This approach was tried for many years. For example, people with visual perceptual problems were taught to trace complex figures to try to increase their ability to interpret complex visual information. We now know that for an academic skill to improve, a student needs to receive direct instruction in that academic skill.

Fallout

If learning problems are not dealt with during school years, they may persist. Some adults with LD may continue to struggle with reading, writing, spelling, and computing. Others may struggle with social skills, or may feel vulnerable, afraid their hidden disability will be revealed. Fearful that they will be discovered as illiterate, they are embarrassed, afraid of criticism, or reminded of the hurt they experienced as children. They may worry about the reactions of co-workers, friends, strangers. Others lash out in anger at family, friends, and spouses, paying the world back for their misery. Some become violent. Others become depressed and withdrawn, leading lonely and limited lives. Others drive themselves mercilessly to prove they are worthy of respect.

Despite their intelligence and their often outstanding gifts, people with learning disabilities do not have a reservoir of success to replenish them after they have failed a task. The experience of repeated failure throughout their early school years can keep them from taking risks.

Yet many succeed. They grow beyond their hurts and disappointments, they find help and support, and they learn to appreciate and develop their strengths.

They discover that their learning disability is only part of their selves—a part that they can learn to manage. Their disability is no longer disabling.

What We Know about Successful Adults with Learning Disabilities

> "I found out I was learning disabled when my two sons were diagnosed. I think of my brain as being like an outdated computer when it comes to listening to a conversation. It can do anything a modern computer can do; it just takes longer. I have to get there earlier and stay longer but I will succeed. I have written a few books. I have developed a writing friend. I fix his teeth and he fixes my grammar. The relationship works well for both of us."
>
> *(A successful dentist with LD)*

Whether on the job, in college, or in their personal life, adults with learning disabilities are more successful if:

1. They are aware of their learning style and needs.

2. They are able to compensate and make modifications for those needs.

3. They can advocate for themselves, requesting the support and assistance they need.

By accepting themselves and understanding their learning disabilities, by compensating and coping, adults with LD accept their differences and build on their strengths. They work harder than others on tasks that touch on weaknesses. They learn to use technological tools such as word processors, spell checkers, tape recorders, and electronic organizers. They build positive support systems.

For an excellent overview of the challenges that confront adults with LD and strategies to overcome them, you might want to read the book *Exceeding Expectations: Successful Adults with Learning Disabilities,* listed at the end of this chapter.

Conclusion: The Future

In the past, efforts to assist individuals with learning disabilities have emphasized *remediation*—efforts to correct the problem. This approach has worked for many, but for others, it has led to more frustration.

This book looks at learning disabilities as a condition to be understood and overcome. The underlying theme is that everyone has unique ways of learning and that modifications (accommodations) should be developed that support each individual's unique learning strengths and weaknesses, as well as his self-appreciation.

Dr. Mary Poplin, a well-known educator, summarizes this philosophy most eloquently. She speaks of the often-overlooked creativity of people with learning disabilities. These individuals may be talented in music, poetry, dance, art, mechanics, computer programming, or athletics, but their abilities are usually forgotten or lost by "deficit driven" approaches. Dr. Poplin challenges us to "reject our . . . focus on disability, and courageously change our emphasis to abilities and talents."

Resources

BOOKS

Most of the books listed in **Unlocking Potential** can be found in libraries, or purchased or ordered through bookstores or online services such as Amazon.com or BarnesandNoble.com. In some cases it may be easier or quicker to order directly through the publisher, so contact information for publishers is given.

Adults with Dyslexia: Aspiring and Achieving, 1997
Author: Joan R. Knight
The International Dyslexia Association,
8600 LaSalle Road,
Chester Building, Suite #382
Baltimore, MD 21286-2044
Phone: (800) ABCD123 (222-3123)
Phone: (410) 296-0232
Fax: (410) 321-5069
E-mail: info@interdys.org
http://www.interdys.org

Basic Facts about Dyslexia: What Everyone Ought to Know, 1993
Authors: Angela Wilkins, Alice Garside, and Mary Lee Enfield
International Dyslexia Association
See address above.

Bridges to Practice: A Research Based Guide for Literacy Practitioners Serving Adults with Learning Disabilities, Guidebook 1: Preparing to Serve Adults with Learning Disabilities, 1999
University of Kansas
Institute on Research and Learning Disabilities and
Academy for Educational Development
1875 Connecticut Ave., NW
Washington, DC 20009-1202
Phone: (800) 953-2553
Fax: (202) 884-8400
E-mail: admin@aed.org
http://www.aed.org

Disability Awareness Packet, 1996
Beach Center on Families and Disabilities
3111 Haworth Hall
University of Kansas
Lawrence, KS 66045
Phone: (913) 864-7600
Fax: (913) 864-7605
E-mail: beach@dole.lsi.ukans.edu
http://www.lsi.ukans.edu/beach/beachhp.htm

Dyslexia: Research and Resource Guide, 1996
Authors: Carol Sullivan Spafford and George S. Grosset
Allyn and Bacon
160 Gould Street
Needham Heights, MA 02194-2315
Phone: (800) 852-8024
Fax: (781) 455-8024
E-mail: AandBpub@aol.com
http://www.abacon.com

Exceeding Expectations: Successful Adults with Learning Disabilities, 1997
Authors: Henry B. Reiff, Paul J. Gerber, and Rick Ginsberg
Pro-Ed, Inc.

8700 Shoal Creek Blvd.
Austin, TX 78757-6897
Phone: (800) 897-3202
Fax: (800) 397-7633
Email: info@proedinc.com
http://www.proedinc.com

Frames of Mind: The Theory of Multiple Intelligence, 1993
Author: Howard Gardner
Zephyr Press
P.O. Box 660066-OL
Tucson, AZ 85728-6006
Phone: (800) 232-2187
Fax: (520) 323-9402
E-mail: zephyrmi@aol.com
http://www.zephyrpress.com

Guide to Disability and Rehabilitation Periodicals, 1994
National Rehabilitation Information Center (NARIC)
8455 Colesville Road, Suite #935
Silver Spring, MD 20910-3319
Phone: (800) 346-2742
Fax: (301) 587-1967
E-mail: naric@capacess.org
http://www.naric.com/naric

Helping Children Overcome Learning Difficulties, 3rd edition, 1993
Author: Jerome Rosner
Academic Therapy Publications
20 Commercial Blvd.
Novato, CA 94949
Phone: (800) 422-7249
Fax: (415) 883-3720
E-mail: atpub@aol.com
http://www.atpub.com

Language-Related Learning Disabilities: Their Nature and Treatment, 1993
Author: Adele Gerber
Paul H. Brookes Publishing Company
P.O. Box 10624
Baltimore, MD 21285-0624

Phone: (800) 638-3775
Fax: (410) 337-8539
E-mail: custserv@pbrookes.com
http://www.pbrookes.com

LD: Basic Concepts, Assessment Practices and Instructional Strategies,
4th edition, 1990
Authors: Patricia Meyers and Donald Hamill
Pro-Ed, Inc.
8700 Shoal Creek Blvd.
Austin, TX 78757-6897
Phone: (800) 897-3202
Fax: (800) 397-7633
E-mail: info@proedinc.com
http://www.proedinc.com

Learning Disabilities, 1995
NIH Publication No. 95-3611
NIMH Public Inquiries
6001 Executive Blvd.
Room 8184 MSC 9663
Bethesda, MD 20892-9663
Fax: (301) 443-4279
E-mail: nimhinfo@nih.gov
http://www.nimh.nih.gov/publist/puborder.
cfm#953611

Many Ways to Learn: Young People's Guide to Learning Disabilities, 1996
Authors: Judith Stern and Uzi Ben-Ami
Magination Press/American Psychological Association
750 First Street, NE
Washington, DC 20002
Phone: (800) 374-2721
Fax: (202) 336-5502
E-mail: Books@apa.org
http://www.maginationpress.com

Perspectives on Learning Disabilities: Biological, Cognitive, and Contextual, 1998
Editors: Robert Sternberg and Louise Spear-Swerling
Westview Press/Harper Collins
10 East 53rd Street

New York, NY 10022
Phone: (800) 242-7737
Fax: (800) 822-4090
http://www.harpercollins.com

Seven Pathways of Learning: Teaching Students and Parents about Multiple Intelligence, 1994
Author: David Lazear
Zephyr Press
P.O. Box 66006-OL
Tucson, AZ 85728-6006
Phone: (800) 232-2187
Fax: (520) 323-9402
E-mail: zephyrmi@aol.com
http://www.zephyrpress.com

Succeeding with LD: 20 True Stories about Real People with LD, 1997
Author: Jill Lauren
Free Spirit Publishing
400 First Avenue North, Suite 616
Minneapolis, MN 55401-1724
Phone: (800) 735-7323
Fax: (612) 337-5050
E-mail: help4kids@freespirit.com
http://www.freespirit.com

They Speak for Themselves: A Survey of Adults with Learning Disabilities, 1996
Learning Disabilities Association
4156 Library Road
Pittsburgh, PA 15234-1349
Phone: (412) 341-1515
Fax: (412) 344-0224
E-mail: ldanatl@usaor.net
http://www.ldanatl.org

The Tuned-In Turned-On Book about Learning Disabilities, 1994
Author: Marnell L. Hayes
High Noon Books
Academic Therapy Publications
20 Commercial Blvd.
Novato, CA 94949

Phone: (800) 422-7249
Fax: (415) 883-3720
E-mail: atpub@aol.com
http://www.atpub.com

Understanding Learning Disabilities: International and Multidisciplinary Views, 1995
Author: Drake Duane
Plenum Press
233 Spring Street
New York, NY 10013
Phone: (800) 221-9369
Fax: (212) 807-1047
E-mail: info@plenum.com
http://www.plenum.com

FACT SHEETS

ABC's of LD/ADD: Learning Disabilities and Attention Deficit Disorder, 1998
Publisher: LDOnline
http://www.ldonline.org/abcs_info/articles-info.html

Adult Learning Disabilities
National Center for Learning Disabilities (NCLD)
381 Park Avenue South, # 1401
New York, NY 10016
Phone: (888) 575-7373
Fax: (212) 545-9665
http://www.ncld.org/brochures/adult_ld.html

Characteristics of Adults with Specific Learning Disabilities, 1998
Office of Vocational and Adult Education/U.S. Dept. of Education
400 Maryland Avenue, SW
Washington, DC 20202
Phone: (800) 227-0216
http://www.ldonline.org/ld_indepth/adult/index.html

General Information about Learning Disabilities, 1997
Fact Sheet Number 7 (FS7)
Publisher: KidSource
http://www.kidsource.com/NICHCY/learning_disabilities.html

General Information Packet on Learning Disabilities
National Center for Learning Disabilities (NCLD)
381 Park Avenue South, #1401
New York, NY 10016
Phone: (888) 575-7373
Fax: (212) 545-9665
http://www.ncld.org/brochures/geninfo.html

Learning Disabilities, # E516
Author: Jean Lokerson
Council for Exceptional Children
ERIC Clearinghouse on Handicapped and Gifted Children document
1920 Association Drive
Reston, VA 22091
Phone: (703) 620-3660
Fax: (703) 264-9494
http://www.ldonline.org/ld_indepth/general_info/eric_ldgen.html

Tell Me the Facts about Learning Disabilities
Publisher: LDOnline
http://www.ldonline.org/abcs_info/articles-info.html

What Are Some Common Signs of Learning Disabilities?
Publisher: LDOnline
http://www.ldonline.org/abcs_info/articles-info.html

What Is Meant by "Learning Disabilities"?
Children and Adults with Attention Deficit/Hyperactivity Disorder (CHADD)
8181 Professional Place, Suite 201
Landover, MD 20785
Phone: (800) 233-4050
Fax: (301) 306-7090
Email: national@chadd.org
http://www.chadd.org/doe/doe_ld.htm

WEBSITES
Internet Resources for Special Children (IRSC)
This nonprofit website has links to useful resources for persons with various disabilities.
http://www.irsc.org

Internet Special Education Resources

This site is a directory of professionals serving persons with disabilities for students, parents, and professionals.

http://www.iser.com

LD Online (The Learning Disabilities Project)

This site is filled with information, links, chatrooms, listservs, and bookstores for consumers, educators, counselors, and students.

http://www.ldonline.org

Roads to Learning

This organization works to teach the general public about disabilities through public libraries.

http://www.ala.org/roads

Special Education Resources on the Internet

This is filled with numerous links dealing with definitions, issues, and studies of disabilities. It has links for legislative information as well as teaching and learning.

http://www.hood.edu/seri/serihome.htm

Teens Helping Teens

This site is a wonderful resource for students with dyslexia, run by students with dyslexia. Includes information about the disorder, support, and study tips. Funded by the NY State chapter of the International Dyslexia Association.

http://www.ldteens.org

BUSINESSES, ORGANIZATIONS, AND GOVERNMENT OFFICES

Contact these groups for further information. Addresses are given in the back of the book, beginning on page 347.

- Association on Higher Education and Disability (AHEAD)

- Beach Center on Families and Disability

- Clearinghouse on Disability Information

- Council for Exceptional Children

- Council on Learning Disabilities

- Disabilities Studies and Resource Center

- ERIC Clearinghouse on Disability & Gifted Education

- The Federal Resource Center for Special Education

- Higher Education And The Handicapped—HEATH Resource Center

- The International Dyslexia Association

- Internet Special Education Resources

- LDA (Learning Disabilities Association of America)

- National Association for Adults with Learning Difficulties (NAALD)

- National Center for Learning Disabilities (NCLD)

- The National Institute on Disability and Rehabilitation Research (NIDRR)

- National Joint Committee on Learning Disabilities

- National Network of Learning Disabled Adults (NNLDA)

- National Organization on Disability

- National Parent Network on Disabilities

- National Parent to Parent Support and Information Service (NNPSIS)

- NICHCY (National Information Center for Children and Youth with Disabilities)

- Roads to Learning

2

ATTENTION DEFICIT/ HYPERACTIVITY DISORDER

Challenges and Benefits

IN THIS CHAPTER:

- Overview
- Defining AD/HD
- Causes, Concepts, and Theories of AD/HD
- Treatment for AD/HD
- Positives to AD/HD

John Staba & Juliana M. Taymans

"I could only read a page in a book and then my mind would wander."

"My energy level sometimes helped me accomplish what I needed to get done."

"I couldn't focus on my work."

"Sometimes I can totally focus and get amazing amounts of work done."

"I couldn't keep up. I am so disorganized."

"I always thought I wasn't smart enough."

"In class I usually feel restless and hyper."

Overview

Do these comments sound familiar? Have you ever made a similar statement? Feelings like these are often expressed by individuals with attention deficit/hyperactivity disorder (AD/HD).

Living with AD/HD is a challenge. Some people compare it to driving a car without brakes. At times you can feel exhilarated and focused, and at other times you can feel frustrated and panicked. Likewise, if you have conquered high school, the thought of attending more school can be exciting, but also overwhelming and intimidating.

We know that at least 3-5 percent of school-age children in the United States have AD/HD. Some estimates go as high as 20 percent. We also know that some people with AD/HD also cope with anxiety, depression, other psychological disorders, and learning disabilities. Many more boys are identified with AD/HD than girls. However, as teachers, doctors, and college learning specialists become more aware that AD/HD does not have to be linked to hyperactivity and impulsivity, more girls are being identified and treated.

At least one-third to two-thirds of children with AD/HD continue with it into adulthood. There are an estimated two million adults with AD/HD in the United States. If you are one of those adults, that does not mean you cannot enjoy success in postsecondary education, employment, and your personal life. You will definitely benefit, however, from learning to find and use supports individualized to your unique strengths and weaknesses. This chapter will help you get started by explaining the nature of AD/HD and helping you understand how it can affect you.

Defining AD/HD

Attention deficit/hyperactivity disorder is a condition that affects individuals from infancy through adulthood. AD/HD affects three areas of behavior:

1. maintaining attention,

2. controlling impulses, and

3. managing activity level.

Often children with AD/HD experience trouble in school, while adults experience trouble with work. Getting along with family and friends can also be a challenge. For older adolescents and adults, difficulties with organization and time management can be barriers to success.

The American Psychiatric Association publishes the "official" criteria for a diagnosis of AD/HD in its *Diagnostic and Statistical Manual of Mental Disorders.* This manual currently lists characteristics of three possible subtypes of attention deficit hyperactivity disorder:

1. inattentive;

2. hyperactive-impulsive; or

3. a combination of inattentive and hyperactive-impulsive.

Inattentive Subtype

One type of AD/HD is called Attention Deficit/Hyperactivity Disorder - Inattentive Type. Table 2.1 *(below)* shows the nine possible symptoms. To be diagnosed, you must show six or more symptoms for at least six months.

TABLE 2.1—SYMPTOMS OF INATTENTION

- often fails to give close attention to details or makes careless mistakes in schoolwork, work, or other activities

- often has difficulty sustaining attention in tasks or play activities

- often does not seem to listen when spoken to directly

- often does not follow through on instructions and fails to finish schoolwork, chores, or duties in the workplace (not due to oppositional behavior or failure to understand instructions)

- often has difficulty organizing tasks and activities

- often avoids, dislikes, or is reluctant to engage in tasks that require sustained mental effort (such as schoolwork or homework)

- often loses things necessary for tasks or activities (e.g., toys, school assignments, pencils, books, or tools)

- often easily distracted by extraneous stimuli

- often forgetful in daily activities

Reprinted with permission from the Diagnostic and Statistical Manual of Mental Disorders, Fourth Edition. Copyright 1994 American Psychiatric Association.

Students with this type of AD/HD have trouble concentrating on the task at hand. In school, this can mean trouble paying attention to an in-class reading assignment, teacher presentation, or discussion. Students can drift off into their own thoughts or get distracted by other activities going on around them—the noise of a lawnmower, a conversation among other students, pictures on the wall. Avoiding difficult tasks, procrastinating, or beginning but having trouble completing work is also part of this type of AD/HD.

Consider Coreen. Coreen is preparing for a test in American History tomorrow. She dreads studying for the test because it means reading, memorizing, and organizing information and ideas. She is in her room, which is a mess. She can't find the study guide her teacher handed out yesterday. She knows she wants to study for short periods of about 20 to 30 minutes and then take breaks to call friends or listen to music, but she has already spent 20 minutes looking for the study sheet.

Coreen's mother calls to her to remind her that it is Thursday, and she is responsible for setting the table and helping in the kitchen. Coreen feels stressed and overwhelmed and decides to ignore her mother so they don't end up in another argument. She thinks, "How am I ever going to get ready for this test? Why didn't I start studying last night to give myself more time?" Coreen's thoughts get more and more negative about herself. Her mother keeps calling for her help with dinner. Coreen sits in her room feeling angry, depressed, and helpless.

Coreen is like many people with the inattentive subtype of AD/HD. She is often unable to find what she needs, or to fulfill others' expectations. She procrastinates and then feels that she doesn't have the time to get organized. Frequently, as happened today, the stress of studying is compounded by her mother's (or others') anger. All of this stress frustrates Coreen and makes her feel like a failure whose life is out of control.

Hyperactive-Impulsive Subtype

This subtype of AD/HD is diagnosed if someone has six or more of these symptoms of hyperactivity-impulsivity for at least six months.

Hyperactivity is probably the most obvious characteristic of this type of AD/HD. This action-orientation can be seen as restlessness or over-activity. While sitting or standing, the person may wiggle a foot, tap a pencil, or shift position often. Hyperactivity can also mean sleep difficulties, a constant quest for something to do, or talking too much. Hyperactivity can be an advantage when it is directed and focused.

Impulsivity means acting without thinking about the consequences of your behavior. This quick acting leads to problems completing school tasks, performing well on the job, and interacting with others. In school, impulsive students may answer questions on a test without completely reading directions or thinking about all the possible answers. On the job, impulsive employees may respond too quickly to a request without all the needed information. In interpersonal situations, impulsive individuals can interrupt conversations or do things without considering others' desires or feelings. We probably all know people who are shy or withdrawn and who seem to have difficulty getting involved in activities. These people help us see that a little impulsivity can make life interesting and fun. For people with AD/HD, the challenge is to be aware of the impulses and to then make a rational decision to act or not.

TABLE 2.2—SYMPTOMS OF HYPERACTIVITY-IMPULSIVITY

Hyperactivity

- often fidgets with hands or feet or squirms in seat

- often leaves seat in classroom or in other situations in which remaining seated is expected

- often runs about or climbs excessively in situations in which it is inappropriate (in adolescents or adults, may be limited to subjective feelings of restlessness)

- often has difficulty playing or engaging in leisure activities quietly

- is often "on the go" or often acts as if "driven by a motor"

- often talks excessively

Impulsivity

- often blurts out answers before questions have been completed

- often has difficulty awaiting turn

- often interrupts or intrudes on others (e.g., butts into conversations or games)

Reprinted with permission from the Diagnostic and Statistical Manual of Mental Disorders, Fourth Edition. Copyright 1994 American Psychiatric Association

Impulsivity combined with hyperactivity can be a recipe for trouble. Impulsive buying can turn into a habit. For example, a woman who loved red bought 20 pairs of red slacks in one year. Impulsivity combined with an action orientation can lead to quick thinking and quick acting that alienates others, results in criminal acts, or leads to alcohol and drug abuse.

For example, Martin is a person who is always on the go. The first time he got into trouble at school was in third grade when he impulsively pulled the fire alarm while changing classes. In middle school, his athletic ability allowed him to make sports teams but he would either quit or be asked to leave due to rule breaking or angry outbursts. In high school, Martin started smoking and drinking. After an argument with his father, he took the family car and left town for a weekend. Martin's parents informed the police, and he was arrested. Martin and his parents then entered family counseling, where they all learned about Martin's AD/HD.

Martin's diagnosis helped him get counseling, school support services, and medication—all of which enabled him to make it through high school and be ready for college. Through this process, he learned that his quick thinking, good reading, and strong verbal skills could be strengths he could use once he learned to focus and control his impulsivity.

Combined Subtype—Inattention and Hyperactive-Impulsive

This subtype of AD/HD includes individuals who display both inattention and hyperactivity-impulsivity. An individual must have six symptoms of inattention and six symptoms of hyperactivity-impulsivity to be diagnosed with AD/HD-combined subtype.

Alex was not diagnosed with AD/HD until his freshman year in college. In high school, he couldn't read more than a page without his mind starting to wander. His friends would do the reading and tell him what was in the textbooks. He excelled in dramatics, and his desire to perform in school plays motivated him to keep his grade point average at the minimum acceptable level. Throughout school, Alex felt that he was always out of sync with what he was supposed to be doing. He was unable to trust his own ideas, so he relied on teachers, friends, and family for direction. His parents were constantly reminding him to complete tasks. His friends, amazed at his disorganization, helped him remember what he needed to do to get by in school. Although this hurt his self-confidence, he was able to make jokes about it. His sense of humor also helped people accept some of the opinions that he would blurt out.

When Alex entered college, he had not developed the study skills he needed to pass his college courses. He was overwhelmed by the amount of reading required. Just sitting for two hours in a class was challenging, much less paying attention to lectures. He excelled in his social life. He loved staying up talking until the early morning hours with dorm friends. He partied on the weekends. He tried to find quiet places to study, but he just didn't know how to keep himself focused. After he was placed on academic probation, he knew he had to find help. This led to his AD/HD diagnosis and to work with a learning specialist. He began to develop a support system and to keep the schedule he needed to succeed in his classes. At the age of 20, he was beginning to develop self-understanding and self-control.

Causes, Concepts, and Theories of AD/HD

Although AD/HD symptoms have been identified since the mid-1800s, only in the past 20 years has the term attention deficit/hyperactivity disorder emerged.

Researchers are studying brain function and structure and finding evidence that AD/HD may be caused by differences in the size, shape, and activity levels of certain areas of the brain. For example, some studies have shown differences in the size of the frontal lobes and basal ganglia in the brains of people with AD/HD. Other researchers have found evidence that one cause of AD/HD may be lack of certain chemicals in the brain. Many experts also believe that AD/HD may have genetic or biological causes, since it often can be found in more than one family member. For example, many adults find out they have AD/HD during the process of having their child diagnosed. The more we learn about the causes of AD/HD, the more effective physicians and diagnosticians can be in managing AD/HD.

Russell Barkley, a leading researcher and writer on AD/HD, has developed a theory that explains AD/HD in terms of difficulty controlling thoughts and actions. Cognitive researchers call this function of the brain *executive control*. Executive control is what enables people to plan, work through, and evaluate what we do.

When faced with a task such as writing a paper or giving a party, a person with AD/HD can have trouble planning, organizing, and sequencing the many steps it takes to accomplish the task. Her impulsiveness may interfere with her ability to follow steps to complete the task. And even if she makes a plan, she may have difficulty sticking with the plan. In addition she may have trouble regulating her actions by using *self-talk*—that is, by telling herself what to do in her mind.

The final part of executive control is to evaluate what we have done and learn from our successes and mistakes. People with AD/HD may skip this reflection or assess what they have done in an overly positive or negative way. Barkley believes that these problems with executive control are more troublesome for individuals with AD/HD than problems with inattention.

Treatment for AD/HD

An appropriate diagnosis is the first step to getting treatment for AD/HD. After that, an individualized treatment plan can be developed. Often, treating AD/HD requires medical, psychological, and educational intervention, as well as behavior management techniques. Treatment approaches include:

- parent training in behavior management;

- individual and family counseling, when needed;

- a support system;

- medication when required.

Parent Training in Behavior Management

Parenting a child with AD/HD is different from parenting a child without this condition. Parents often feel guilty about or responsible for their children's AD/HD behaviors. Once the burden of guilt is lifted, and they understand that they did not cause the AD/HD, they are able to look more objectively at their child and to participate more effectively in behavior management.

Parents usually benefit from guidance on how to effectively communicate, support, and guide a child with AD/HD. Parent training programs and support groups can be found through local Children and Adults with Attention Deficit/Hyperactivity Disorder (CHADD) chapters, school systems, and community agencies such as YMCAs. Guidebooks and Web sites on AD/HD often provide information specifically written for parents. (See the Resources section at the end of this chapter.)

Consistency, structure, and limit setting are crucial in managing behavior. A behavior management system that defines clear and reasonable consequences for unacceptable behavior can keep stressful times manageable for both parents and child. The period of adolescence to young adulthood is a stressful transition time for parents and children. When parents have strategies they can use to control their anger, frustration, and anxieties, more positive and productive communication is usually the result.

Individual and Family Counseling

Counseling may be desirable or necessary, depending on the needs within a family. Family counseling can serve a number of purposes. It can help all members of the family learn about AD/HD and develop strategies to support the family member with AD/HD. By learning how to communicate in a positive, functional, and honest way family members can reduce everyone's stress.

Some parents find couple therapy necessary. This may be important if stress has developed between husband and wife in figuring out how to guide their child with AD/HD without blaming each other or the child. In addition, some parents are coping with challenges of their own, such as AD/HD or clinical depression. Couple therapy can help parents better understand themselves, support their relationship, and help them relate more effectively to their child with AD/HD.

Many adolescents and young adults with AD/HD also can benefit from psychological intervention. One-on-one therapy can help young people develop insight into strengths and needs and how to more effectively make decisions and interact with others. Cognitive-behavioral therapies can provide interventions aimed at slowing down thinking, being less impulsive, and controlling anger. Understanding and accepting a disability is an important foundation to healthy adult living. This self-understanding can be a turning point in taking control of challenges and turning them into advantages.

Individuals with AD/HD can also experience other psychological and learning challenges such as oppositional defiant disorder, behavior or conduct disorders, substance abuse, obsessive-compulsive disorder, anxiety, and depression. It is important to sort out which, if any, of these problems are present and to understand and find ways to take control of these multiple challenges. This takes time and requires help from a professional who is experienced in working with adolescents and adults with AD/HD. Working with a number of professionals can help provide the medical, psychological, and educational interventions and supports that lead to success.

A Support System

College learning specialists report that students with AD/HD often have different educational needs from students with LD. Students with LD have gaps in basic academic or information processing skills. For example, a student may be a good reader but struggle with writing. Or a student may learn well when information is presented orally but not graphically. These students need educational interventions that help them compensate for their areas of weakness. In contrast, many students with AD/HD struggle with performance issues—in using what they know rather than dealing with gaps in what they know.

David Parker and Hane Byron, two postsecondary learning specialists, have developed some specialized approaches for students with AD/HD. In their book, *Rethinking AD/HD: A Guide for Fostering Success with AD/HD at the College Level*, they tell us that many students with AD/HD know what they need to do but can't get themselves to do it. These learning specialists report that it is often helpful for students with AD/HD to get help from a coach.

Professionals who work with individuals with AD/HD often act as coaches. In fact, the American Coaching Association is a national organization that provides information and guidance on coaching individuals with AD/HD. The supportive relationship is focused on the life areas of greatest concern to the individual with AD/HD. Students often work with coaches to get support in structuring their work through a semester, completing major assignments, and communicating with peers and teachers. Adults who are not in school might work with coaches on time and money management, organizational needs at home and work, and communication skills. Coaching often works best when combined with focused work sessions and follow-up contact. Once the coach and student have developed a plan on how to work through the task, then shorter check-in contacts are used. E-mail, voice mail, and phone conversations can provide the support and structure without the need for a lot of face-to-face meetings.

Some colleges have support groups for students with AD/HD. Once students feel comfortable talking about their AD/HD, sharing their difficulties with others who are in the same boat can naturally extend the support network.

Medication

Psychostimulants are the most widely used medication for the management of AD/HD symptoms. Between 70-80 percent of individuals with AD/HD find that their symptoms improve with the help of these medications. These medications decrease impulsivity and hyperactivity, increase attention and, in some people, decrease aggression. In over 50 years of use, stimulants have been given to hundreds of thousands of people with no evidence of significant harm or long-term risk.

In the United States, 90 percent of individuals who take medicine for AD/HD take Ritalin™. Other psychostimulants that may be prescribed include Dexedrine™ and Cylert™. Antidepressant medications, such as imipramine, are effective for between 60–80 percent of individuals with AD/HD. Lastly, Catapres™ (clonidine) is sometimes used to decrease hyperactivity and impulsivity, as well as improve attention span. This medication was originally developed to treat high blood pressure.

Graduation from high school often means that students must now take control of their medication. It is important to work with a doctor to schedule medication that supports your school or work schedule. Some students schedule themselves so they can take their medication before attending their most challenging classes. Students can also take medication just before study time. Many need to be careful not to take caffeine in the form of coffee, soft drinks, and chocolate with stimulant medication. This combination can cause feelings of jitteriness and irritation. Finding the right medication, class, study, and exercise schedule along with a healthy diet is a good start for post-secondary success. Table 2.3 *(below, continued on pages 36-37)* provides a guide for making your medications work for you.

TABLE 2.3—FAST FACTS FOR COLLEGE STUDENTS REGARDING MEDICATION FOR AD/HD

1. **Know the name of your medication and how it works.** Ritalin (methylphenidate) and Dexedrine or Adderall (amphetamines) are the most commonly prescribed medications for ADD/AD/HD. Ritalin and Dexedrine are available as either short-acting (usually 4 hours) and longer-acting (6-12 hours) preparations. Short-acting medications take effect in 20 minutes while long-acting medications may take up to an hour to be fully effective. Both medications work on correcting the neurobiochemistry of the brain thought to be the cause of the symptoms seen in AD/HD. These medications enhance brain receptor functioning, inhibit breakdown of certain neurotransmitters in the brain, and can themselves act as false transmitters.

2. **If you needed stimulant medication to concentrate in high school, you most likely will need medication to concentrate in college.** Stimulants are the treatment of choice for AD/HD. They increase concentration and focus while decreasing distractibility and impulsivity. Approximately 70 percent of individuals with AD/HD continue to have problems with attention throughout their life span.

3. **Stimulants improve cognitive functioning but you will still have to put in time studying and attending classes.** Taking medication before classes

(Continued on next page.)

TABLE 2.3—FACTS FOR COLLEGE STUDENTS . . . *(Continued)*

can help you concentrate and enhances information gathering. You can also use your medication dosage times to establish a schedule for studying. You should know how long your medication will be effective and therefore determine how much focused study time you have available. Set up a schedule for studying accordingly and stick to it.

Stimulants can also help you stay focused while you are reading and thus improve your reading comprehension. Students frequently report that they read all of the materials assigned, but have no clue as to what they have just read because they weren't paying attention. To solve this problem, be sure your stimulant medication is in effect while you are reading.

4. **AD/HD affects all aspects of life: social, home, athletics, and employment.** As you probably already know, you don't just need to concentrate and be focused in class. You also need to focus on what your friends are saying or instructions on the job. Focus and concentration are important in sports, whether you are playing tennis or catching a football. Often being distracted and/or acting impulsively can get you in trouble with your friends or—when you are driving—the law. Therefore, it is important for you to assess how much of the symptoms of your AD/HD affect your functioning, and to take your medication accordingly. Improved concentration may improve the quality of your life in many ways.

5. **It is important to take medications as prescribed for you by your physician. Don't self-medicate.** Many students have a mistaken notion that if one pill works well, two pills will work better. While this may be true for some other medications, that is not the case with stimulants. For them, there is something called the "window of efficacy." This term refers to the amount of medication that is the most effective for your particular brain chemistry. The amount of medication you need does not depend on body weight or on the severity of your symptoms, but rather on what works for you. That is why you may need to periodically reassess whether your medication is still functioning at optimum effectiveness.

Many students come to college on the same dose of medication that worked for them in elementary or high school. That's fine if that determination has been made after a recent, careful review of your needs and is demonstrated by the continued effectiveness of that particular dosage level.

6. **It is illegal to distribute (share) your prescription medication.** Stimulant medications are controlled substances. The law states that all medications

should be kept in their original container and labeled with your name, and name and dosage of the medication inside. It is important not to transfer your stimulant medication to another bottle for any reason.

It is against the law for you to distribute a controlled substance. This means not sharing your medication with a friend who needs to study for that big test or concentrate in class or a sport. Many students carry their medications with them at all times to avoid leaving them unattended in their rooms, where they may be more accessible to others.

7. **Drugs and alcohol do not mix with stimulants.** Your AD/HD is caused by a chemical imbalance in your brain. You are taking stimulant medication to try to correct that imbalance. If you use other drugs such as marijuana that also affect brain dopamine, you wreak havoc with an already imbalanced system. Your medications will not be as effective and your functioning will be more impaired. Taking stimulants also affects the metabolism of alcohol in the body, and can result in higher blood alcohol levels, thus increasing the risk of alcohol poisoning. Mixing cocaine and stimulants can kill!

8. **Checkups are important. Check in with the health center on campus when you arrive and monthly after that.** As a controlled substance, stimulant prescriptions need to be refilled monthly. When you arrive on campus, it is important for you to visit the health center and set up a mechanism to receive your medication prescriptions regularly. If you depend on other systems, they may break down at some point and you may be left without medication. This usually occurs at critical times such as while studying for finals or during exams. It is also important for the staff to become familiar with you, so that if questions arise about dose or side effects, they can be answered more readily. You can also have your weight checked monthly, to make sure that you are getting enough calories and not losing weight, because you are not hungry or forget to eat.

9. **See your primary physician at least once a year for an examination and blood tests if necessary.** As with all chronic conditions and medications that are taken routinely, it is important to have a regular checkup. Blood tests that assess liver functioning are important if you are on certain medications. Your physician back home is likely the one that diagnosed your AD/HD and knows you the best. Be sure you check in with him or her from time to time to assess how things are going.

These facts are taken from RE-THINKING AD/HD: A Guide for Fostering Success in Students with AD/HD at the College Level, *edited by Patricia Quinn and Anne McCormick, Advantage Books (888-238-8588), Bethesda, MD, 1998. These three pages may be reproduced for personal use.*

Positives to AD/HD

Yes . . . there *are* positives to having AD/HD. When the challenges of AD/HD are managed, then the strengths and resources associated with AD/HD can be enjoyed and used to their fullest. M. Susan Roberts and Gerard J. Jansen have identified the following positive AD/HD characteristics in their book *Living with AD/HD: A Workbook for Adults with Attention Deficit Disorder.* Think about which ones might apply to you.

- **Creativity** - This can take the form of flexible thinking, great brainstorming abilities, and abstract thinking. Creativity can be expressed in many different ways such as music, conversation, art, design.

- **Sense of humor**—If you have a good sense of humor, you can see things in unusual and interesting ways. It also means that you 'get' jokes. Humor can be an invaluable coping skill.

- **Lack of inhibition**—If you are not inhibited, you may blurt out thoughts or do things that others might think twice about and repress. Although uninhibited behavior can cause problems when unregulated, it also opens up new experiences. Trying new things, meeting interesting people, and asking questions that others may be unwilling to ask can make life more interesting.

- **High-energy level**—Energy focused on a worthwhile end can be a real strength. Not everyone can put in the long hours it takes to begin a business, juggle two jobs, or get the job done on a tight timeline—but many individuals with AD/HD can.

- **Ability to hyperfocus**—Hyperfocusing means that you are able to give your entire attention to a topic or activity that you find interesting. Hyperfocusing can be pleasurable and productive.

- **Willingness to take risks**—The inclination to jump into an activity rather than sit on the sidelines can help you get new ideas off the ground. It can also help you take action even when you feel unsure.

- **Other strengths**—Other strengths professionals have often observed when working with individuals with AD/HD include resourcefulness, loyalty, tenacity, forgiveness, and the ability to see through a facade.

Conclusion

Although young people with AD/HD often face challenges when preparing for life after high school, they can also be highly successful. Some keys to making the transition to a fulfilling adulthood include:

- Know the strengths and weaknesses that go along with your own AD/HD.

- Develop the support network needed to be successful.

- Learn about options and seek out the assistance available.

The rest of the book offers many practical strategies to help you achieve these important goals.

Resources

BOOKS

ADD and Adults - Strategies for Success from CH.A.D.D., 1999
CHADD
8181 Professional Place, Suite 201
Landover, MD 20785
Phone: (800) 233-4050
Fax: (301) 306-7090
E-mail: national@chadd.org
http://www.chadd.org/doe/doe_ld.htm

ADD and the College Student: A Guide for High School and College Students with Attention Deficit Disorder, 1994
Editor: Patricia O. Quinn, MD
Magination Press/American Psychological Association
750 First Street, NE
Washington, DC 20002
Phone: (800) 374-2721, x 5510
Fax: (202) 336-5502
E-mail: books@apa.org
http://www.maginationpress.com

ADD Success Stories, 1995
Author: Thom Hartmann
Underwood Books
P.O. Box # 1609
Grass Valley, CA 95945
Fax: (530) 274-7179
E-mail: 76702.2425@compuserve.com
http://www.underwoodbooks.com

ADHD and the Nature of Self-control, *1997*
Author: Russell A. Barkley
Guilford Press
72 Spring Street
New York, NY 10012
Phone: (800) 365-7006
Fax: (212) 966-6708
E-mail: info@guilford.com
http://www.guilford.com

ADHD & Teens: A Parent's Guide to Making It through the Tough Years, 1995
Authors: Colleen Alexander-Roberts and Paul Elliott
Taylor Publishing Company
1550 Mockingbird Lane
Dallas, TX 75235
Phone: (800) 677-2800
Fax: (214) 819-8580
http://www.taylor.com

Adolescents and ADD: Gaining the Advantage, 1995
Author: Dr. Patricia Quinn
Magination Press/American Psychological Association
750 First Street, NE
Washington, DC 20002
Phone: (800) 374-2721, x 5510
Fax: (202) 336-5502
E-mail: books@apa.org
http://www.maginationpress.com

Attention Deficit Disorder: A Different Perception, 1997
Author: Thom Hartmann
Underwood Books

P.O. Box # 1609
Grass Valley, CA 95945
Fax: (530) 274-7179
E-mail: 76702.2425@compuserve.com
http://www.underwoodbooks.com

Attention-Deficit Hyperactivity Disorder in Adults, 1998
Author: Paul Wender
Oxford University Press
2001 Evans Road
Cary, NC 27513
Phone: (800) 451-7556
Fax: (917) 677-1303
http://www.oup-usa.org/order/index.htm

A Comprehensive Guide to Attention Deficit Disorder in Adults, 1995
Author: Kathleen Nadeau
Tayor and Francis/Brunner-Mazel Publishers
47 Runway Road
Levittown, PA 19057
Phone: (800) 821-8312
Fax: (215) 785-5515
http://www.bmpub.com/fager/index.htm

Diagnostic and Statistical Manual of Mental Disorders, 4th edition,1994
American Psychiatric Association
1400 K. St., NW
11th Floor
Washington, DC 20005
Phone: (800) 368-5777
Fax: (202) 682-6850
E-mail: csdept@appi.org
http://www.appi.org

Driven to Distraction: Recognizing and Coping with Attention Deficit Disorder from Childhood through Adulthood, 1994
Authors: Edward M. Hallowell and John J. Ratey
Touchstone/Simon & Schuster
200 Old Tappan Road
Old Tappan, NJ 07675
Phone: (800) 223-2336

Fax: (800) 445-6991
http://www.simonsays.com

Dr. Larry Silver's Advice to Parents on Attention-Deficit Hyperactivity Disorder, 1999
Author: Dr. Larry Silver
Times Books
201 E. 50th St.
New York, NY 10022
Phone: (800) 733-3000
Fax: (212) 572-4949

Living with ADD: A Workbook for Adults with Attention Deficit Disorder
Authors: Susan Roberts and Gerard J. Jansen
New Harbinger Publications
5674 Shattuck Avenue
Oakland, CA 94609-1662
Phone: (510) 652-0215
E-mail: nhhelp@newharbinger.com
http://www.readersndex.com/imprint/000002h/imprint.html

Making the Grade: An Adolescent's Struggle with ADD, 1992
Authors: Harvey Parker and Roberta Parker
Specialty Press/ADD Warehouse
300 NW 70th Avenue, # 102
Plantation, FL 33317
Phone: (800) 233-9273
Fax: (954) 792-8545
E-mail: sales@addwarehouse.com
http://www.addwarehouse.com

Re-thinking ADHD: A Guide for Fostering Success in Students with ADHD at the College Level, 1999
Authors: Patricia Quinn and Anne McCormick
Advantage Books
4400 East-West Highway, # 816
Bethesda, MD 20814
Phone: (888) 238-8588

Succeeding in College with Attention Deficit Disorders: Issues & Strategies for Students, Counselors, & Educators, 1996
Author: Jennifer Bramer

Specialty Press/ADD Warehouse
300 NW 70th Avenue, # 102
Plantation, FL 33317
Phone: (800) 233-9273
Fax: (954) 792-8545
E-mail: sales@addwarehouse.com

Teenagers with ADD: A Parents' Guide, 1995
Author: Chris Zeigler Dendy
Woodbine House
6510 Bells Mill Road
Bethesda, MD 20817
Phone: (800) 843-7323
Fax: (301) 897-5838
E-mail: info@woodbinehouse.com
http://www.woodbinehouse.com

Think Fast! The ADD Experience, 1996
Authors: Thom Hartmann and Janie Bowman
Underwood Books
P.O. Box #1609
Grass Valley, CA 95945
Fax: (530) 274-7179
E-mail: 76702.2425@compuserve.com
http://www.underwoodbooks.com

You Mean I'm Not Lazy, Stupid or Crazy?! (Adults and ADD), 1996
Authors: Kate Kelly and Peggy Ramundo
Simon & Schuster
200 Old Tappan Road
Old Tappan, NJ 07675
Phone: (800) 223-2336
Fax: (800) 445-6991
www.simonsays.com

FACT SHEETS
ABC's of LD/ADD, 1998
Publisher: LDOnline http://www.ldonline.org/abcs_info/articles-info.html

ADD: The Race Inside My Head
George Washington University

Association on Higher Education and Disability (AHEAD)
P.O. Box 21192
Columbus, OH, 43221-0192
Phone: (614) 488-4972
Fax: (614) 488-1174
E-mail: ahead@postbox.acs.ohio-state.edu
http://www.ahead.org

ADHD: Building Academic Success, 1995
Author: Gregg Soleil
Publishers: Appalachian Educational Laboratory, Inc.
P.O. Box 1348
Charleston, WV 25325
Phone: (800) 624-9120
Fax: (304) 347-0487
E-mail: aelinfo@ael.org
http://www.ael.org/index

ADHD: Legal Responsibilities for Schools, 1994
Publisher: Appalachian Educational Laboratory
See above for address.

Attention Deficit Disorder: Adding Up the Facts, 1994
Department of Education
600 Independence Avenue, SW
Washington, DC
Phone: (800) 424-1616
Fax: (301) 470-1244
http://www.ed.gov

Attention Deficit Hyperactivity Disorder: National Institute of Mental Health Decade of the Brain, 1998
NIMH Public Inquiries
6001 Executive Blvd.
Room 8184 MSC 9663
Bethesda, MD 20892-9663
Fax: (301) 443-4279
Email: nimhinfo@nih.gov
http://www.nimh.nih.gov/publist

Series: Children and Adults with Attention Deficit/Hyperactivity Disorder, CHADD

FACT 1-The Disability Named ADD

FACT 2-Parenting a Child with ADD

FACT 3-Medical Management of Attention Deficit Disorders

FACT 4-Educational Rights for Children with ADD

FACT 5-Attention Deficit Disorders: An Educator's Guide

FACT 6-Controversial Treatments for Children with ADD

FACT 7-Attention Deficit Disorders—Not Just for Children

FACT 8-All about CH.A.D.D

FACT 9-Attention Deficit Disorder Predominantly Inattentive Type

Children and Adults with Attention Deficit/Hyperactivity Disorder, CHADD

8181 Professional Place, Suite 201

Landover, MD 20785

Phone: (800) 233-4050

Fax: (301) 306-7090

E-mail: national@chadd.org

http://www.chadd.org

LISTSERV

Adults with Attention Deficit Disorders

Send subscription request to: ADDULT@SJUVM.STJOHNS.EDU

WEBSITES

ADD and Challenged Individuals

An informative site with additional links for persons with ADD or ADHD.

http://www.concentric.net/~skiplac/challeng.html

American Coaching Association

This site has information on the benefits of coaching and information on locating a coach or becoming trained as one.

http://www.americoach.com

Internet Special Education Resources

This site is a directory of professionals serving persons with disabilities for students, parents, and professionals.

http://www.iser.com

Kennedy Krieger Institute

Provides information concerning patient care, education, and research on disabilities.

http://www.kennedykrieger.org

One A.D.D. Place: The Attention Deficit Disorder Community Hub
This site has numerous links for ADD and ADHD: information, resources, treatment, and legislation.
http://www./oneaddplace.com

Resources on ADD
An informative web page on AD/HD.
http://aace.virginia.edu/curry/dept/cise/ose/categories/add.html

Businesses, Organizations, and Government Offices
Contact information for the following useful organizations can be found beginning on page 347.

- American Coaching Association

- American Psychiatric Association

- Association on Higher Education and Disability (AHEAD)

- Center for Mental Health Services

- Office of Consumer, Family, and Public Information

- Children and Adults with Attention-Deficit/Hyperactivity Disorder (CHADD)

- Clearinghouse on Disability Information

- Council for Exceptional Children

- ERIC Clearinghouse on Disability & Gifted Education

- Higher Education and the Handicapped - HEATH Resource Center

- Internet Special Education Resources

- National Association of School Psychologists

- National Attention Deficit Disorder Association (National ADDA)

- National Parent Network on Disabilities

- NICHCY (National Information Center for Children and Youth with Disabilities)

- NIMH Public Inquiries

- YMCA of the USA

3

THE LEGISLATION AND TRANSITION FROM HIGH SCHOOL

What You Need to Know

IN THIS CHAPTER:

- The Individuals with Disabilities Education Act (IDEA)
- Section 504 of the Rehabilitation Act (Workforce Investment Act)
- Americans with Disabilities Act (ADA)

Carol A. Kochhar-Bryant

This chapter provides a summary of three laws that can help you make a successful transition to postsecondary education and employment:

1. the Individuals with Disabilities Education Act (IDEA),

2. Section 504 of the Rehabilitation Act of 1973,

3. and the Americans with Disabilities Act (ADA).

While you are in high school, you will ideally work together with your parents and teachers to understand how these laws apply to you and to make sure their provisions are used to your advantage. Once you leave high school, however, it will be largely up to you to ensure that schools and other agencies are providing the rights, protections, and benefits you are entitled to under the law. It is essential for you to understand the basics of these laws so that you know which services you are entitled to receive from school and community agencies, as well as how to obtain them.

The Individuals with Disabilities Education Act (IDEA)

The Individuals with Disabilities Education Act (Public Law 105-17) guarantees all students with disabilities under the age of 22 a free, appropriate public education. IDEA defines a free, appropriate public education as an education that:

- is free—provided at no cost to students or their parents;

- is appropriate—meaning that it benefits the student and meets his specific educational needs; and

- includes preschool, elementary school, or secondary school education.

Under IDEA, a free, appropriate education includes:

- special education—specially designed instruction, at no cost to parents, to meet the unique needs of a child with a disability;

- related services—services that support the development of a student with a disability or enable him to benefit from his education or to be identified as having a disability. Examples of related services include speech-language therapy, physical or occupational therapy, counseling services, rehabilitation counseling, and diagnostic medical services.

The law is written to ensure that special education and related services are provided *in addition to the general education curriculum*, not separate from it.

Who is Eligible?

To be eligible to receive special education, a student must be found to have one of the thirteen qualifying disabilities listed in IDEA. Students with learning disabilities most often qualify under the label of "specific learning disabilities." Students with AD/HD can receive services under the category of "other health impaired" if their AD/HD significantly affects their ability to perform academically at school.

To determine whether you have one of these qualifying disabilities, you must be evaluated by a team of professionals. This evaluation is provided free of charge by the school district, and usually includes:

1. review of existing evaluation information about you as a student;

2. information provided by your parents;

3. new evaluations and observations completed by your teachers or related service providers, if necessary.

Once the evaluation is complete, your results are compared with the criteria used by your school district to determine whether a learning disability or AD/HD is present.

The evaluation process can be set in motion at any time during your elementary or high school years. You or your parents may request an evaluation through your classroom teacher or a special education coordinator or consultant in the school. Your parents may call or write the school and request an evaluation.

The Individualized Education Program (IEP)

If you are found eligible for special education, a team will meet to develop an individualized education program (IEP) for you. The IEP document developed will serve as a roadmap for your education. It:

- Identifies your strengths, needs, and skill areas to be addressed (based on recent evaluations, observations, and input from you, your parents, and school personnel).

- Defines measurable annual goals (i.e., what you can reasonably achieve in a year), and short-term objectives, to help you reach those goals.

- Lists services that will be provided by the school to help you meet your goals and objectives (see below).

- Lists modifications (accommodations) that will be made to instructional methods, the classroom, or materials to help you succeed (see below).

- Explains how you will be involved in the general education curriculum, non-academic, and extracurricular activities. Under IDEA, all students are required to be educated in the "least restrictive environment" (LRE). This means the classroom where they will have the maximum contact with typically developing students and the regular education curriculum while still being able to meet their goals. For students with LD and/or AD/HD, the LRE is often the regular classroom, with or without some time spent in a resource room to work on especially problematic goals.

- Describes how district and state assessments of achievement will be modified to enable you to participate in these assessments.

- Helps you, your parents, and your team to determine your progress toward your individualized goals. This is done by identifying your levels of performance in academic, social, vocational, and other areas.

- Explains how the school will regularly inform your parents about your progress toward your annual IEP goals.

Once you reach the age of 14, your IEP must also include an Individualized Transition Plan (ITP) to help you prepare for life after high school. The ITP documents how your disability affects your involvement and progress in the general curriculum and in relevant career-vocational and community-based experiences. It also lists the resources the IEP team decides are necessary to enable you to receive needed transition services and supports. See the section below on "The Individualized Transition Plan" for more information.

The IEP Meeting

The participants in your meeting should include your parents, teachers, transition services personnel, and other individuals who know you and work with you. If you are participating in general education classes, your IEP team must include at least one of your general education teachers. In addition, representatives that have traditionally provided post high school services should be involved in transition planning as part of your IEP meeting. You and your parents may bring other people to the meeting who can be helpful in providing information (e.g., friends, neighbors, or specialists).

Remember that the IEP meeting is a way for you, your parents, and school personnel to communicate. The IEP meeting is about you and your future. You should have a say in what is planned for you and you should help evaluate how well your school program fits your desires and needs.

You and your parents have a right to a copy of your IEP. You and your parents should also be informed that your family can appeal the team's decisions if they disagree. The IEP process first allows your family and the team to resolve any differences in viewpoints through discussions. If the team cannot make a decision you and your family agree with, then there are *due process* procedures that allow you get opinions beyond your IEP/ITP team. *Due process* means that the school has to follow a procedure that brings other people into the disagreement between you and the school. In addition, the school must offer you and your parents the option to go to mediation to try to resolve differences.

Services and Accommodations

During your IEP meeting, team members may decide that you need modifications, supplementary services, or related services to help you achieve your goals.

Modifications. Modifications are changes in school or classroom routines that can help you learn. Some common accommodations are: simplifying instruction, using alternative texts, using visual tools and computer instruction, providing special seating arrangements, and modifying tests. Many more examples are described in Chapter 9.

Supplementary Aids and Services. Supplementary services are provided to help you do your best and succeed within the general education classroom, to participate in extracurricular activities, and to be educated and participate with other students (with and without disabilities). They do not necessarily modify, but supplement or add to the regular classroom routines. For example, an in-class teacher assistant can work with you to help you learn study skills or how to organize your books and materials so you can complete an assignment or project. Or a work-study teacher may help you with time management skills and work behaviors on the job.

Related Services. Related services provide assistance you need to help you meet your IEP goals and benefit from your education. They may be provided for you within your school or by an agency outside your school. Examples of related services that students with LD or AD/HD might need include:

1. speech-language and audiology services, if there are related communication or hearing difficulties;

2. counseling services, including rehabilitation counseling, if the student needs counseling to adjust to the classroom or work setting;

3. medical services for diagnostic and evaluation purposes;

4. social work services, if there are family problems that contribute to difficulties at school;

5. psychological services, if there is a need for behavioral support services.

The professionals who provide related services are often part of the IEP team when the service they provide is being discussed.

The Individualized Transition Plan (ITP)

As mentioned above, your IEP must include a plan to help you prepare for life after high school starting when you are 14. This part of the IEP is known as the Individualized Transition Plan (ITP). By the time you are 14, your IEP must plan for your "course of study" as it relates to the transition to adult life. Depending on your interests and abilities, this could be participation in advanced placement courses, a vocational education program, or standard high school courses. The purpose of this requirement is to focus attention on how your secondary school program can be planned to help you make a successful transition to life after secondary school.

At age 16, the ITP must include a plan of specific transition services to assist you to achieve your transition goals and to adjust to life after secondary school. Transition services are defined as a coordinated set of activities to help you leave high school prepared to be a successful adult. These coordinated activities should be based on your individual needs and take into account your skills and interests.

Career-vocational and transition services can include any of the following:

- vocational-technical education—specially designed instruction that meets your individual needs, is provided at no cost to your parents, and is an organized educational program offering a sequence of courses that directly prepares you for paid or unpaid employment. Schools often organize vocational-technical programs into these areas:

- agricultural education (e.g., welding technology);

- marketing and cooperative education (e.g., business management and ownership);

- occupation, family, and consumer services (e.g., early childhood care provider or culinary arts);

- trade and industrial/technology education (e.g., auto technology and electronics),

- health education (e.g., medical assistant);

- business education (e.g., office technology);

- applied technology education (e.g., computer aide, multimedia technology, drafting and design, laser/photonics);

- community-based work experience;

- instruction in daily living skills; and

- vocational assessment and evaluation

Vocational education planning can be coordinated with special education and rehabilitation agencies and must be consistent with your IEP/ITP. Your career-vocational teachers should be involved in your IEP/ITP development and review. By age 14, you should begin the process of career counseling and vocational assessment. This will enable you to have the information, experiences, and courses that will help support your decisions about what you will do after high school.

Prior to the eleventh grade, or as early as ninth grade if necessary, career exploration and counseling should be provided if you need additional time for pre-employment training, or are experiencing particular difficulties in your school program. These services may be very helpful if you think you are interested in identifying, selecting, or reconsidering your interests, goals, and career majors. Your needs for career-vocational education services—with or without modifications—should be included in your IEP/ITP.

Receiving Transition Services from Non-school Agencies

A recent change to IDEA is that many non-school agencies are now required to provide services to support your transition from school to postsecondary education and employment. For example, if you need transition support services, they may be provided by vocational rehabilitation agencies, employment services, Job Training Reform Act programs, School-to-Work Opportunities Act programs, Workforce Investment Act programs, supported employment projects, or Projects with Industry.

Your IEP/ITP should contain a statement of interagency responsibilities or any "linkages"—relationships between your school and community agencies that are required to ensure that you receive the transition services you need. In addition, your IEP/ITP coordinator must invite representatives from those agencies to attend the meetings. This new requirement for interagency collaboration and shared responsibility means that:

- Schools must develop a seamless system of supports, if needed, to assist you in making a successful transition to postsecondary life.

- You and your family should participate in transition planning well before graduation.

- There must be formal interagency agreements between schools and cooperating agencies.

Reaching the Age of Majority

IDEA includes a procedure for transferring parental rights to the student when he or she reaches the "age of majority." This age differs from state to state, but is typically age 18. Under this provision, one year before you reach the age of majority, the IEP/ITP must include a statement that you have been informed of the rights that transfer to you when you reach the age of majority. These include:

- the right to provide informed consent for services or an educational program;

- the right to decide your own post-school goals and objectives;

- the right to make your own plans for the future.

This transfer of rights is an enormous step toward your independence and your participation in the decision making for your education and future planning. You may want to ask your teachers for more information to help you understand and take on this responsibility.

What Can You Expect after High School?

Once you graduate from high school, IDEA will no longer cover you. You will not be eligible for services provided by the school system and will not have an IEP/ITP. However, if you have been receiving career or vocational services from Rehabilitation Services as part of your transition plan, you can continue to receive them. You will have an Individual Written Rehabilitation Plan (IWRP) and may be eligible for services such as employment assistance, postsecondary education, counseling, and vocational evaluation and assessment. And assuming you have reached the age of majority, Rehabilitation Services (and any other service agency) will now deal directly with you, rather than your parents. See the section on "504 Protections Beyond High School" on page 57 for more information about IWRPs.

After you "age out" of IDEA, you are still covered by Section 504 of the Rehabilitation Act and the Americans with Disabilities Act (see below). It is especially important to learn what protections they offer you as you prepare to embark on postsecondary education or employment.

Section 504 of the Rehabilitation Act (Workforce Investment Act)

Before passage of IDEA, Section 504 of the Rehabilitation Act of 1973 established many important rights for students with disabilities. Today, it still provides important protections for high school students who are not covered by IDEA, as well as students with disabilities in colleges, universities, technical schools, and other postsecondary programs.

Section 504 is a nondiscrimination clause in the Rehabilitation Act that states:

No otherwise qualified individual with disabilities . . . shall solely by reasons of his disability, be excluded from the participation in, be denied the benefits of, or be subjected to discrimination under any program or activity receiving Federal financial assistance.

Although the Rehabilitation Act does not provide funds for states to provide education for students with disabilities (as IDEA does), the law does make it illegal for any program receiving federal funding to discriminate against any student on the basis of disability. This means that educational institutions must be prepared to make accommodations and adaptations (such as extended time to take tests) so that students with disabilities are able to participate fully in all activities.

Eligibility

Section 504 applies to individuals of all ages who have, or have a record of having, "physical or mental impairments which substantially limit one or more of the major life activities." The major life activities include caring for one's self, performing manual tasks, walking, seeing, hearing, speaking, breathing, learning, and working. Since "learning" is a major life activity, students with LD and AD/HD are covered under the Act.

504 Plans

Sometimes students with learning disabilities or AD/HD are not affected significantly enough by their disability to qualify under IDEA's stringent eligibility guidelines. And yet they still struggle with academics or behavior due to the effects of their disability. Often these students can qualify for Section 504 protection instead. Every school system must have a written procedure for determining which students are eligible under Section 504.

If you qualify under 504, but not IDEA, then you can have a 504 plan developed instead of an IEP. This plan should detail the adaptations that will be made to help you succeed at school. Often 504 plans include fairly minor accommodations for students, such as being able to take short breaks during class, sitting in the front of the room, receiving extended time to take tests, or using a computer instead of writing by hand. Under Section 504, all accommodations provided must be "reasonable." This means that they can be provided without placing an "undue financial and administrative burden" on the school system and are necessary for a student to benefit from his education.

Every school system is supposed to have a 504 Coordinator on staff to answer questions and concerns from families and assist in developing 504 plans. Some individual schools have 504 Coordinators to assist students.

As with IEPs, students are no longer eligible for 504 plans after graduation from high school. They still qualify for 504 protections, however, as discussed in the next section.

504 Protections Beyond High School

In 1997, amendments to the Rehabilitation Act strengthened and clarified the Act's role in supporting people with disabilities during their transition to adult life.

First, the amendments require that, during your final two years of high school, you receive information about available services and providers that can help you make the transition to employment or college. Rehabilitation services such as early assessment for eligibility for services, vocational assessments, and counseling in work behaviors are now available to you in your final years of high school, and after graduation. If you have not been referred to vocational rehabilitation before graduation, then you may be referred upon graduation to be assessed for eligibility and assistance with employment or postsecondary education.

Second, the amendments clarify that colleges, universities, and other educational institutions that receive government funding must comply with Section 504 of the Rehabilitation Act. This means that students with LD and/or AD/HD are entitled to accommodations to help them succeed in a postsecondary program. Chapters 9 and 10 describe accommodations that are frequently used in these settings. Students who qualify for 504 protections are responsible for making their disability known and for asking for the accommodations they need.

Third, the 1997 Amendments strengthened the role of rehabilitation agencies in providing services to help students make the transition to employment. The State Vocational Rehabilitation unit must create and annually update a plan to work with students with disabilities transitioning from high school—whether or not they have an IEP or a 504 plan. This plan must be developed in cooperation with the secondary school. This provision links the IEP and the Individual Written Rehabilitation Plan (IWRP) in accomplishing rehabilitation goals prior to high school graduation. IWRP's are plans that describe services you will receive that are supported by vocational rehabilitation.

Vocational rehabilitation can provide funds for eligible students with LD and AD/HD to attend postsecondary education or technical education programs. However, under the 1997 Amendments, the emphasis is on rehabilitation services for individuals with more significant physical and cognitive disabilities. The kinds of services that might be provided for students with AD/HD and LD include vocational assessment, job placement assistance, job coaching, and sometimes tuition support for postsecondary technical training.

Americans with Disabilities Act (ADA)

The Americans with Disabilities Act of 1990 (ADA, Public Law 101-336) prohibits discrimination against people with disabilities, including individuals with LD and/or AD/HD. This law requires public and private institutions to make accommodations for persons with disabilities in the areas of education, employment, transportation, public accommodations, state and local governments, and telecommunications.

In high school, the ADA requires that schools provide reasonable accommodations to students with disabilities—much as Section 504 does. In contrast to Section 504, however, ADA does not just apply to schools receiving federal funding. Even private schools that receive no federal funds cannot deny reasonable accommodations to students with disabilities (although they do not have to provide special education programs). In addition, ADA requires that accommodations be provided to students with disabilities in public and private postsecondary schools—colleges and universities, postsecondary vocational-technical schools, employer-based training programs, and other private training programs. (Previously, under Section 504, postsecondary schools only had to provide accommodations if they were receiving federal funding.)

Eligibility

Anyone with a "qualified" disability is protected by the ADA. The term disability refers to an individual who:

1. has a physical or mental impairment that substantially limits one or more of the major life activities;

2. has a record (history) of such impairment; or

3. is regarded by others as having a disability.

ADA Protections in Postsecondary Education

ADA prohibits discrimination against students with disabilities in the application process and in their education programs once they are admitted. Although you still need to meet entrance criteria such as test scores and GPA, your disability cannot be used as a reason for denying you admittance to a school.

Once you are admitted to a school, you may request reasonable accommodations to help you participate in courses, exams, and other activities. Your school will probably want you to provide diagnostic proof that these accommodations are needed, such as a letter from your doctor or an evaluation report.

In most colleges and universities, students apply for and receive support services from a department or office with a title such as *disability support services*. Students who qualify for accommodations are not given an IEP or 504 plan. Instead, most students communicate with their instructors on their own to get the accommodations they need. For example, here is how one college student with LD describes the accommodations he has worked out:

> *Professors have provided me with extra feedback on my writing, have allowed me extensions of time when taking tests, and have allowed me to tape record lectures to compensate for missed information. Professors and students have withheld their pre-judgements and given me the same opportunities as all students have to participate, speak in front of the class, and complete all projects and assignments.*

Chapter 9 lists many other types of accommodations available under both Section 504 and ADA.

There are also a few types of accommodations not generally supported by ADA. These include:

- Changes in the type of exams required for courses: For example, a degree program may mostly require multiple choice tests. Requesting an essay exam may be viewed as changing the essential way the field of study wants students to store and demonstrate information.

- Requesting extended time for practical exercises (such as giving a physical exam): This may not be allowed since completing a task in a specified amount of time may be an essential skill that cannot be modified.

Colleges have much more flexibility in complying with ADA requirements than secondary schools have in complying with IDEA. This means that they are not required to give you exactly what you ask for if they can accommodate you some other way.

The ADA and Employment

If you are working your way through school or finished with your formal education, the ADA can help you with finding and keeping a job. Employers who have 15 or more employees are prohibited from discriminating against workers with disabilities. The ADA says:

- Employers may not discriminate against qualified individuals with a disability when hiring and promoting employees. This means that if you have the skills and experiences needed for the job, employers cannot use your disability as a reason for not hiring you.

- Employers can ask you about your skills to perform a job, but they cannot ask you whether you have a disability or test you to see if you have a disability.

- Employers need to offer reasonable accommodations if you need them. This could include restructuring a job to match your strengths. It could also include getting you equipment or other aids to help you do the job.

- Employers do not need to provide accommodations that are an "undue hardship" for them. An undue hardship means taking an action that may be very expensive or difficult to do.

Conclusion

Successful transition is a process that requires you to actively participate in planning for your future. Knowing about your legal rights to education and employment opportunities is therefore essential to your transition from high school to adulthood. The three most important laws for you to know about are IDEA, Section 504 of the Rehabilitation Act, and the ADA. These laws can be the key to helping you reach your education and employment goals.

Resources

BOOKS

Accommodations in Higher Education under the Americans with Disabilities Act, 1999
Editors: Michael Gordon and Shelby Keiser
Guilford Press
72 Spring Street
New York, NY 10012
Phone: (800) 365-7006
Fax: (212) 966-6708
Email: info@guilford.com
http://www.guilford.com

Free Appropriate Public Education: The Law and Children with Disabilities, 4th edition, 1993
Author: H. Rutherford Turnbull III
Love Publishing Company
9101 E. Kenyon Avenue, Suite # 2200
Denver, CO 80237
Phone: (303) 221-7333
Fax: (303) 221-7444
E-mail: LovePublishing@compuserve.com

The Law
Office of Special Education and Rehabilitative Services (OSERS)
U.S. Department of Education,
400 Maryland Avenue, SW
Washington, DC 20202-0498
Phone: (800) USA-LEARN
E-mail: CustomerService@inet.ed.gov
http://www.ed.gov/offices/OSERS/IDEA

The Law and Special Education, 1997
Author: Mitchell Yell
Prentice-Hall Publishers
P.O. Box 11071
Des Moines, IA 50336
Phone: (800) 947-7700
http://www.viacom.com

Negotiating the Special Education Maze: A Guide for Parents and Teachers, 1997
Authors: Winifred Anderson, Stephen Chitwood, and Deidre Hayden
Woodbine House
6510 Bells Mill Road
Bethesda, MD 20817
Phone: (800) 843-7323
Fax: (301) 897-5838
Email: info@woodbinehouse.com
http://www.woodbine.com

Special Education Law, 1995
Author: Laura F. Rothstein
Addison-Wesley
1185 Avenue of the Americas
New York, NY 10036
Fax: (800) 284-8292
E-mail: exam@aol.com

Student Access—A Resource Guide for Educators: Section 504 of the Rehabilitation Act of 1973
CEC's Council of Administrators of Special Education
1920 Association Drive
Reston, VA 22091
Phone: (800) CEC-SPED

Fax: (703) 620-3660

http://www.cec.sped.org

Summary of Existing Legislation Affecting People with Disabilities

Office of Special Education and Rehabilitation

Education Publications

P.O. Box # 1398

Jessup, MD 20794-1398

Phone: (877) 433-7827

Fax: (301) 470-1244

http://www.ed.gov/pubs/edpubs.html

PAMPHLETS

Disability Law Highlights

N. Neal Pike Institute on Law and Disability

Boston University School of Law

Email: pikeinst@bu.edu

http://www.bu.edu/pike/highlights/highlights.html

Learning about the Americans with Disabilities Act and Title II

The Arc

500 E. Border St., Ste. 300

P.O. Box 1047

Arlington, TX 76010

Phone: (800) 433-5255

Fax: (817) 277-3491

http://www.TheArc.org/welcome.html

E-mail: thearc@metronet.com

A Primer on IDEA 1997 and Its Regulations

LDOnline

http://www.ldonline.org/ld_indepth/special_
education/cec_idea_primer.html

To Tell or Not To Tell: Self-identification, Self-advocacy, and Civil Rights in Employment and Postsecondary Education, 1996

Author: Glenn Young

LDOnline

http://www.ldonline.org/ld_indepth/adult/index.html

WEBSITES

Americans with Disabilities Act Home Page

U.S. Department of Justice

An explanatory website that also has government and organization links.

http://www.usdoj.gov/crt/ada/adahom1.htm

Council of Parent Attorneys and Advocates

This association's website offers wonderful
legal, emotional, and informative resources, as well as links to state organizations that also promote advocacy for persons with disabilities and their families.

http://www.copaa.net

Disability Rights Education Defense Fund

With legal summaries and notices, this site is an asset for persons with disabilities and their families.

http://www.dredf.org

Federal Resource Center for Special Education

This site has information concerning special education technical assistance programs, as well as publications, links, and disability information.

http://www.dssc.org/frc/index.htm

FedWorld

U.S. Government Network

National Technical Information Service (NTIS)

E-mail: helpdesk@fedworld.gov

http://www.fedworld.gov

Individuals with Disabilities Education Act, Amendments of 1997 (IDEA)

This site is run by the U.S. Department of Education, and includes information as well as links.

http://www.ed.gov/offices/OSERS/IDEA

National Association of Protection and Advocacy Systems

This national association, which represents state programs that are federally mandated to protect the rights of persons with disabilities, provides information concerning legal issues, technical assistance, advocacy, and training programs, as well as links to other helpful sites.

http://www.protectionandadvocacy.com

National Health Law Program
This site provides legal information concerning federal and state health-oriented legislative issues.
http://www.healthlaw.org

Thomas: Legislative Information on the Internet
Brought to the public by the Library of Congress. It has links to all branches of government (judicial, legislative, and executive) in addition to good summaries of pertinent issues.
http://thomas.loc.gov

GOVERNMENT ASSISTANCE CENTERS
ADA Mediation Program
U.S. Department of Justice
950 Pennsylvania Ave., NW
Washington, DC 20530
Phone: (800) 514-0301
http://www.usdoj.gov/crt/ada/mediate.htm

ADA Technical Assistance Program
U.S. Department of Justice
950 Pennsylvania Ave., NW
Washington, DC 20530
Phone: (800) 514-0301
http://www.usdoj.gov/crt/ada/taprog.htm

Americans with Disabilities Information Line
U.S. Department of Justice
950 Pennsylvania Ave., NW
Washington, DC 20530
Phone: (800) 514-0301
http://www.usdoj.gov/crt/ada/infoline.htm

Clearinghouse on Adult Education
Division of Adult Education
Office of Vocational and Adult Education
U.S. Department of Education
400 Maryland Avenue, SW
Washington, DC 20202
Phone: (800) 227-0216

Clearinghouse on Disability Information
Office of Special Education and Rehabilitative Services (OSERS)
U.S. Department of Education
400 Maryland Avenue, SW
Washington, DC 20202-2524
Phone: (202) 205-8241
http://www.ed.gov/OFFICES/OSERS

Consumer Information/Federal Communications Commission (FCC)
445 12th Street, SW
Washington, DC 20554
Phone: (888) 225-5322
E-mail: fccinfo@fcc.gov
http://www.fcc.gov

Disability and Business Technical Assistance Centers
National Institute on Disability & Rehabilitation Research (NIDRR)
400 Maryland Avenue, SW
Washington, DC 20202
Phone: (800) 949-4232
http://www.adata.org

Employment and Training Administration
Office of Public Affairs
U.S. Department of Labor
200 Constitution Ave., NW
Room S4206
Washington, DC 20210
Phone: (202) 219-6871

Information and Publication Requests
U.S. Internal Revenue Service (IRS)
Phone: (800) 829-1040
http://www.irs.ustreas.gov

Library of Congress
101 Independence Avenue, SE
Washington, DC 20540
Phone: (202) 707-5000
http://www.loc.gov

National Transportation Library
U.S. Department of Transportation
400 7th St., SW
Washington, DC 20590
Email: ntl@bts.gov.
http://www.bts.gov/ntl/

Office for Civil Rights National Office
Department of Education, Room # 5000
400 Maryland Avenue, SW
Washington, DC 20202
Phone: (800) 421-3481
Fax: (202) 205-9862
Email: OCR@ED.Gov
http://www.ed.gov/offices/OCR

Office of Special Education Programs (OSEP)
Office of Special Education and Rehabilitative Services (OSERS)
400 Maryland Avenue, SW
Washington, DC 20202
Phone: (800) 872-5327
Fax: (202) 260-0416
http://www.ed.gov/offices/OSERS/OSEP

Office of Special Education & Rehabilitative Services (OSERS)
U.S. Department of Education
400 Maryland Avenue, SW
Washington, DC 20202
Phone: (800) 872-5327
Fax: (202) 205-9252
http://www.ed.gov/offices/OSERS

Office on the Americans with Disabilities Act
Civil Rights Division
U.S. Department of Justice
P.O. Box 66118
Washington, DC 20035-6118
Phone: (202) 514-0301

Protection and Advocacy of Individual Rights
Rehabilitation Services Administration (RSA)

U.S. Department of Education
400 Maryland Avenue, SW
Washington, DC 20202
http://www.ed.gov/offices/OSERS/RSA/PGMS/pair.html

Rehabilitation Services Administration
Office of Special Education and Rehabilitation
U.S. Department of Education
400 Maryland Avenue, SW
Washington, DC 20202
http://www.ed.gov/offices/OSERS/RSA/rsa.html

U.S. Architectural & Transportation Barriers Compliance Board, ATBCB
Technical Assistance Line
Phone: (800) 872-2253
http://www.access-board.gov

U.S. Department of Education
400 Maryland Avenue, SW
Washington, DC 20202
Phone: (800) 872-5327
Fax: (202) 401-0689
http://www.ed.gov

U.S. Dept. of Health and Human Services
200 Independence Avenue, SW
Washington, DC 20201
Phone: (877) 696-6775
http://www.hhs.gov

U. S. Department of Housing & Urban Development (HUD) Distribution Center
451 7th Street, SW
Washington, DC 20410
Phone: (800) 767-7468
Fax: (202) 708-2313
http://www.hud.gov/fairhsg1.html

U.S. Department of Justice
950 Pennsylvania Ave., NW
Washington, DC 20530
Phone: (800) 514-0301
http://www.usdoj.gov

U. S. EEOC Technical Assistance and Training Programs
U.S. Equal Employment Opportunity Commission (EEOC)
1801 L Street, NW
Washington, DC 20507
Phone: (800) 669-4000
http://www.eeoc.gov/taps.html

U.S. House of Representatives
U. S. Capitol
Phone: (202) 224-3121
http://www.house.gov

U.S. Senate
Phone: (202) 225-3121
http://www.senate.gov

U.S. Social Security Administration
Phone: (800) 772-1213
http://www.ssa.gov/

ORGANIZATIONS

Contact information for the following useful organizations can be found beginning on page 347.

- American Congress of Community Supports & Employment Services

- The Arc

- Disability Rights Education and Defense Fund, Inc. (DREDF)

- Job Accommodation Network

- National Council on Disability

- PACER Center

- TASH—Disability Advocacy Worldwide

4

DIAGNOSIS

Now What?

Pamela Leconte & Jeanne Embich

Overview

Diagnosis plays a vital part in postsecondary planning for students with disabilities. In a sense, it is a "ticket" to appropriate and effective services. Most colleges require that a student be diagnosed with a specific disability before plans can be made for course work accommodations. Typically, diagnostic documentation (results of tests indicating the presence of a disability) must be submitted. A professional employed at the school who provides support services for students with disabilities then looks at this documentation to determine whether a student qualifies for and needs support services.

When the diagnostic process is completed, it should be possible to get a helpful answer to the simple question: "Now what?" The answer should provide you with down-to-earth guidance and recommendations for making choices. Are academic and career goals realistic? Is your current educational program too hard? In what ways? Where do specific problems lie? What are your aptitudes and abilities? How can you incorporate strengths into learning and work situations? How can you compensate for areas of difficulty? Would counseling help you to deal with problems and personal adjustment?

Assessment and diagnosis can take place at any time in a person's life. Some people participate in diagnostic testing many times in their school career. Others may not have their first diagnostic tests until adulthood. Getting a diagnosis of LD and/or AD/HD as an adult can be a powerful and positive experience. Beginning to understand your hidden disability can be an important step to appreciating your strengths and working effectively with your areas of need.

This chapter outlines the uses of diagnosis in planning appropriate postsecondary education experiences. This information can be used in a variety of postsecondary settings, such as work, vocational rehabilitation, colleges, adult education courses, and trade and technical programs. Additionally, this information may be used by students, parents, diagnosticians, support personnel, or counselors.

The Basics

Getting a complete diagnosis involves skilled observation, interviews, and formal and informal tests to assess your aptitudes, verbal and nonverbal strengths and needs, and preferred ways of learning.

Tests that might be used to document and understand your disability include: a standardized IQ test, standardized achievement tests in the areas of reading, spelling, math and language, and specialized testing in the area of disability (i.e., within language or information processing). Table 4.1 *(at right)* defines some key words that are important to understanding the diagnostic process.

Which tests you will be given and by which professionals will depend on whether you are believed to have a learning disability, AD/HD, or both, as explained below.

Do You Have a Learning Disability?

If you are being evaluated for a learning disability, the individual or team of professionals you are working with should have training and experience in as-

TABLE 4.1—DEFINITIONS

Assessment: This is the process of finding out what a person knows and can do; the process of gathering relevant information to make decisions. Many different techniques can be used to gather such information, including observations and testing.

Diagnosis: This information-gathering process is designed to find out if a learning disability (LD), Attention Deficit/Hyperactivity Disorder (AD/HD), or other disability is affecting a person's ability to perform. This process also assesses a student's strengths and may indicate how a student compensates for areas of difficulty. Put simply, it is a means of discovering how a student learns and where he or she may need support to learn.

Aptitudes: This is a term often used in assessment reports and means that a person shows the potential or possesses the ability to learn something or to perform a task. For example, Jess shows the aptitude to follow multi-step directions. Terry, with the proper training, has the aptitude to succeed in graphic arts.

Achievement: This term is also used in assessment reports and refers to an individual's academic performance—what an individual has already learned. Standard (norm-referenced) achievement tests measure a particular student's performance compared to performances of students of similar age and grade. For example, diagnostic achievement tests may help determine the process a student is using to solve a math problem or decode a reading passage. These tests may also help determine why a student is not performing at the level of other students.

sessing adolescents and adults with LD. The diagnostic process may be carried out by clinical or educational psychologists; school psychologists; neuropsychologists; or learning disabilities specialists.

Some typical questions that will guide the diagnostic process include:

- Is there a discrepancy between potential and achievement?

- Are cognitive indicators (such as IQ scores) high, but are grades low?

- Is academic performance uneven? For example, do you earn A's & B's in some subjects and fail others?

- Can you reason well, yet not remember words?

- Can you understand a subject, but not be able to organize the answers for an exam?

- How do your grades compare with personal aptitude?

If discrepancies are found between potential and achievement, the diagnostician will gather evidence to verify learning disabilities as the cause. In the process, he or she may eliminate the possibility of physical disability, mental retardation, emotional disturbance, and visual or hearing impairment as primary causes of discrepancies.

If the diagnostic process results in the identification of learning disabilities, then the specific types of learning disabilities should be identified and explained. For example, a specific diagnosis would be dyslexia in contrast to a non-specific diagnosis of a "reading problem."

Do You Have ADHD?

Attention Deficit/Hyperactivity Disorder (AD/HD) requires diagnosis by a physician, psychiatrist, psychologist, or neuropsychologist. You may work with a team of clinical professionals from education, medicine, and counseling. Again, it is important to make sure the professionals you work with have specialized training and experience in working with adolescents and adults with AD/HD. The diagnosis is often completed in coordination with family members, teachers, and the student.

Some typical questions that will guide the diagnostic process include:

- Is there evidence that you begin several tasks and rarely complete them?

- Do you often overlook or forget important details?

- Do you blurt out answers before questions are completed?

- Do you avoid or dislike tasks that require sustained mental effort?

- Is there evidence that academic achievement is not on par with ability as a result of an inability to focus attention?

The diagnostician should also investigate whether you have any medical or psychiatric conditions such as depression, anxiety, or thyroid problems that could cause AD/HD-like symptoms.

To be diagnosed with AD/HD, you must meet criteria identified in the *Diagnostic and Statistical Manual (DSM)-IV,* which is published by the American Psychiatric Association. Key parts of this definition are included in Chapter 2. Examples of specific ADHD diagnosis are also explained in Chapter 2.

How and When to Request an Evaluation

If you are entering a postsecondary program and know or suspect that you will need accommodations, you will need to present current assessment data. This means that formal assessments should be conducted within the last two years of high school.

If you are in high school and have a current Individualized Education Program (IEP) or a Section 504 Plan, be sure that the documentation (testing results, teacher reports, etc.) is sufficiently detailed. Just having an IEP or Section 504 Plan is not enough documentation for you to receive accommodations at college.

If you are in high school and have never been evaluated for LD or AD/HD, ask your guidance counselor how to initiate the diagnostic process. Most schools require that parents make written requests for diagnostic testing. When conducted through the school system, this testing can be provided at no cost to the family. If you experience uncommon delays, you can contact the special education department or director in the central office of the school system for help.

If you discover or suspect problems after you enroll in a postsecondary program, you are responsible for initiating the diagnostic process. You are also responsible for paying for your diagnosis, unless Rehabilitation Services agrees to pay for it (see Table 4.2 on page 74). To begin, try contacting the office responsible for providing support services to students with disabilities. This office often maintains a list of diagnostic services and facilities. If they do not, other campus offices may have the information: Student Affairs, Student Life, Study Skills Center, Career Center, and/or the Counseling Department. If those offices do not have the needed information, there are a number of other resources described in the table below.

The Diagnostic Process

Screening

Once the contact with a diagnostician has been made, the first step is screening. Screening is an assessment process that explores possible causes for students' academic difficulties. You should be prepared to answer these questions:

TABLE 4.2—WHERE TO GO FOR DIAGNOSIS

State or Local Chapters of Disabilities Associations:
The Learning Disabilities Association (LDA), Children and Adults with Attention Deficit Hyperactive Disorder (CHADD), and the International Dyslexia Association often have local chapters. Parents, professionals, or members of a youth or adult affiliate might be able to recommend practitioners who have been helpful. To find the chapter closest to you, get in touch with the national office (see the Resources at the end of the chapter).

State or Local Rehabilitation Services Offices:
These offices either arrange for testing through their own agency or make a referral to one who can. Higher Education And The Handicapped (HEATH) keeps a directory of state rehabilitation services contacts. Also, the Rehabilitation Services Administration (RSA) of the U.S. Department of Education has state agency contacts on their web site. For more information on Rehabilitation Services, see Chapter 5.

State Departments of Education—Special Education Divisions:
These offices have resource personnel who can help families and students in elementary, middle, and high school locate local diagnostic resources. Many states also have hot lines for "Child Find" services.

Information and Referral Services:
Check with city hall and/or the county administrator's office for listings or directories. This information may also be available on your town's websites.

University Special Education Departments:
Universities may have diagnostic facilities. Additionally, they may be able to make referrals to qualified professionals who diagnose learning disabilities.

Guidance Counselors:
Check with counselors at local high schools or community colleges. These individuals are likely to have information about diagnostic practitioners who work primarily with adolescents and adults.

- What is the problem?

- When did it start?

- How has the school system tried to deal with it?

- What are the possible reasons for the problems?

This historical information is very important in identifying AD/HD in particular, since there must be evidence that it was present in early childhood and that it affects more than one part of your life.

Gathering background information is another important part of screening. You can expect to be asked questions in the following areas:

- **Educational history.** This includes finding out about learning problems during early grades, previous educational diagnoses, special education placement, and how well you have learned to compensate for specific problem areas.

- **Family history.** In gathering information, the interviewer may look for signs of dyslexia or learning and attention problems in other family members.

- **Medical history.** A thorough medical checkup should evaluate vision and hearing, injuries or illnesses, allergies, birth trauma, low birth weight, or related medical conditions, such as epilepsy.

- **Psychosocial history.** The evaluator must investigate all the possible reasons for your problems. It is important to rule out psychiatric conditions as the underlying cause of the learning problems.

- **Samples of academic work.** Screening often includes examining examples of projects, papers, exams, and other student products of performance. Handwriting samples may also be used to detect possible learning disabilities.

The screening stage itself may lead to helpful interventions. For example, you may decide to try the campus writing center or learning lab, to drop one heavy reading course, or to get tutoring. Change does not have to wait until all the results of a full-scale diagnosis are received. Some students may not actually require further diagnosis but can work out their problems on their own or with the assistance of an advisor.

Formal Assessment

Based on the results of the screening, the diagnostician will decide which formal tests might be helpful in diagnosing your disability and in determining your strengths and needs.

Tests of Cognitive Abilities. The *Wechsler Intelligence Scale for Children—third revision* (WISC-III) and the *Wechsler Adult Intelligence Scale—third revision* (WAIS-III) are the instruments (tests) most frequently used to assess the aptitude (i.e., ability to learn; cognitive ability) of students with and without disabilities. One of the following tests of aptitude may be used in addition to the WISC-III or WAIS-III: *Woodcock-Johnson Psycho-Educational Battery—Revised: Tests of Cognitive Ability, the Kaufman Adolescent and Adult Intelligence Test, or the Stanford-Binet Intelligence Test* (latest edition).

Achievement Tests. To understand academic achievement, the diagnostician will gather information about current levels of functioning in reading (decoding and comprehension) and mathematics, as well as oral and written language. The *Woodcock-Johnson Psycho-Educational Battery—Revised: Tests of Achievement* is used most frequently to assess academic achievement. Other instruments used include the *Scholastic Abilities Tests for Adults* (SATA), the *Stanford Test of Academic Skills*, and the *Wechsler Individual Achievement Test* (WIAT). Specific achievement tests may include the *Nelson-Denny Reading Skills Test,* the *Stanford Diagnostic Mathematics Test,* the *Test Of Written Language* (TOWL-3), and the *Woodcock Reading Mastery Tests - Revised*. These types of tests are important because their results can be contrasted with cognitive tests to see if there is a discrepancy between cognitive ability and school achievement.

Information Processing Tests. Information processing is also known as psychological processing. It refers to your ability to perceive and interpret visual and auditory stimuli (sights and sounds). Difficulties in processing information are not the same as the visual and auditory acuity problems that are experienced by people with hearing or visual impairments. Instead, they are difficulties that you might experience in organizing and interpreting what you see or hear.

Typical instruments used to assess information processing include the *Detroit Tests of Learning Aptitude-3* (DTLA-3), the *Detroit Tests of Learning Aptitude—Adult* (DTLA—A), and the *Beery Developmental Test of Visual-Motor Integration, 3rd Revision*. Information from subtests on the WAIS-R, WISC-II, and Woodcock-Johnson Psycho-educational Battery, Part I—Revised, as well as other relevant instruments, can be used also.

Reporting of Test Results. Most test results are reported with standardized scores and percentiles. A standard score is based on the "bell curve," in which a score of 100 is usually considered average. A percentile expresses what percentage of students at your age or grade level would score lower than you on the same test. These scores can be difficult to understand so both written and oral interpretations of scores are important. Diagnosticians are responsible for explaining and interpreting results in person. Don't be afraid to ask questions and insist that reports be written in clear language that everyone can understand. For more help in understanding test scores and percentiles, there are a number of additional resources: staff at the college Disability Support Services office, parent guidelines for special education from each state department of education (special education division), and/or the local school system.

Information gathered from cognitive ability, academic achievement, and/or perceptual motor testing, alongside observation, may answer many questions about learning challenges.

Table 4.3 on pages 78 and 79 provides key information concerning the most commonly used diagnostic instruments.

Controversy about Testing

It is important to point out that some techniques of diagnosis are controversial. There is no universal agreement about how to assess potential, how to diagnose learning disabilities, what tests to use, or who should do the testing. Although tests have been developed and are available for use with children, adolescents, and adults, some tests are more useful than others.

Intelligence tests are a particular focus of controversy. Testing for potential usually involves getting an Intelligence Quotient (IQ). The IQ is widely used to estimate one's ability to learn. But, an intelligence test is only one sample of behavior at a given time and reflects the test author's own definition of intelligence. An IQ score is not the last word about what a student can do. In fact, recent theories about students having multiple intelligences (see Chapter 1), cause people to question traditional intelligence tests. In many instances, IQ tests measure how well a student is able to learn in a traditional classroom, not her innate intelligence. Many factors, such as anxiety, language problems, and limited experiences, can lower a score and give a false picture. Also, results can be distorted by underlying visual or auditory perceptual problems.

Despite these controversies, most school systems require IQ testing as part of the diagnostic evaluation process. This is because they rely on a formula for

TABLE 4.3—COMMONLY USED ASSESSMENT INSTRUMENTS

Test	Components and Subtests
Wechsler Adult Intelligence Scales R (WAIS R) ages: 16-17 years, adults, and older adults *and* **Wechsler Intelligence Scales for Children III (WISC III)** ages: 6-16 years	**Common Subtests:** Information, Comprehension, Arithmetic, Similarities, Digit Span, Vocabulary, Block Design, Picture Arrangement, Picture Completion, and Object Assembly. **WAIS only Subtests:** Digit Symbol. **WISC only Subtests:** Coding, Symbol Search, and Mazes.
Woodcock-Johnson Psycho-Educational Battery, Revised Tests of Cognitive Abilities Standard Battery ages: 2-17 years, adults, and older adults	**Subtests:** Memory for Names, Memory for Sentences, Visual Matching, Incomplete Words, Visual Closure, Picture Vocabulary, and Analysis-Synthesis.
Woodcock-Johnson Psycho-Educational Battery, Revised Tests of Cognitive Abilities Supplemental Battery ages: 2-17 years, adults, and older adults	**Subtests:** Visual-Auditory Learning, Memory for Words, Cross Out, Sound Blending, Picture Recognition, Oral Vocabulary, Concept Formation, Delayed Recall-Memory for Names, Delayed Recall-Visual Auditory Learning, Numbers Reversed, Sound Patterns, Spatial Relations, Listening Comprehension, and Verbal Analogies.
Woodcock-Johnson Psycho-Educational, Revised Tests of Achievement-Standard Battery ages: 2-17, adults, and older adults	**Subtests:** Letter-Word Identification, Passage Comprehension, Calculation, Applied Problems, Dictation, Writing Samples, Science, Social Studies, and Humanities.
Woodcock-Johnson Psycho-Educational, Revised Tests of Achievement-Supplemental Battery ages: 2-17 years, adults, and older adults	Subtests: Word Attack, Reading Vocabulary, Quantitative Concepts, Proofing, and Writing Fluency.
Developmental Test of Visual-Motor Integration, 3rd Revision (Beery-Keith-E) ages: 3-17 years and adult	Twenty-four geometric designs
Bender-Gestalt Test Bender-Lauretta ages: 5-17 years and adult	Nine geometric designs
Detroit Tests of Learning Aptitude, third edition (DTLA-3) ages: 6-17 years	**Subtests:** Word Opposites, Design Sequences, Sentence Imitation, Reversed Letters, Story Construction, Design Reproduction, Basic Information, Symbolic Relations, Word Sequences, Story Sequences, and Picture Fragments.
Behn-Rorshach Test Adolescent Apperception Cards ages: 5-17 and adult	Draw-A-Story Draw-A-Person Tasks of Emotional Development Test Thematic Apperception Test

* Note: Assessment of Social and Emotional Development. A student with social or emotional problems may or may not have underlying LD and/or ADHD. This is one of many issues a diagnostician may need to investigate. Inappropriate or immature behavior, low self-esteem, anxiety about competition, and other symptoms may all have their origins in learning disabilities. Careful study of family, school, and medical histories and perceptive diagnostic

Cognitive Ability Can provide specific information on verbal ability, capacity to think conceptually, ability to exercise judgment, visual memory, ability to think sequentially, orientation to time and space, understanding of the whole in relation to its parts, distractibility, motor control, and motivation.
Cognitive Ability, Scholastic Aptitude, and Achievement Long- and short-term memory ability, auditory and visual processing and speed, reasoning ability, and comprehension ability. Knowledge achievement. Reading, mathematics, written language, and cognitive aptitude.
Cognitive Ability, Scholastic Aptitude, and Achievement Long- and short-term memory ability, auditory and visual processing and speed, reasoning ability, and comprehension ability. Knowledge achievement. Reading, mathematics, written language, and cognitive aptitude.
Academic Achievement Reading, mathematics, written language, and knowledge achievement.
Academic Achievement Reading, mathematics, written language, and knowledge achievement.
Visual-Motor Integration Samples behavior in order to measure a student s ability to integrate visual and motor skills.
Maturation, Visual Perception, Degree of Eye Injury, Psychological Issues A work sample measuring ability to perceive and reproduce geometrical designs to reflect perception of reality.
General Intelligence, Cognitive Ability, and Aptitude Measures present mental abilities to predict future performance.
Social and Emotional Development *

interviewing are part of assessing emotional well-being. The diagnostician may also arrange for some formal testing, ask for additional professional consultation, or evaluate the results of some formal tests.

determining whether LD or AD/HD is present. This formula requires an individually administered test of cognitive ability and scores from standardized achievement tests. Formulas vary from school district to school district, but a "significant" discrepancy is often defined as a difference of 15 points or more between the IQ and achievement test scores. More information about these tests can be found in Table 4.3.

Students with LD and/or AD/HD, as well as other students, frequently have the potential for learning in unique ways not measured by traditional IQ tests. A single test is not enough to determine a student's intelligence. Diagnostic assessment therefore involves seeking information from a variety of sources and sifting the results of different tests, work samples, interviews, and observations. Student portfolios, which are gaining popularity in schools, can be particularly useful as evidence of performance. In fact, portfolios can show different aspects of intelligence that cannot be assessed by tests. They often include writing samples and other products that show student progress. However, it is important to remember that postsecondary schools and employers need documentation of a disability from the standard tests discussed in this chapter.

Who Conducts the Diagnosis?

The diagnostic team may be composed of psychologists, educational diagnosticians, and LD/AD/HD specialists/teachers. If your assessment is being conducted by the school system, they will select the members of the team. If you are paying for the assessment yourself, you will be doing the choosing.

Before hiring someone to conduct the assessment, it is important to ask certain questions. First, inquire about their training, credentials, and experience, as suggested in Table 4.4. Most importantly, the professional should be experienced in working with adolescents and adults with LD and/or AD/HD. Next, ask how they conduct the evaluation. Their response to this question should include routine questions they ask as they work with you. For example, many diagnosticians believe that accurate scoring of answers is not enough; it is equally important to note *how* a person arrives at an answer or solves a problem.

Diagnosticians find clues to your needs by observing you as you answer questions and take tests. Picking up subtleties of behavior is part of the diagnostician's expertise. These are typical questions diagnosticians attempt to answer:

- How hard do you work to answer questions?

- Which questions seem to cause you the most concern?

- Do you show nervousness or anxiety when taking certain tests?

- Do you answer before hearing the entire question?

- Do you understand verbal questions?

- Can you describe your strengths and needs in an understandable way?

The Association for Higher Education and Disability and the Educational Testing Service offer the recommendations in Table 4.4 on how to get the most useful information from the assessment process.

Getting the Results

Results of the diagnosis should be explained as simply and clearly as possible. You need to know what the terms *learning disabilities (LD)* and *attention deficit/hyperactivity disorder (AD/HD)* mean and how the condition is affecting your performances. You should have the opportunity to ask questions, and, above all, to know what your strengths are. You should also be able to describe how these strengths can support learning and what accom-

TABLE 4.4—RECOMMENDATIONS FOR CONSUMERS

1. **Finding a qualified professional:**

   a. Contact the disability services coordinator at the institution you attend or plan to attend to discuss documentation needs;

   b. Discuss your future plans with the disability services coordinator. If additional documentation is required, seek assistance in identifying a qualified professional;

   c. Ask others who have gone through the process where they went for the assessment process; and

   d. Call local professional associations who may know individuals qualified and experienced in the assessment process.

2. **Selecting qualified professionals:**

   a. Ask for his or her professional credentials and/or degrees;

   b. Ask what experiences and training he or she has had working with adults and adolescents with LD and AD/HD;

   c. Ask if he or she has ever worked with the service provider at your institution or with the agency to which you are sending material;

   d. Ask for the cost of the assessment;

   e. Ask how long the assessment process will last;

   f. Ask if you will receive a full written report with clear explanations of findings; and

   g. If you are being assessed for AD/HD, ask whether the person has training in evaluating the full range of psychiatric disorders.

3. **Working with the professional(s):**

   a. Take a copy of these guidelines to the professional;

   b. Encourage him or her to clarify questions with the person who provided you with these guidelines;

   c. Be prepared to be forthcoming, thorough, and honest with requested information;

   d. Provide the professional with any anecdotal information that may explain and clarify difficulties in order to form an appropriate or useful recommendation; and

   e. Know that professionals must maintain confidentiality with respect to your records and testing information.

4. **As follow up to the assessment by the professional:**

   a. Request a written copy of the assessment report;

   b. Request the opportunity to discuss the results and recommendations;

   c. Request recommendations for coping strategies;

   d. Request additional resources if you need them; and

   e. Maintain a personal file of your records and reports.

This chart is adapted from both AHEAD's Appendix A: Recommendations for Consumers and ETS's Appendix A & B, Policy Statement for Documentation of a Learning Disability in Adolescents and Adults. See http://www.ahead.org/ldguide.htm#appendixa and http://www.ets.org/distest/ldpolicy.html

modations you need. You will need to describe these to instructors, employers, friends, and others.

Many people who have been diagnosed with LD and/or AD/HD feel great relief. The years of frustration are finally explained, and they learn there are ways to compensate. Although diagnosis can give a sense of a new beginning, it can also be difficult news to accept and understand. It takes more than one explanation to understand and use the information positively. It is very helpful to have the opportunity for follow-up with the diagnostician, an educational specialist, or a therapist. You may need to ask more questions or need help in planning for the future.

Providing Assessment Data to Schools

Most postsecondary institutions require that students be formally diagnosed with a disability before arrangements can be made for needed accommodations. If you have been diagnosed with AD/HD or LD it is important to report to the Disability Support Services (DSS) office on campus *before or upon enrollment*. Remember, after high school it becomes your responsibility to request services. If you choose not to do this, the school is under no obligation to provide support.

Diagnostic test results indicating the presence of a disability must be submitted to the school's DSS office. A DSS professional reviews the results of diagnostic tests to determine whether you:

a. meet the qualifications as an individual with disabilities as defined by the Americans with Disabilities Act and Section 504 of the Rehabilitation Act,

b. have the potential for meeting academic or vocational standards, or

c. need support services.

Under the Individuals with Disabilities Education Act of 1990 (and as amended in 1997), a current IEP with transition goals can be used to determine appropriate accommodations, but cannot be used as the sole means for determining a disability (see Chapter 3 for more information).

The Association on Higher Education and Disability (AHEAD) is the organization for professionals who provide support services for postsecondary students with documented disabilities. According to AHEAD guidelines, most colleges and universities require the following assessment documentation:

1. a formal evaluation report, including a summary of a comprehensive diagnostic interview (a diagnostic interview might include a description of the presenting problems, developmental, medical, psychosocial, and employment histories, family history, and discussion of dual-diagnosis, when necessary);

2. results of a diagnostic battery of tests;

3. evidence of a substantial limitation to learning or other major life activity which includes, at minimum, the categories of aptitude, academic achievement, and information processing.

As noted above, it may also be useful for you to provide the most current IEP, including transition goals and specific recommendations for accommodations that have been successful.

Vocational Assessment

If you are still in high school, another type of assessment that can be very useful is the vocational assessment. It can help you to clarify career goals and decide whether to go on to college or to a postsecondary vocational education program. This part of stocktaking includes a review of work experiences (work-study programs; summer, holiday, or part-time jobs; or volunteer placements), interests, and vocational aptitudes, transition needs, and career goals. As in any evaluation, the more input from the person tested and significant others, the more realistic recommendations can be.

In some school systems, students have the opportunity to receive rehabilitation services such as transition planning and vocational assessment. Rehabilitation counselors can be involved in transition planning, and in some cases they may be able to arrange for a vocational evaluation before the end of high school. See Chapter 5 for more information about rehabilitation services.

In other school systems, schools provide their own vocational assessment and evaluation services. In these instances, the vocational evaluation staff should provide you with copies of their results and recommendations. If you have difficulty obtaining these services, contact the director of special education for your school district.

A thorough vocational evaluation can take several days or weeks and is administered by specially trained vocational evaluators. To assess your abilities to do specific types of jobs, you may be given:

- standardized tests to measure career-related aptitudes, interests, and achievement;

- work samples (e.g., if you were interested in auto mechanics, an evaluator might watch you diagnose an electrical problem with an ignition system);

- work tryouts (an unpaid work experience arranged by a vocational evaluator—for example, doing data entry with employed data entry clerks), and, in some cases;

- community-based assessments that replicate actual working conditions.

Hands-on experiences are particularly appropriate for students with LD and/or AD/HD.

If you have this assessment early in high school, there are more opportunities to plan an appropriate curriculum and work-study program. However, this type of vocational evaluation is useful whenever a person is considering a career choice. After the evaluation, results should be shared with all of the involved professionals.

If your school does not provide vocational evaluation services, remember you can contact the director of special education (or the director of career and technology education) in your school district. You could also decide to obtain a private evaluation, as discussed in the next section. Vocational or career assessment professionals work for state rehabilitation services programs, Social Security, in local community rehabilitation agencies, public schools, some community colleges, and in private practice. Contact the national Vocational Evaluation and Work Adjustment Association or the national Commission on Certification of Work Adjustment and Vocational Evaluation Specialists (CCWAVES) to locate qualified professionals in your community, listed at the back of this book.

A word of caution: Before selecting an agency or practitioner to conduct a private vocational evaluation, be sure to check on qualifications and reputation, costs, ratio of students to evaluators, variety of occupational fields that will be sampled, and how the sampling will be done. Make sure that you will receive a comprehensive, written report of all findings and specific recommendations.

Career Assessment Assistance

If you desire more assessment information—to help you decide what you want to do and can do in future careers—you can seek assistance from vocational or career assessment professionals. Career or vocational assessment services help students and adults identify their:

- goals and interests,

- learning style preferences (an individual's most comfortable way of receiving or processing information),

- skills (vocational, academic, transferable—those that can be used in a variety of tasks),

- worker traits and habits (i.e., punctuality, working as a team member)

- temperaments (preferences for careers that involve mostly working with data/information, people, or things),

- accommodations that are helpful in academic and work settings (e.g., modified work schedules, directions provided in writing, assistive technology), and

- other personal attributes or characteristics.

The goal of career assessment is to match a person's attributes with various career, occupational, and work requirements, environments, and demands. Career and vocational assessment help students make informed decisions about their current and future plans and goals. When personal attributes and career demands are compatible, students can feel more confident about your short- and long-term decisions. For instance, after you have participated in hands-on career or work experiences through assessment, you will have a better idea about your preferences for the realities of work. Assessment can also help you decide on appropriate courses and majors in college. This type of assessment process helps you make an eventual career match that will be both satisfying and successful. If you are unsure how your skills, abilities, and areas of need match up to types of careers, this type of evaluation can be very helpful.

Conclusion

A comprehensive diagnosis can give you and your advisors a basis for understanding and decision making. As you begin your postsecondary education, assessment results can help you understand: a) academic areas that need strengthening, b) compensatory skills that should be taught, and c) types of accommodations and support that may be needed.

Since the responsibility for getting your special needs met shifts to your shoulders after high school, it is crucial for you to understand your own diagnosis. If diagnostic results are not written in everyday, functional terms, you may need to meet with the diagnostician to discuss results more than once. Remember: the more you understand diagnosis and assessment, aptitude and achievement, and where to go for assistance, the greater opportunity you have for success.

Resources

BOOKS

Assessment in Special Education: An Applied Approach, 1995
Author: Terry Overton
Prentice-Hall Publishers
P.O. Box 11071
Des Moines, IA 50336
Phone: (800) 947-7700
http://www.viacom.com

Assessment of Children, 1992
Author: Jerome M. Sattler
Jerome M. Sattler, Publisher, Inc.
P.O. Box 3557
La Mesa, CA 91944-3557
Phone: (888) 815-2898
Fax: (619) 460-2489
E-mail: jsattler@psychology.sdsu.edu
http://sd02.znet.com/sattler

Assessment of Children: WISC-III and WPPSI-R Supplement, 1992
Author: Jerome M. Sattler
Jerome M. Sattler, Publisher, Inc.
See address above.

Attention Deficit Hyperactivity Disorder: A Handbook for Diagnosis and Treatment, 2nd edition, 1998
Author: Russell A. Barkley
Guilford Press
72 Spring Street
New York, NY 10012

Phone: (800) 365-7006
Fax: (212) 966-6708
Email: info@guilford.com
http://www.guilford.com

Attention, Memory, and Executive Function, 1995
Editors: G. Reid Lyon and Norman A. Krasnegor
Paul H. Brookes Publishing Company
P.O. Box 10624
Baltimore, MD 21285-0624
Phone: (800) 638-3775
Fax: (410) 337-8539
Email: custserv@pbrookes.com
http://www.pbrookes.com

Bridges to Practice: Guidebook 2 The Assessment Process, 1999
The Academy for Educational Development
1875 Connecticut Ave., NW
Washington, DC 20009-1202
http://www.aed.org

Children's Psychological Testing: A Guide for Nonpsychologists,
3rd edition, 1997
Author: David L. Wodrich
Paul H. Brookes Publishing Company
P.O. Box 10624
Baltimore, MD 21285-0624
Phone: (800) 638-3775
Fax: (410) 337-8539
E-mail: custserv@pbrookes.com
http://www.pbrookes.com

**Complete Learning Disabilities Resource Library: Ready-to-Use Information
and Materials for Assessing Specific Learning Disabilities**, 1996
Authors: Joan Harwell and Colleen Duffy Shoup
Center for Applied Research in Education
Phone: (800) 947-7700
Fax: (515) 284-2607
http://www.viacom.com

Diagnosis and Management of Learning Disabilities, 3rd edition, 1996
Authors: Frank Brown, Elizabeth Aylard, and Barbara Keogh
Singular Publishing Group
401 West A. Street
San Diego, CA 92101
Phone: (800) 521-8545
Fax: (619) 238-6789
E-mail: singpub@singpub.com
http://www.singpub.com

Diagnostic and Statistical Manual of Mental Disorders, 4th edition,1994
American Psychiatric Association
1400 K. St., NW
11th Floor
Washington, DC 20005
Phone: (800) 368-5777
Fax: (202) 682-6850
E-mail: csdept@appi.org
http://www.appi.org

Foundations of Intellectual Assessment: The WAIS-III and Other Tests in Clinical Practice, 1998
Author: Robert Gregory
Allyn and Bacon
160 Gould Street
Needham Heights, MA 02194-2315
Phone: (800) 852-8024
Fax: (781) 455-8024
E-mail: AandBpub@aol.com
http://www.abacon.com

Handbook on the Assessment of Learning Disabilities: Theory, Research and Practice, 1991
Author: H. Lee Swanson
Pro-Ed
8700 Shoal Creek Blvd
Austin, TX 78757-6897
Phone: (800) 897-3202
Fax: (800) 397-7633
E-mail: info@proedinc.com
http://www.proedinc.com

Intelligent Testing with the WISC-III, 1994
Author: Jerome Sattler
John Wiley and Sons, Inc.
1 Wiley Drive
Somerset, NJ 08875-1272
Phone: (800) 225-5945
Fax: (732) 302-2300
E-mail: bookinfo@wiley.com
http://www.wiley.com

LD: Basic Concepts, Assessment Practices, and Instructional Strategies,
4th edition, 1990
Author: Patricia Myers
Pro-Ed
8700 Shoal Creek Blvd.
Austin, TX 78757-6897
Phone: (800) 897-3202
Fax: (800) 397-7633
E-mail: info@proedinc.com
http://www.proedinc.com

Learning Disabilities: New Directions for Assessment and Intervention, 1994
Authors: Nancy Jordan and Josephine Goldsmith-Phillips
Allyn and Bacon
160 Gould Street
Needham Heights, MA 02194-2315
Phone: (800) 852-8024
Fax: (781) 455-8024
E-mail: AandBpub@aol.com
http://www.abacon.com

Learning Disabilities: Theories, Diagnosis, and Teaching Strategies,
7th edition, 1997
Author: Janet Lerner
Houghton Mifflin Company
1900 S. Batavia Avenue
Geneva, IL 60134
Phone: (800) 733-2828
Fax: (800) 733-2098
Email: storemanager@hmco.com
http://www.schooldirect.com

The Nature of Learning Disabilities: Critical Elements of Diagnosis and Classification, 1995
Lawrence Erlbaum Associates, Inc.
10 Industrial Ave.
Mahwah, NJ 07430-2262
Phone: (800) 926-6579
Fax: (201) 236-0072
Email: orders@erlbaum.com
http://www.erlbaum.com

Special Educator's Complete Guide to 109 Diagnostic Tests: How to Select and Interpret Tests, Use Results in IEP's, and Remediate Specific Difficulties, 1998
Authors: Roger Pierangelo and George Giuliani
Center for Applied Research in Education
Phone: (800) 947-7700
Fax: (515) 284-2607
http://www.viacom.com

Test Scores and What They Mean, 1991
Author: Howard Lynn
Prentice-Hall Publishers
P.O. Box 11071
Des Moines, IA 50336
Phone: (800) 947-7700
http://www.viacom.com

Testing: Critical Components in the Identification of Dyslexia, 1997
Author: Joan R. Knight
International Dyslexia Association
8600 LaSalle Road,
Chester Building, Suite #382
Baltimore, MD 21286-2044
Phone: (800) 222-3123
Fax: (410) 321-5069
http://www.interdys.org

FACT SHEETS
Adults with Learning Disabilities, 1998
ERIC Digest # 189
LDOnline
http://www.ldonline.org/ld_indepth/adult/index.html

AHEAD Guidelines for Documentation of a Learning Disability
Author: Jane E. Jarrow
Association on Higher Education and Disability (AHEAD)
P.O. Box 21192
Columbus, OH 43221-0192
Phone: (614) 488-4972
Fax: (614) 488-1174
E-mail: ahead@postbox.acs.ohio-state.edu
http://www.ahead.org/ldguide.htm

Assessing Children for the Presence of a Disability, 1994, News Digest 4
NICHCY
P. O. Box 1492
Washington, DC 20013
Phone: (800) 695-0285
Fax: (202) 884-8441
E-mail: nichcy@aed.org
http://www.nichcy.org

Questions to Ask When Selecting a Professional to Assess or Treat ADHD
Parents' Education Resource Center, (PERC)
1660 South Amphlett Blvd., # 200
San Mateo, CA 94402-2508
Phone: (800) 471-9545
Fax: (650) 655-2411
E-mail: perc@perc-schwabfdn.org
http://www.perc-schwabfdn.org

WEBSITES
American College Testing
This site offers information on applying for extended or special testing options when taking the ACT. It also permits online registration for the ACT.
http://www.act.org

Buros Institute of Mental Measurements
An informative website about assessment and its tools. It has descriptions of tools and of assessment.
http://www.unl.edu/buros

The Buros Test Review Locator
Information on tests as well as test publishers. This site also has its own bookstore.
http://ericae.net/testcol.htm#trev

The Cognitive Processing Inventory (CPI)

Assesses information-processing skills and learning styles while also providing information for their impacts on school life. It is produced by Scott L. Crouse, a psychologist.

http://www.hopkins.k12.mn.us/Pages/North/LD_Research/cpi1.htm

Educational Testing Service (ETS)

This site provides information about ETS tests (SAT, GRE), as well as policy and requirements concerning accommodations.

http://www.ets.org

ERIC Clearinghouse on Assessment & Evaluation: Assessment & Evaluation on the Net

This site is a database with information on assessment, evaluation, statistics, and educational research. It includes reviews of tests and has a bookstore and a library.

http://ericae.net

General Educational Development (GED) Testing Service

This site has statistics, tips, and information concerning policy and procedures for taking tests produced by GED. Additionally, it has valuable links related to adult learning and credentials.

http://www.acenet.edu/Programs/CALEC/GED/home.html

Internet Special Education Resources (ISER)

This site covers the basics of assessing LD and AD/HD and also allows you to search for a professional who can diagnose LD and AD/HD.

http://www.iser.com/steps.html

Psychology Test Library

In alphabetical order, this site has explanations of numerous, commonly ad-ministered tests.

http://www.bhs.mq.edu.au/lib/testref.html

Tests in Print

Provides important information about specific tests such as purpose, intended audience, and scoring.

http://www.unl.edu/buros/howtotip.html

Yahoo: Education: Standards and Testing

This site changes often but always consists of links to test explanations, pro-ducers, and informational articles.

http://www.yahoo.com/Education/Standards_and_Testing

Yahoo: Education: Statistics

This site has links to sites concerning education and statistics, as well as organizations.

http://www.yahoo.com/Education/Statistics

COMPUTERIZED INFORMATION DELIVERY SYSTEMS AND PRODUCERS

Educational Testing Service

Corporate Headquarters

Educational Testing Service

Rosedale Road

Princeton, NJ 08541 USA

Phone: (609) 921-9000

Fax: (609) 734-5410

E-mail: etsinfo@ets.org

http://www.ets.org

ExPan

Producer: College Board Admission and Enrollment Services

Phone: (800) 927-4302

E-mail: info@aes.collegeboard.org

Program for Assessing Your Employability

Producer: Educational Testing Service

Rosedale Road

Princeton, NJ 08541

Phone: (609) 921-9000

Fax: (609) 734-5413

E-mail: etsinfo@ets.org

http://www.ets.org

ORGANIZATIONS

Contact information for the following useful organizations can be found beginning on page 347.

- Association on Higher Education and Disability (AHEAD)

- American Association of University Affiliated Programs for Persons with Developmental Disabilities

- American Psychiatric Association

- Association for Career and Technical Education (ACTE), *formerly American Vocational Association (AVA)*

- Beach Center on Families and Disability

- CCWAVES: Commission on Certification of Work Adjustment and Vocational Evaluation Specialists

- Children and Adults with Attention-Deficit/Hyperactivity Disorder, CHADD

- Clearinghouse on Disability Information

- Council for Exceptional Children

- Educational Testing Service (ETS)

- ERIC Clearinghouse on Assessment & Evaluation

- General Education Development (GED)

- Internet Special Education Resources

- LDA (Learning Disabilities Association of America)

- National Association of School Psychologists

- National Association of Vocation and Education Special Needs Personnel (NAVESNP)

- National Occupational Information Coordinating Committee (NOICC)

- National Rehabilitation Information Center (NARIC)

- PACER Center

- Rehabilitation Services Administration

- Vocational Evaluation and Work Adjustment Association (VEWAA)

5

KNOWING WHERE YOU WANT TO GO AND HOW TO GET THERE

Self-Determination and Transition Planning

IN THIS CHAPTER:

- Overview: What is Self-determination?
- Developing Self-determination Skills
- Using Self-advocacy Skills for Transition Planning
- The Self Advocate at the IEP Meeting
- Problem Solving to Reach Desired Goals
- Guidelines and Timelines
- The Family's Role in Creating a Self-Advocate
- Vocational Rehabilitation Services

Bob Rahamin, Stephanie Corbey, Michael Ward, & Lynda West

Overview: What Is Self-determination?

During high school I learned how to take charge of my IEP meetings because my special education teacher taught me how to do it. I sent out invitations to my teachers and guidance counselor, and made sure that my parents were prepared for the meeting. At the meeting I would discuss the progress I had made each year, and the accommodations that were most helpful in each class. My teachers would share their records of my specific progress and my parents would discuss how well I was able to keep myself organized at home. This was great preparation for college and being a successful employee. I am able to tell people how my learning disabilities and attention deficit disorder affect me. I have a lot of trouble with oral directions and my spelling is horrible. But if I can see things in writing and have time to proof my work, I do fine. I have lots of energy and like to work in short, intense spurts. I have a part-time job with a messenger service, which is perfect. I read maps well, and like having my job broken up with different delivery trips. I have started classes at the local community college studying computer graphics, which helps me use my strong visual memory. My goal is to save money and finish my degree at a four-year college away from home.

—Carlos, college student with LD and AD/HD

From the short introduction Carlos has given us, we could say that he is a self-determined individual. Simply put, self-determination is the ability to define and achieve goals based on knowing and valuing yourself.

Self-determination skills are extremely useful as you make the transition to adult life. First, self-determination can ensure that your wishes, desires, needs, and goals are considered in the transition planning process. Second, self-determination allows you to build and maintain relationships with people who can offer you help and support. Third, self-determination can assist you in developing decision-making skills. Finally, self-determination allows you to ask for the services and supports that you need.

Self-determination is a skill that should ideally be developed as a part of your high school program. Self-determination skills should be incorporated into your Individualized Educational Program (IEP) or Section 504 plan. There are two ways you can make sure this happens: 1) by being an active participant in the meeting, and 2) by including self-determination skills as part of your IEP.

Sharon Field and Alan Hoffman, university researchers in the field of special education, have developed a high school curriculum that teaches self-determination skills. Their program outlines a five-stage model for developing self-determination, described below.

Developing Self-Determination Skills

Stage 1: Know Yourself

To know yourself, you need many different experiences to help you figure out what you do well and what you don't do as well. School is just a part of life, and being a student is just one role you play. Participating in out-of-school activities like sports, clubs, volunteering, helping out at home, and part-time jobs helps you know yourself in different roles. This helps you learn about what you like and don't like to do. The more you know about your strengths and preferences, the easier it is to determine the types of careers that may interest you. This helps you stay focused on how school can help you prepare for activities you may enjoy pursuing after high school. Look back at what Carlos had to say: what does he know about himself?

Stage 2: Value Yourself

To value yourself means that you accept your strengths and areas of need. This self-acceptance makes it easier to explain your disability to friends, teachers, and employers. When you are able to discuss your disability, it is easier for others to understand and appreciate you for who you are. Valuing yourself also helps you take care of yourself so you stay mentally and physically healthy. What does Carols value about himself?

Stage 3: Plan

In order to plan you must first have a goal. Self-determined individuals look ahead, set goals, and then plan steps that will help them reach their goals. One reason it is so important for you to be actively involved in your IEP meetings is that it helps you learn about setting and monitoring yearly plans. It also sets up a support system to help you meet educational goals.

Being focused on goals and planning is a challenge for many people. The ability to plan is a skill. The more you observe others setting goals and following plans, the more you will learn about the process. Many students need direct instruction in planning skills and then support from parents, teachers, or coaches. What goal does Carlos have?

Stage 4: Act

Once you have a plan, you need to take steps to achieve your plan. Achieving most of our goals involves some type of communication with other people. Developing communication and social skills that encourage others to be supportive and helpful is crucial for young people who are trying to be successful in school and work. Refer to the sidebar below for information about communication styles that can help or harm you.

Stage 5: Experience Outcomes and Learn

The final stage is to self-assess. Have you met your goal? If so, what steps were most helpful? If you haven't met your goal, why not? Taking time to self-reflect is important. Talking to others about successes, near misses, and failures can help you figure out the reasons for each. The key is to celebrate successes and learn from mistakes.

COMMUNICATION STYLES

Are you a passive, aggressive, or assertive communicator? And what does your communication style tell others about you?

- **Passive** people let others tell them what to do. They stay quiet even when they don't agree. Passive people may feel angry or upset, but don't say anything. They may feel guilty if they don't do what others want them to do. They think others can read their minds.

- **Aggressive** people think they can get what they want by yelling at other people. They talk in a loud and angry manner. They do not think about other people's feelings. It is hard to get the help you need if you yell and scream. It makes others angry and they will not listen or want to help.

- **Assertive** people tell others what they want and need. They do not demand things. They respect the rights and feelings of others. They talk about their ideas with other people and ask questions to get help. They then make up their own minds about what to do and do not let other people tell them what to do. You are much more likely to get your needs met if you are an assertive communicator.

Using Self-advocacy Skills for Transition Planning

A self-determined person is able to use self-advocacy skills. Self advocacy means speaking or acting on your own behalf to improve the quality of your life. Many parents have had to develop advocacy skills when dealing with schools to help their children get the services and accommodations they need. During the transition planning years (ages 14-21), it is important that students learn to develop these skills for themselves in preparation for life after high school.

If you have an IEP, the law requires that your school and your family formally plan for your transition to adult life. This transition planning process offers you an excellent opportunity to develop and hone self-advocacy skills. This is because IDEA states that transition services must be developed based on *the student's* needs, taking into account his or her preferences and interests. You are a crucial member of the team of people setting goals and planning experiences to help you prepare for life after high school.

To be a good self advocate, you need to understand your strengths, weaknesses, and preferences. You need to have a complete understanding of your disability and how it affects present and future situations. Much of this information can be learned through the diagnostic process described in Chapter 4. In addition, community experiences and applied academics provide a "hands on" approach to learning this information.

The Self Advocate at the IEP Meeting

As mentioned above, the IEP process provides many opportunities for you to identify and work on self-advocacy skills that you will need as an adult. It gives you the chance to think about what you would like to accomplish in high school and beyond, and to persuade your parents and teachers to support your goals. With practice, you may even be able to lead the IEP meeting, or guide it in the direction you would like it to go.

Preparing for Your IEP Meeting

IEP meetings are held at least once each school year, and more often if requested by any member of your IEP team—including your teachers, parents, or yourself. One of the best ways to learn to advocate for yourself is to consciously prepare yourself for these meetings. You can do this by thinking about your goals for the future, as well as the questions and problems that need to be resolved for you to meet your goals.

To help you prepare, you might want to write down some of the following information and bring it to the IEP meeting with you:

- a list of your likes and dislikes, strengths, or skills that you know need work;

- a list of questions you have about your future;

- a list of opportunities or experiences you would like to have before you leave high school:

    - practice interviewing for a job,

    - visits to various businesses to observe different work environments,

    - practice role playing or problem solving real-life scenarios,

    - practice communicating with strangers.

In addition, you may want to come to your IEP meeting with a list of objectives that you would like to see included on your IEP. For example, here are some objectives you could request to help you learn to be a better self advocate:

- to improve listening skills;

- to learn how to communicate without aggression;

- to improve eye contact;

- to demonstrate the ability to summarize conversations;

- to improve the ability to respond orally to questions;

- to learn how to seek others' opinions.

As you begin to take a more active role in the IEP meeting, you will begin to gain more confidence in speaking up on your own behalf. You will realize that you are the real expert on your hopes and dreams and that you should play a major role in decisions about your future.

Leading an IEP Meeting

With preparation, you can lead your IEP meetings. You can set the time, place, and date for the meeting along with identifying the team members to be invited. You may choose team members based on who is currently providing support, who will be providing you with support in the future, and family and friends who are important in helping you achieve your life goals. At the meeting you may identify where team members sit by having name cards on the table. You may then introduce the team members to each other and thank them for attending the meeting. The purpose for the meeting will be explained and an outline of the meeting agenda will help you address the items to be discussed. A positive method for beginning the IEP meeting is for you to share with the team your accomplishments since the last meeting.

There are several skills needed for you to run the IEP meeting. These skills include:

- reviewing past goals and performance,
- asking relevant questions,
- asking for input and feedback,
- dealing with differences of opinion,
- deciding whether there are other services needed from non-school providers, and
- ending the meeting by summarizing the decisions.

Taking charge of this process might seem like a lot to expect. But it is possible for many students to learn to do this over time by building on skill acquisition starting at age 14. The more you prepare and practice being your own self-advocate, the more successful you will be. To make it easier, you might choose to invite a friend to attend your IEP meeting and then attend theirs in turn. Once you experience some success or see others succeed, you will feel more in control and able to successfully direct your own IEP.

Problem Solving to Reach Desired Goals

Students in transition from school to adult life need to learn the difference between short-term objectives and long-term goals. One obvious reason is that IEPs require you to identify long-term goals and the short-term objectives that will help you reach them. But even beyond the classroom, it is important to understand that setting realistic short-term objectives can lead to accomplishing long-term goals, even if they seem very far away. Having distinct short-term objectives can also provide a pause along the way to evaluate the direction or strategies you have been using to reach the long-term goal.

Short-Term Objectives	Long-Term Goals
To take math courses; To take industrial trade courses; To job shadow; To lead an informational interview with a carpenter; To visit career centers to learn about work conditions, wages, job responsibilities, skills, union/apprenticeship.	**To be a carpenter**
To complete high school course work To identify and use necessary accommodations To identify and use assistive technology that helps me complete my coursework To talk to four-year colleges about services for students with LD or AD/HD	**To be admitted to a four-year college**

There are several activities you can try to improve your ability to set personal goals. One activity is to talk to friends who have AD/HD or LD about some of the transition goals from your IEP meeting. Compare your goals with theirs and describe problems you have encountered along the way. Discuss possible solutions to these problems. Questions to discuss include:

- What do I want or need?

- What people or resources can help me get what I need?

- What are some possible obstacles?

- What if my plan doesn't work?

- What fears may hold me back from reaching my goal?

Another useful activity is to identify a situation you would like to change—for example, not feeling comfortable making an accommodation request, or difficulty getting organized to write a term paper. Ask a teacher, guidance counselor, or classmate to help you develop a plan to make a positive change.

Guidelines and Timelines

Preparing for the world beyond high school requires advance planning, not only for you, but for your family as well. The more planning involved, the smoother the transition will be. The following suggestions for planning for your future have been summarized and adapted from various guides. The exact timelines you follow may vary according to your life circumstances, readiness, and the amount of support needed from your school, community, and home.

Ninth Grade

- Begin exploring postsecondary options (e.g., search out information online or at your high school career center).

- Participate in a comprehensive assessment of your abilities and limitations, including vocational assessment (see Chapter 4).

- Understand the differences between expectations in high school and postsecondary education.

- Prepare for and attend your IEP meetings.

- Participate in your IEP meetings.

- Schedule meetings with your guidance counselor to discuss your career interests/goals and to determine courses that will help you prepare for postsecondary education/training programs.

- Join clubs and participate in extracurricular activities.

- Ask for postsecondary resource materials (start folders to collect and organize information).

- Ask about study skills courses in your high school.

Tenth Grade

- Be able to describe your strengths, abilities, and disabilities.

- Know which supports you need because of your LD and/or AD/HD.

- Prepare for and attend your IEP meeting.

- Participate in the IEP process.

- Make contact with a rehabilitation services case worker to determine eligibility (see below for information about rehabilitation services).

- Attend college fairs and meet representatives.

- Work on goal setting and self-advocacy skills.

- Get information on entrance exams such as the SAT® Test.

- Discuss postsecondary plans with your guidance counselor.

- Continue to participate in extracurricular school activities.

- Participate in community service or service learning activities

Eleventh Grade

- Prepare for and attend your IEP meeting.

- Participate in your IEP meeting.

- Discuss postsecondary plans with your guidance counselor.

- Search for colleges or postsecondary programs that have the courses and supports you need.

- Watch for announcements about college entrance exam dates.

- Make campus visits and meet with Disability Support Service (DSS) personnel to discuss how support services are accessed.

- Watch for announcements about financial aid opportunities.

- Attend seminars, college nights, and future fairs.

- Talk to college students with LD and/or AD/HD to learn about demands and expectations.

- If possible, work during the summer to earn money and develop employment skills.

- Talk to teachers about obtaining recommendations.

Twelfth Grade

- Make sure you have recent diagnostic assessment information documenting your LD and/or AD/HD.

- Obtain admission testing dates.

- Schedule necessary tests.

- Make arrangements for testing accommodations (e.g., taped tests, longer time, large print, quiet area).

- Prepare for and attend your IEP meeting.

- Conduct and/or participate in your IEP meting.

- Narrow your choices of college or other postsecondary training programs.

- Talk to guidance counselors about interviews, references, applications, etc.

- Apply for financial aid.

- Meet all deadlines, including housing, admissions, and registration.

- Send thank you notes to all who helped.

The Family's Role in Creating a Self-advocate

Parents arrive at the transition phase of their child's life with much experience. Up until now, they are the ones who have been responsible for making decisions and communicating with school personnel. Often, they have had negative experiences with school personnel and other service providers. They may fear that something will go wrong and stay close to catch their children if they fail. Although this feeling is understandable, it is also important that families understand the need for their children to become self advocates and to assist with the transition process. Parents need to help their son or daughter understand not only personal strengths and weaknesses but also how to take responsibility for making decisions.

Before mapping out a postsecondary plan, parents need to be aware of how their unspoken expectations might affect planning. Most children want to make their parents proud; they want to live up to family expectations. By pushing for unrealistic goals, parents can unwittingly set their children up to fail. The more open-minded parents are, the more wisely they can evaluate the appropriateness of postsecondary programs. Parents should also trust their special knowledge and understanding of their child. Report cards and evaluations do not tell the whole story.

If expectations are reasonable, a parent's perspective is invaluable in figuring out directions and goals. Parents know what their child likes to do outside of school, and what activities provide a sense of achievement and success. These activities could even be indicators for a career.

Whatever a young person's interests or talents, the more experiences he has with them, the better. Parents can encourage their children to join clubs and participate in community activities. They can guide their children to take courses that would help develop skills further. No matter which hobby or interest develops, it is not so much the particular interest that counts at any one moment (this can change from year to year), but the overall trend. By weighing all of these factors and balancing them with academic and vocational strengths and needs with the help of the IEP team, parents may begin to see some themes and develop ideas for making postsecondary plans.

During this transition time a solid IEP team, including adult service providers, should be combining resources, information, and efforts to help out a student's future. The information that parents share with each of the service providers facilitates this collaboration. Parents can also turn to guidance counselors, since they are knowledgeable about various postsecondary programs, including admission and academic requirements. They are a good source of information concerning special programs or additional resources.

For parents of students who were not identified as having a disability in high school, it is not too late to request an evaluation if you think your son or daughter may have a disability. See the preceding chapter for information about obtaining an evaluation.

Vocational Rehabilitation Services

Vocational Rehabilitation Services is a nationwide employment training program funded jointly by federal and state governments. It can be a link to educational and other services needed to prepare young people with LD or AD/HD for employment and independence. Depending on the employment goal, these services can include assistance and support for the following:

- vocational evaluation to determine if you have the ability, aptitude, and interest to do certain jobs;

- job training;

- prevocational, academic, social, or daily living skills training;

- adult education courses (e.g., in computer skills, interview skills, personal finance)

- attending a trade or technical school to develop job-specific skills; and

- a wide range of other public or private services.

If college is a way to achieve an employment goal, services may, in some instances, include financial assistance for tuition or to cover costs of needed equipment, such as tape cassettes.

LD, AD/HD, and Vocational Rehabilitation Services

LD and AD/HD have only recently been recognized as disabling conditions eligible for vocational rehabilitation (VR) services. Some, but not all, VR counselors are trained to evaluate and develop plans for individuals with LD and/or AD/HD. Also, since VR services are provided first to individuals with the most severe disabilities, there may not be enough resources to provide services to people with LD and/or AD/HD.

When making the initial contact, ask if there is a VR counselor on the staff who is specifically trained to address the needs of people with LD and/or ADHD, or if the area has a learning specialist. Ideally, you will meet a vocational rehabilitation counselor during the transition planning process. If this does not occur while you are in high school, you can contact the Division or Department of Rehabilitation Services (DRS) after you finish high school.

When meeting with a vocational rehabilitation counselor, you should bring along documentation of your disability, such as recent school records and test results. DRS will then determine whether you qualify for services, as described in Steps 2 and 3 below.

If accepted for services, you will work with the counselor on an Individual Plan for Employment (IPE). The plan is based on your interests, abilities, and aspirations; the results of evaluation; and the availability of resources. You may seek out input from others, such as parents, teachers, and other professionals to help draw up a meaningful plan of action.

Accessing Vocational Rehabilitation Services

Here are some guidelines for accessing the Department or Division of Rehabilitation Services (DRS) for assistance in the transition planning process:

Step 1: Apply for Services

Contact the DRS office nearest your home and arrange for an interview with a counselor. Vocational rehabilitation offices are located in or near every city. However, they are known by different names in different states. If you can't find your local office in the phone book under state government listings, try the city, county, or state information service, the library, the school system, or the nearest chapter of the Learning Disabilities Association (LDA). Or write to the HEATH Resource Center for its state agency listing (see Resources at the back of the book).

Ideally, you should apply for services at least two years before graduating from high school, but you can do so at any time that you are considering employment training.

Step 2: Interview

Meet with a counselor, who will explain the rehabilitation application process. You should bring relevant medical, educational, and employment information to this meeting. If copies of the information are not available, names and addresses of your doctors, schools, and employers should be provided so the counselor can request the reports. You will have to give the counselor permission to do so by signing a release of information request. The counselor will also obtain additional information needed to determine your eligibility.

Step 3: Are You Eligible?

You are eligible for rehabilitation services if:

- You have a physical or mental impairment that results in a substantial barrier to employment; and

- The services provided should result in employment; and

- You need rehabilitation services to prepare for, engage in, or keep employment.

If you are not eligible for services, the counselor will explain why and recommend other agencies that may be able to help. The counselor will also inform you of your right to appeal this decision for eligibility.

Step 4: Plan

Additional assessments such as a vocational evaluation may be needed to help you and your counselor develop an Individual Plan for Employment (IPE). Then, you and your counselor will write an IPE that will include:

- an employment goal (e.g., a career in computer technology);

- the services DRS will arrange to assist you reaching your goal (see "Get Services" below for examples);

- an agreement as to who will pay for the services;

- the ways that you and your counselor will determine if the services are helping;

- a description of your rights and responsibilities, such as the right to choose between the several service options to reach your goal.

You and your counselor will sign and date the IPE. You will then receive a copy.

Step 5: Get Services

DRS may arrange one or more of the following services for you:

- Vocational Counseling to help with working toward your goals;

- Physical and Mental Rehabilitation Services, such as personal counseling, for limited periods;

- Rehabilitation Technology Services such as voice recognition, computer software, or tape recorder;

- Job Skills Training and Placement to help you find a job;

- Follow-up Services once you are working to make sure you and the employer are satisfied;

- Other support services that may be needed.

DRS payment for services will depend upon your income. In some cases, you may be asked to pay something toward the cost of services received. DRS will pay the remainder of the costs if other sources of payment are not available.

Step 6: Achieve Your Goal

From the first day you enter the counselor's office, the services you receive are directed toward helping you achieve your employment goal. Together you and your counselor will work to prepare you for and locate appropriate employment. After you reach your goal, your counselor can provide additional services to help you keep the job or maintain independence. You can also reapply for DRS services if problems develop or additional assistance is needed down the road.

Handling Disputes

If you ever disagree with your counselor's recommendations, and the problem cannot be resolved, you can contact your Client Assistance Project (CAP) and ask to speak to an ombudsman. Ombudsmen investigate complaints for consumers who think they have wrongly been denied services, or are dissatisfied with the type or amount of services they receive. The addresses and phone numbers of the nearest CAP are available from the local vocational rehabilitation office.

Tips for Finding Other Options

Vocational rehabilitation may or may not be an option for you. Unfortunately, there is no single system that is responsible for providing the combination of daily living skills, academic skills, and prevocational and vocational skills needed by many young people with LD or AD/HD. You need to be alert and search out other services. You need to ask others for ideas to help you find the services you need. Your district school system may know where some of these services exist.

Networking with other people in the same situation is often the way to find information. One way to reach experienced and knowledgeable individuals with LD or AD/HD and their families is through state or local chapters of the Learning Disabilities Association (LDA) or Children and Adults with Attention Deficit/Hyperactivity Disorder (CHADD). The national offices of these organizations can help you locate the nearest chapter. (See the Resources.)

Parent Training and Information Centers, organized and run by parents, are another source of help. Centers throughout the country have received federal funds to assist them in carrying out information and training activities. For information about local or regional centers, contact your local school system or the U.S. Department of Education, Division of Personnel Preparation, Office of Special Education and Rehabilitative Service (OSERS).

Summary

As you prepare for postsecondary education and employment, both you and your family need to adjust to the fact that you are moving into the adult world. To make a successful transition, it is essential that you know the following:

- what you can do independently,

- what assistance is available,

- what assistance you need,

- what you have to contribute, and

- what your action plan is for the next three to five years.

These issues, and resources to address them, are described throughout this book.

Resources

BOOKS

Advocacy: Self-Advocacy and Special Needs, 1995
Editors: Philip Garner, Richard Joss, and Sarah Sandow
Open University Press/Taylor & Francis Inc.
47 Runway Road,
Levittown, PA 19057
Phone: (800) 821-8312
Fax: (215) 269-0363
E-mail: enquiries@openup.co.uk
http://www.taylorandfrancis.com/BOOKS

Complete Guide to Special Education Transition Services: Ready-to-Use Help and Materials for Successful Transitions from School to Adulthood, 1998
Authors: Roger Pierangelo and Rochelle Crane
Center for Applied Research in Education
P.O. Box 11071
Des Moines, IA 50336-1071
Phone: (800) 947-7700
Fax: (515) 284-2607
http://www.viacom.com

Counseling Secondary Students with Learning Disabilities: A Ready-To-Use Guide to Help Students Prepare for College and Work, 1998
Authors: Michael Koehler and Marybeth Kravets
Center for Applied Research in Education
See address above.

Falling through the Cracks: Rehabilitation Services for Adults with LD, 1992
Author: J. Osgood Smith
Learning Disabilities Association
4156 Library Road
Pittsburgh, PA 15234-1349
Phone: (412) 341-1515
Fax: (412) 344-0224
E-mail: ldanatl@usaor.net
http://www.ldanatl.org

Making It Happen: Student Involvement in Education Planning, Decision Making, and Instruction, 1998
Editors: Michael L. Wehmeyer and Deanna J. Sands
Paul H. Brookes Publishing Company
P.O. Box 10624
Baltimore, MD 21285-0624
Phone: (800) 638-3775
Fax: (410) 337-8539
E-mail: custserv@pbrookes.com
http://www.pbrookes.com

Self-Determination Across the Life Span: Independence and Choice for People with Disabilities, 1998
Editors: Deanna J. Sands and Michael L. Wehmeyer
Paul H. Brookes Publishing Company
P.O. Box 10624
Baltimore, MD 21285-0624
Phone: (800) 638-3775
Fax: (410) 337-8539
E-mail: custserv@pbrookes.com
http://www.pbrookes.com

Self-Determination Strategies for Adolescents in Transition
Authors: Sharon Field, Alan Hoffman, and Shirley Spezia
Pro-Ed
8700 Shoal Creek Blvd.
Austin, TX 78757-6897
Phone: (800) 897-3202
Fax: (800) 397-7633
E-mail: info@proedinc.com
http://www.proedinc.com

Teaching Self-Determination to Students with Disabilities: Basic Skills for Successful Transition, 1997
Authors: Michael L. Wehmeyer, Martin Agran, and Carolyn Hughes
Paul H. Brookes Publishing Company
P.O. Box 10624
Baltimore, MD 21285-0624
Phone: (800) 638-3775
Fax: (410) 337-8539
E-mail: custserv@pbrookes.com
http://www.pbrookes.com

Transition and School-Based Services: Interdisciplinary Perspectives for Enhancing the Transition Process, 1999
Editors: Sharon DeFur and George Patton
Pro-Ed
8700 Shoal Creek Blvd.
Austin, TX 78757-6897
Phone: (800) 897-3202
Fax: (800) 397-7633
http://www.proedinc.com

Transition and Students with Learning Disabilities: Facilitating the Movement from School to Adult Life, 1996
Author: James R. Patton and Ginger Blalock
Pro-Ed
See address above.

Transition to Employment, 1998
Author: Craig Michaels
Pro-Ed
See address above.

Young Person's Occupational Outlook Handbook
JIST Works, Inc.
720 North Park Avenue
Indianapolis, IN 46202-3490
Phone: (800) JIST-USA
Fax: (800) 547-8329
E-mail: Jistmktg@aol.com
http://www.jist.com

VIDEO
Self-Advocacy: Taking Charge, 1995
Transition Plus Services
Minneapolis Public Schools
Minneapolis, MN 55413
Phone: (612) 627-2260
http://www.mpls.k12.mn.us

FACT SHEETS
10 Steps to Independence: Promoting Self-Determination in the Home
The Arc
500 East Border Street, Suite 300
Arlington, TX 76010
Phone: (817) 261-6003
Fax: (817) 277-3491
E-mail: thearc@metronet.com
http://www.thearc.org

Directory of Self-Advocacy Programs
The Arc's Self-Advocacy Committee
500 East Border Street, Suite 300
Arlington, TX 76010
Phone: (817) 261-6003
Fax: (817) 277-3491
E-mail: thearc@metronet.com
http://www.thearc.org

Helping Youth Gain Independence, 1994
The National Center for Youth with Disabilities
University of Minnesota
Minneapolis, MN 55455
Phone: (612) 626-1212
E-mail: cyfcec@maroon.tc.umn.edu
http://www.cyfc.umn.edu/Youth/chhealth.html

Linkages—Self-Advocacy: Empowerment for Adult Learners with Learning Disabilities and
Linkages—Transitions Issues for the Adult Learner with Learning Disabilities
National Adult Literacy and Learning Disabilities Center (ALLD)
1875 Connecticut Ave., NW

Washington, DC 20009-1202
Phone: (800) 953-2553
Fax: (202) 884-8422
E-mail: info@nalldc.aed.org
http://www.ld-read.org
go to publications

Self-determination, 1988
NICHCY
P.O. Box 1492
Washington, DC 20013
Phone: (800) 695-0285
Fax: (202) 884-8441
E-mail: nichcy@aed.org
http://www.nichcy.org

CURRICULA

Become Your Own Expert: Self-Advocacy for Individuals with Learning Disabilities, 1995
Author: Winnelle D. Carpenter
Cognitive Learning Consultants
P.O. Box 202065
Bloomington, MN 55420
Phone: (612) 854-4935

Choice Maker: Self-Determination Transition Curriculum
Center for Educational Research
University of Colorado Springs
Division of Continuing Education
P.O. Box 7150
Colorado Springs, CO 80933-7150
Phone: (719) 593-3364

HIRE Learning Workbook Series
(Setting Your Career and Life Direction, Succeeding in Your Work and Community)
Authors: Patricia Duffy & T. Walker Wannie
JIST Works, Inc.
720 North Park Avenue
Indianapolis, IN 46202-3490
Phone: (800) JIST-USA
Fax: (800) 547-8329

E-mail: Jistmktg@aol.com

http://www.jist.com

The Self-Advocacy Strategy for Education & Transition Planning, 1994
Authors: Anthony K. Van Reusen, Candace S. Bos, Jean B. Schumaker, and
Donald Deshler
Edge Enterprises, Inc.
P.O. Box 1304
Lawrence, KS 66044
Phone: (913) 749-1473
Fax: (913) 749-0207

Tools for Transition
Authors: Jean Ness and Elizabeth Aune
American Guidance Services (AGS)
4201 Woodland Road
P.O. Box 99
Circle Pines, MN 55014-1796
Phone: (800) 328-2560
Fax: (800) 471-8457
E-mail: agsmail@agsnet.com
http://www.agsnet.com

ORGANIZATIONS

Contact information for the following useful organizations can be found beginning on page 347.

- American Congress of Community Supports & Employment Services

- The Arc

- Association for the Advancement of Rehabilitation Technology (RESNA)

- Beach Center on Families and Disability

- Clearinghouse on Disability Information

- Disability Rights Education and Defense Fund, Inc. (DREDF)

- Educational Testing Service, Inc.

- Higher Education and The Handicapped (HEATH) Resource Center

- LDA (Learning Disabilities Association of America)

- National Center for the Study of Postsecondary Educational Supports, Rehabilitation Research & Training Center (RRTC)

- National Clearinghouse of Rehabilitation Training Materials (NCHRTM)

- The National Institute on Disability and Rehabilitation Research (NIDRR)

- National Rehabilitation Information Center (NARIC)

- Office of Special Education & Rehabilitative Services (OSERS)

- PACER Center

- Rehabilitation and Disability Services/ABLE DATA

- The Rehabilitation Resource Center

- Rehabilitation Services Administration

- Technical Assistance on Training about the Rehabilitation Act (TATRA)

- YMCA of the USA

6

MAKING EDUCATIONAL CHOICES

Arden Boyer-Stephens

CHAPTER 6-A—Overview: Making Choices

"I needed a year of remedial classes so I could handle reading, English, and math better."

"I was too immature and angry to handle college the first time. I had to bottom out before I could figure out what my problems were and how to handle them."

"I fell in love with the college I went to. It was an art school, and for the first time I could concentrate on what I was good at."

"I took time off in the Marine Corps before I tackled college."

"High school was enough for me . . . I said to myself, 'There's a world out there and you can make it. You don't need college to make it.'"

"I had no idea what we would do when my son finished high school. How would he ever get ready for a job? Would he just sit at home and watch TV?"

What's ahead after high school? These words spoken by adults and parents reveal that there are no simple answers. For some, colleges or technical schools are the best possibilities. For others, going to work or getting into a job training or apprenticeship program are the best next steps. Others need extra time to set their goals.

Students graduating from high school are not the only ones who need to make decisions about postsecondary education. Many adults with learning disabilities (LD) and/or Attention Deficit/Hyperactivity Disorder (AD/HD), now in the working world, want to return to school. Some may have dropped out in their teens. Others never knew they had LD and/or AD/HD and settled for jobs below their potential. They may want to learn computer skills, to read music, or to become a social worker, a practical nurse, a carpenter, etc.

Many students need a period of transition following high school before they are ready for a formal postsecondary education program. They may need time to mature, to develop socially, to learn skills of independent living. Some may need counseling to overcome self-defeating attitudes. Others may need job experience to gain self-confidence and help clarify career goals. Extra time and well-planned activities can lay the groundwork for success. You will need to decide what direction you need to take next.

Keep an open mind and a flexible attitude; these are essential in planning your future. Decisions need not be considered permanent. You, like other students, may choose one route at one stage and another at a later time. The motivation that comes from achievement, self-awareness, and support from others can lead to the acceptance of new challenges or the willingness to take risks.

Getting Ready

How to begin? Transition planning during high school can be very helpful in setting a direction. If you are no longer in high school, you will want to seek guidance from parents, friends, and counselors to help get different perspectives on your skills, interests, and special talents. The best decisions are made after gathering information. This chapter offers you information on a range of postsecondary education options. The more knowledgeable parents, students, and advisors are about possible options, the better the chance for a successful match.

Gathering Information about Career Options

Deciding on the best secondary education option for you will depend on a variety of factors, as discussed above. One of the biggest deciding factors, of course, is the kind of career you think you might be interested in. Some careers require a college education, some require a technical school education, and some require other combinations of education and experience.

Chapters 3 and 5 discuss some of the activities that can be written into your IEP to help you learn about careers during the high school years. For example, perhaps you have an interest in working with small children. You might ask to have your IEP specify that you will volunteer at a day care center for 50 hours during the school year (or summer). And Chapter 5 discussed how vocational services might help you examine career options. But there are also activities you can do on your own or after you have graduated from high school to help you narrow down possible career interests. They include:

- part-time, summer, or volunteer work experiences;

- work-study programs;

- talking to people about their jobs.

Of course, not every student enters a postsecondary program with a career goal in mind. It's perfectly OK if you fall into this category. In fact, it's important to know whether you don't know what you want to be "when you grow up." That might mean that going to college, where you can sample many course offerings, is a good option for you. Or it might mean that taking time off from school to work for a year or two might be best....

Work Experiences

Working is a way to sample and screen career fields. Perhaps you did not like your summer job flipping hamburgers at the local restaurant, or did enjoy selling clothes or helping people select hardware or plants. Maybe that volunteer job in the hospital helped you feel useful and needed. Each job experience, no matter how unskilled, can teach us about our likes and dislikes, about settings in which we feel comfortable or uncomfortable, and about chances for learning and advancement.

Working can also provide opportunities to mature. By working with adults, you can observe and learn work habits. In addition, you can learn social skills and specific skills that are the key to successful employment. Self-expression is also easier in settings where adults are accepting and eager to help a youngster without being as judgmental as your peers. Service learning and employment during high school help students learn more about themselves and can broaden how they see themselves.

Work-Study Programs

A work-study program usually involves going to school in the morning for the required courses and going to work in the afternoon. Although these jobs may be low paying and hard work, they can expose a teenager to the real world. For some students, this can be a rude awakening; for others, it can be a welcome relief and a boost to their morale. For still others, it may be a motivator to seek advanced training.

A work-study program during the last two years of high school can sometimes break a cycle of boredom and failure, provide career awareness and motivation for postsecondary education, and build self-esteem by giving financial rewards for employment. Perhaps the most valuable by-product is discovering that you can make positive contributions in a non-school setting.

If you decide to participate in a work-study program, be sure that it does not keep you from successfully completing basic courses required to graduate or get into a college. Guidance counselors, special education teachers, and any other relevant school personnel can guide you and your family through this process.

CHAPTER 6-B—The College Option

College offers potential benefits for all students, including those with LD and/ or AD/HD. For some, a two-year or four-year college or university program may lead to a career-entry job. For others, a college degree may lead to advanced graduate or professional training. Stretching one's horizons intellectually and socially can lead to personal growth. Experiences both in and out of classes can help to set a career course. College can provide exposure to new ideas and new people.

Is College an Option for You?

Even if you struggled academically in high school, you may be ready for the challenges in college. Some reasons why:

- In postsecondary institutions, you are more likely to have a choice of teachers

- So you can choose the one whose teaching style most closely fits your learning style.

- You can arrange your schedule so you are only taking one or two classes that are difficult for you in any given semester.

- You can take classes at the time of day when you are most alert.

- After you choose a major, you can concentrate on courses that are in your areas of strength.

If you are wondering whether college is a realistic option for you, you might want to look into one of the *Summer Pre-College Options* offered by some colleges and universities across the nation. These programs are for high school students who have completed their junior or senior year. They usually offer three units of college credit and include classes in learning strategies, computer lab instruction, and tutoring for one or more regular college classses.

These summer programs are often quite expensive. It is possible that your local Vocational Rehabilitation might provide funding for you to attend such a program, however, so be sure to ask. You can obtain a current listing of these summer programs from:

> HEATH
> One Dupont Circle
> Suite 800
> Washington, DC 20036
> 800-544-3284
> http://www.acenet.edu/About/programs/Access&Equity/HEATH/
>   HotTopics.html

Types of Colleges and Universities

In considering the college option, students with LD and/or AD/HD should not only review types of services available for students with LD and/or AD/HD, but should learn the goals and objectives of each institution and the advantages each offers to students with disabilities. This section reviews the options that are generally available across the United States.

Two-Year Colleges

In the U.S., there are two types of colleges with programs designed to last two years: 1) public community (junior) colleges, and 2) private junior colleges. Although there are some differences between the two, both offer students an opportunity to test the academic waters.

For many students, two-year colleges offer a chance to prepare for further education, to learn an occupational skill, or to change careers. For others, they provide a way to enhance personal development. You can complete these two-year programs, earn an Associate of Arts (AA) degree, and credits can be transferred to a four-year college or university. Some courses of study lead to an Associate of Applied Science (AAS) degree. Those are usually occupation-specific degrees (e.g., automotive technician), taking two years to complete. Some of the AAS degree course work will transfer to a four-year college, but some will not. For courses of study in some occupations (e.g., child care, heavy equipment operator), a certificate, rather than a degree, is awarded. These courses frequently take less than two years to complete.

Public Community Colleges

Publicly funded community colleges can be found in most locations within a reasonable commuting distance. These institutions are committed to serving the educational and training needs of the local communities. Open admission policies make it possible for individuals over 18 years of age to attend even if they do not have a high school diploma. However, most community colleges do require that students taking courses for credit have a diploma or pass a high school equivalency test such as the General Educational Development (GED) Test. Preparation for the GED Test is usually given on campus.

Community colleges offer liberal arts subjects as well as training in specific occupations, such as hotel management, auto mechanics, marketing, computer

TABLE 6.1—ADVANTAGES TO ATTENDING COMMUNITY COLLEGES

- The choice of living at home while making the transition to college

- No admissions requirements (i.e., college entrance exams, grade point average, class rank)

- The chance to increase academic skills through developmental or remedial classes, if necessary

- An opportunity to try out college by taking one or two courses

- A chance to build a better academic record that can be transferred to a four-year college or university for which the student is qualified. A student transferring to a four-year college is not usually required to take entrance examinations, although other entrance requirements must be met

- An opportunity to learn an occupation, to work on academic skills, or to learn ways to accommodate learning problems

- The chance to return to school to upgrade academic and job skills and to work toward improved employment opportunities or a career change

- Lower tuition and other costs than at a typical four-year college

programming, or dental assisting. Most also have remedial or developmental courses for upgrading basic academic skills. Community colleges are becoming increasingly responsive to the needs of students with LD and/or AD/HD, and many are developing excellent support services. To find out what services are available, you should contact the Disability Support Services (DSS) office.

Private Junior Colleges

Most private junior colleges are small residential schools that prepare students for transfer to a four-year liberal arts college. Some offer occupational training. Upon completion of the two-year program, an AA degree is awarded. Entrance examinations are usually required, although in many cases, other criteria, such as work experience and extracurricular activities, are considered.

TABLE 6.2—ADVANTAGES TO ATTENDING JUNIOR COLLEGES

- An opportunity to live away from home in an intimate, supportive environment

- Small classes in which instructors can provide individualized attention

- Opportunities to work on improving reading, writing, and math skills

- A chance to train for a new career after being in the working world

Four-year Colleges and Universities

Four-year colleges and undergraduate university programs, including four-year technical schools, vary in tradition, size, admissions criteria, academic standards, course offerings, student population, location, and cost. All grant bachelors degrees upon completion.

In most colleges or undergraduate university programs, you are expected to sample a variety of courses during the first two years and then focus on your

TABLE 6.3—ADVANTAGES TO ATTENDING A FOUR-YEAR COLLEGE OR UNIVERSITY

- There are over 450 majors offered in American colleges and universities. With appropriate accommodations and services, students with LD and/or AD/HD who have the potential to do college-level work can find many subject areas that are of interest

- Disability Support Services (DSS) Offices are increasingly becoming available

- There are many opportunities to develop talents (e.g., music, art, dance) either by majoring in that field or by attending a specialized four-year college

- Living away from home, either in a dorm or off campus, offers the opportunity to develop independent living skills in a semi-supportive environment

major in the last two years. Requirements for graduation differ, although most colleges require a certain number of credits in English and foreign languages.

A number of colleges are specialized, such as the Massachusetts Institute of Technology, the Juilliard School of Music, and the Rhode Island School of Design. Students are expected to be proficient in their fields but must also take courses in other fields as well. Tuition varies greatly. State-supported institutions tend to be less costly. Some financial aid is usually available.

Graduate and Professional Schools

Opportunities for students with LD and/or AD/HD in graduate and professional schools are increasing as support services develop. Graduate Schools offer master's, specialist's, and doctoral degrees in various subject areas.

Graduate students are entitled to the same types of accommodations and services that are available in undergraduate schools. Graduate students who think they have LD and/or AD/HD can take advantage of campus diagnostic, tutorial, and other support services. If there is a DSS office on campus, this is a logical place to go for assistance. Graduate students, as well as other students, should familiarize themselves with Section 504 of the Rehabilitation Act and the Americans with Disabilities Act to understand their rights on campus. (See Chapter 3.)

Continuing Education Options

Almost all community and junior colleges and many four-year colleges and universities offer classes from their continuing education departments. In most cases, a student does not have to be admitted to the college, but can take these courses

TABLE 6.4—ADVANTAGES TO TAKING CONTINUING EDUCATION COURSES

- Creates a step in the transition process from high school to college

- There are no admission requirements

- Provides a way to explore subject areas

- Provides an opportunity to build academic study skills in context without the stress of grades interfering

- Allows students to explore the choice of college as a possible goal just by signing up and paying the course fee. Some continuing education classes are very academic in nature (like typical college courses), some are taken for continuing education credit to retain certification in a field (e.g., refresher courses for Automotive Technicians), and some classes are taken to pursue leisure and personal interest activities (e.g., scuba diving).

Financial Aid

College tuition varies greatly, with state-supported institutions tending to be less costly. There are usually no specific institutional scholarships for students with LD and/or AD/HD, so they must apply for financial assistance through the traditional channels. Types of financial assistance generally available include:

- **Grants**—assistance in paying college expenses that typically does not have to be paid back, although sometimes strings are attached. For example, you may have to perform a "service" to the school, such as playing in the marching band, or may be expected to work for a certain period of time after graduation in a certain field

- **Loans**—money lent to students by the government, banks, or other agencies, which typically does not need to be repaid until after graduation

- **Scholarships**—gifts of money or other assistance to help with college expenses, awarded to students who meet specified criteria (for example, by achieving certain GPAs or scores on admission tests, by agreeing to major in a certain field, by coming from certain ethnic groups or regions of the country)

- **Work-study programs**—programs in which you are hired by the college to perform needed work on campus, such as clerical or research work, in exchange for an agreed-upon wage

If you are a vocational rehabilitation client, you should check with your counselor to see whether tuition and/or accommodations can be funded by vocational rehabilitation. (See Chapter 5 for more information.) Any applications for funding should be obtained no later than the beginning of your senior year in high school. These applications and information about funding sources are available in high school counselors' offices.

Talent Search and Educational Opportunity Centers are another possible source of assistance. These centers are federally funded programs that were set up to provide counseling and other services to disadvantaged students and students with disabilities. Sometimes they can help students with disabilities negotiate financial assistance with postsecondary institutions. For more information, contact:

Division of Student Service
1250 Maryland Avenue
Portals Building, Suite 600
Washington, DC 20202

When applying to schools, remember to request information about financial aid or to check the general college directories regarding financial aid policies of individual schools. These directories explain eligibility for each school's financial aid program and give application deadlines.

The College Option: In Conclusion

Students with LD and/or AD/HD can succeed in all types of colleges and universities, including the most prestigious. But it is very important to be realistic about the level of support needed and to know in advance if that support is available. Chapter 7 can help you learn how to determine which colleges can offer you the support you need, and how to go about getting it.

CHAPTER 6-C—The Vocational-Technical Education Option

Vocational-technical education is defined as education geared for employment that requires specialized education, but not a bachelor's degree. For some students with LD or AD/HD, postsecondary vocational-technical education can be the key to an independent and productive life. It can provide professional training that leads you to a marketable skill and a job future. It can also fulfill the ultimate goal of education by preparing you to participate in society as a self-sufficient adult.

Vocational-technical education programs are taught in both public and private institutions. Public programs may be offered by technical institutes, community colleges, and area vocational-technical centers. Private (proprietary) programs may be offered by trade, technical, and business schools. These programs teach skills in hundreds of occupational areas including agriculture, health, business, trade, industry, and marketing.

Determining a Career Direction

Tim, a bright student with LD, became adept at using his personal computer while in high school. After graduation, he attended a public postsecondary technical school and received training as a computer technician. He is now employed by a large local retailer as a trainee in its purchasing/inventory control department.

This is not the end of the line for Tim, but is a successful beginning that will lead to additional learning and advancement opportunities. Tim chose his occupational training carefully. He understood his strengths and weaknesses. He knew that his auditory perception problems would not interfere with his ability to work on a computer. He also knew that he was capable of doing the English and math required.

Clearly, a vital part of decision making is determining your individual interests, abilities, and goals. Knowing the variety of occupational possibilities and the settings in which they are taught are also important. If you think that vocational-technical training might be right for you, you can use the strategies outlined under "Gathering Information about Career Options," page 121, to investigate career options and interests.

Selecting a Vocational-Technical Education Program

Once you have chosen an occupational area, the next step is to locate an appropriate school and check on its quality. You need to ask questions about the time involved in completing course work, what degree or certificate is offered, experience of instructors, ability to accommodate students with disabilities, and job placement opportunities.

Locating Programs

Each community has a different array of vocational-technical education programs. They are not always easy to locate, and frequently students are unaware of what their community offers.

Following are some suggestions to assist you in finding appropriate programs:

- Ask about vocational-technical options at state and local chapters of the Learning Disabilities Association (LDA).

- Ask your guidance counselor or the state employment agency about what is available.

- Call the vocational-technical education state office and ask for the individual familiar with support services throughout the state. Each state has a specialist who is usually located within the division of vocational education in the state department of education. One way to locate the address is to request your state's agency list from the Association for Career and Technical Education (ACTE) listed in Resources at the back of the book.

The section on "Types of Vocational-Technical Schools" below will give you an idea of the range of options often available.

Length of Time Required to Complete Course Work

Length of time for completing course work in a vocational-technical education program varies. It depends on the requirements of the occupational area and the level of skill to be attained. Training to be a certified nurse's aide may take ten weeks; to be a geriatric medical assistant, two years. Training to be a broadcast technician can take from ten weeks to two years; to become a veterinarian assistant can take from 28 weeks to 18 months.

Degrees and Certificates Earned

Vocational-technical education students earn either a degree or certificate. After a full two-year course of technical training in an occupational area (such as computer programming, dental assisting, plumbing, air conditioning), a student usually receives an Associate of Applied Science (AAS) or an Associate of Applied Arts (AAA) degree.

Certificate programs have the same requirements for mastery of occupational skills as degree programs, but they do not require the same amount of academic study and usually take one year or less. Possession of a certificate is recognized as an advantage by employers and enhances job possibilities. The certificate can also be used to enter into apprenticeship programs or to obtain more advanced or specialized training. In some cases, students in occupational programs lasting one

TABLE 6.5—QUESTIONS TO ASK ABOUT VOCATIONAL-TECHNICAL EDUCATION PROGRAMS

- What are the minimal academic skills required for entrance into the program? Can any accommodations be made for teaching students at a lower reading or math level (such as providing texts in simpler language)?

- Must all students proceed at the same pace?

- Is there a coordinator of services for students with special needs in the program or a vocational-technical support team? Does the staff have an understanding of LD and AD/HD?

- What basic knowledge of tools is needed for participation in the program?

- What safety rules must be followed for entrance into the program?

- Does training occur in places that closely resemble actual job sites? Is on-the-job training part of the curriculum?

- Do instructors have recent job experience in their fields?

- Will job opportunities be available after training? Will someone at the school help with finding employment?

- If you want to transfer credits to a professional training school or a four-year college or technical institute, is there someone at the school who will help?

year or less are awarded a diploma to signify completion of training. If a license is required in a particular field (such as plumbing, nursing, or electrical engineering), you must do additional work after receiving a degree or certificate.

Types of Vocational-Technical Schools

Vocational-technical education programs are either public or private. The settings range from community colleges to single-specialty schools. Following are descriptions of each type of school, divided into public and private categories.

Public Vocational-Technical Education Programs

State laws that govern public vocational-technical education create different patterns of service in different parts of the country. One state may provide postsecondary vocational-technical education through its community college system; another through technical institutes. Requirements for licenses to practice certain trades or professions also differ from state to state, as do requirements for completing certain courses of study. Despite this diversity, the information in the next few paragraphs can help you to identify the public vocational-technical education services in your community.

Community Colleges. At two-year community and junior colleges, occupational training can be combined with liberal arts. At the end of a two-year program, the student receives an associate's degree. She then has the choice of seeking employment in her chosen occupation, or transferring many or most of her credits to a four-year college and continuing her education.

Two-Year Technical Institutes. Two-year technical institutes, also known as technical colleges, are publicly funded institutions that offer degree programs in skills required to enter and advance in specific occupational fields. Training is provided in numerous technologies. These include:

- business management,

- insurance,

- law enforcement,

- animal health,

- automotive maintenance,

- aviation maintenance,

- graphic communications, and

- social services.

In general, academic courses are related to occupational areas. Math, technical writing, physics, and chemistry may be required for certain courses of study, but not for others. Courses such as communications, English composition, or algebra may be required for all courses of study. Be sure you check catalogs carefully for requirements and electives.

TABLE 6.6—ADVANTAGES TO ATTENDING PUBLIC TWO-YEAR TECHNICAL INSTITUTES

- No admissions requirements other than age (eighteen years or over) and graduation from high school or GED Test, with some exceptions. Entrance exams may be required for certain technical courses of study, such as nursing and engineering

- Availability of DSS office on many campuses. In addition, a vocational support team may be available to help students master specific tasks or skills that present difficulties

- An opportunity to get intensive and highly specialized training in an occupational area

- Preparation for transfer to four-year college or professional school

- Enhanced opportunities for job placement. Programs are usually geared to employment opportunities in the community

- More hands-on work than in a college program, which might be an advantage for some students with LD or AD/HD

Area Vocational-Technical Center/Career Centers. Area vocational-technical centers exist in many states. They are usually run by the public school system or by the community college system. In some states, these centers serve only high school students; in other states, they also serve postsecondary students. These centers usually offer training in a wide range of occupational areas. Time required to complete course work depends on the requirements of specific occu-

TABLE 6.7—ADVANTAGES TO ATTENDING AREA VOCATIONAL-TECHNICAL CENTERS

- No admissions requirement (high school graduation may or may not be required, depending on the course of study)

- Required academics relate to the skills needed in jobs in a particular occupational area

- The opportunity to obtain occupational skills needed in today's job market and to earn a certificate that will be an asset in gaining employment

pational areas. Although these are not usually degree-giving institutions, they award certificates after completion of a course of study.

Single-Specialty Public Vocational-Technical Schools. In some areas of the country, publicly supported schools offer training in single-specialty skills. For example, schools may specialize in such fields as aviation, truck driving, barbering, or cosmetology. The length of programs of study can vary from weeks to 12-18 months. Usually a certificate, rather than a degree, is awarded upon completion of a program.

Private (Proprietary) Schools

Private (proprietary) schools are trade, technical, or business schools that offer training in a variety of occupational skills. They are, for the most part, small, single-purpose schools that specialize in practical training in fields generally requiring two years or less to gain skills needed for employment. Tuition costs are usually higher compared to public trade schools.

Getting Accommodations at a Proprietary School

An increasing number of proprietary schools are becoming aware of issues related to students with LD and/or AD/HD. Vocational rehabilitation agencies are opening up opportunities by placing students with LD and/or AD/HD in proprietary schools and working with administrators and instructors to arrange appropriate accommodations. A school that is a "vendor" for vocational rehabilitation may have gained experience with LD and may be a good choice for students seeking occupational training.

Before you apply to a proprietary school, it is important to find out whether instructors have had experience working with students with LD or AD/HD and types of accommodations that can be made. An inevitable question before enrollment is whether to disclose a disability. Many vocational-technical educators advise students to be honest about their limitations during admissions interviews and to explain their strengths and specific needs very clearly. It can be helpful if you provide simple, printed information about your learning disabilities if you decide to disclose. It is also important to look into a school's reputation, whether it is accredited, and how much help it gives to students in finding jobs. In short, is it worth your investment?

TABLE 6.8—ADVANTAGES TO ATTENDING PROPRIETARY SCHOOLS

- An opportunity to be prepared for a specific job in a wide range of areas such as inhalation therapy, cosmetology, real estate, golf course operation, word processing, etc.

- No admissions requirement at most schools other than the wish to learn. Some programs require that you have a high school diploma or you have passed the GED Test, but others prepare students for the GED Test as part of the program. Some schools may test for aptitude or specific level of reading, writing, or manual dexterity before enrolling students.

The Vocational-Technical Option: In Conclusion

Opportunities for students with disabilities in vocational-technical education are growing. Educators, parents, and adults with disabilities are advocating nationally and locally for appropriate vocational-technical education programs that can prepare people for independence. As with college programs, only you can determine whether a particular program is appropriate for you. See Chapter 7 for further guidance in evaluating your options and choosing the best one for you.

CHAPTER 6-D—Other Options

Although the focus of this book is on postsecondary educational opportunities, many students with LD and/or AD/HD need other options to prepare themselves for employment and independence. Outside of postsecondary education, there are still many options:

- life skills programs,

- apprenticeship and job training programs,

- military service,

- academic skill-building and independent living programs, and

- adult education and vocational rehabilitation services.

Although these options may not be available, appropriate, or accessible for all young people with LD and/or AD/HD, they should be considered as possible alternatives. One option may help you make the transition between high school and further education. Another may help you take those first steps to steady, full-time employment. Or another may help you if you left high school many years ago, but are now looking for ways to achieve greater independence and self-fulfillment. Since many of these programs are in short supply, persistence and imagination may be required to track them down.

Life Skills Programs

Some people with LD and/or AD/HD need more intensive services than a community college, university, or vocational-technical school can offer. There are postsecondary programs designed specifically for young people who need assistance in learning skills for independence. These programs are provided in a residential setting and often offer training in:

- life skills,

- workplace literacy,

- social skills development,

- vocational and career exploration and training,

- time management,

- banking and budgeting.

Examples of such programs include the Independence Center in Los Angeles, California, the Life Development Institute in Phoenix, Arizona, and the Threshold Program of Lesley College in Cambridge, Massachusetts. For a listing of programs, contact HEATH at One Dupont Circle, Suite 800, Washington, DC 20036; 800-544-3284.

Apprenticeship Programs

Apprenticeship programs exist in over 700 "apprenticeable" occupations. Examples include graphic arts, electrical, and plumbing careers. The demand for skilled labor has increased the number of apprenticeship programs in many settings, especially in universities and local and state governments.

In an apprenticeship program, you are hired at entry level to learn a trade or craft from an experienced supervisor. Apprentices learn the skills of one of several trades, including air conditioning and refrigeration, plumbing, carpentry, steam-fitting, temperature control, and automotive mechanics. In addition to holding a 40-hour a week paid job in the trade they are learning, apprentices participate in classroom and lab study each year. Apprentices pay nothing for their training; instead they are paid for their work while they are being trained. How long training lasts depends on the occupation, but usually it extends for several years.

To find out what apprenticeship programs are available in your area, call your nearest state employment office. You can also call the nearest U.S. Department of Labor Bureau of Apprenticeship and Training Office. A list of these offices is posted at: http://www.doleta.gov/bat/sobat.htm.

If you have the aptitude for a specific field and can meet the other eligibility criteria for specific apprenticeship programs, an apprenticeship may be a viable option for you.

Military Service

Some individuals can benefit from the highly structured, repetitive, and physically active regime of military life—if training does not stress skill areas that are impossible to do because of the specific area of disability.

To weigh the pros and cons of enlistment, talk to any service branch recruiter about military life in general and the flexibility in choosing specific training options. Military service can lead to immediate job offers after leaving the service or additional education at the college level. Tuition benefits can be an important benefit of military service.

However, it is important to know that uniformed personnel branches of the military are not covered by Section 504 of the Rehabilitation Act or ADA, which guarantee rights and reasonable accommodations for individuals with disabilities. (See Chapter 3.) No particular accommodations are made for men and women with LD and/or AD/HD, unless they are civilian employees.

Anyone who is interested in enlisting in any branch of the armed forces must first take the Armed Services Vocational Aptitude Battery (ASVAB). This series of tests measures reading, spelling, math, general, and mechanical knowledge and usually screens out individuals who cannot perform adequately in the basic skill areas. One way to prepare for this exam is to get a workbook called *Practice for the Armed Forces Test*.

If someone with learning disabilities passes the ASVAB test, placement in an appropriate training program is not necessarily assured. However, you usually do have some choice of training. Based on your scores on the ASVAB, you will be told what specialties you qualify for, and whether or not there are openings for training in those specialties in the near future. Then you can choose which, if any, of those options you would like.

Military training includes classroom work as well as field experience. Physical demands may be strenuous. Before seriously considering the military as an option, be sure you know what barriers to success exist.

Adult Education

Adult education includes a range of useful learning experiences for people no longer in high school. Courses are designed for adults who wish to obtain a high school diploma, who need educational skills to function more effectively in society, or who simply seek personal enrichment.

The range of possible courses in adult education includes remedial reading and math; general education, such as speed-reading and American history; job skills; hobbies; and parenting, interpersonal communication, and other skills of adult living. Courses are given through county boards of education (at learning centers and in high schools), continuing education departments of colleges, and private programs and schools.

Unfortunately, most states and counties do not realistically have the staff or resources necessary to identify or work extensively with adults who have LD and/or AD/HD. Still, many adult education teachers are becoming more interested in meeting the needs of this group. It may be worth your while to ask whether there are certain teachers within the adult education program who have experience teaching adults with LD or AD/HD.

Local boards of education are good sources of information about adult education programs. Each state has an adult education department that can provide information about instruction for adults. State agency lists are available free from HEATH. (See Resources.)

Adult Basic Education

The Adult Basic Education (ABE) program is an important part of the adult education system. It provides free basic education to people whose reading, writing, and thinking skills have prevented them from getting a high school diploma or getting a well-paying job. Funds for the ABE program are appropriated by the federal government to the states and counties, and priority is given to people at the lowest literacy level.

Getting a High School Diploma

If you are an adult with LD and/or AD/HD who did not complete high school and want to earn a diploma or the equivalent of a diploma, you can look into three possibilities:

1. the General Education Development Test, more popularly called the GED Test;

2. adult high school programs; or,

3. in some states, the External Diploma Program.

GED Test. The GED Test is a timed test that covers reading and writing skills, social studies, science, and mathematics. A passing score on the GED Test is regarded as the equivalent of a high school diploma in many settings. The GED Test is recognized by most employers and many colleges. Some colleges may require a higher GED score for admission than the minimum passing score.

Preparatory courses and pretests are usually available through adult education programs. Books that can help you prepare, such as the *Baron* series, can be obtained in bookstores or libraries. The GED Test can be taken with accommodations, such as extended time, in a separate room, or with a reader. To make these arrangements, contact local or state boards of education.

Adult High School Programs. Adult high school programs are another way to complete high school. Classes are usually small and are held during the day or evening. Students are often more motivated and focused than the typical high school student. This can be to the advantage of older students who were distracted by their peers' behavior when they attended high school in adolescence.

External Diploma. The External Diploma Program is primarily designed for older adults who never finished high school and who now wish to earn a diploma. Adopted by thirteen states (although not in each county), this program is a flexible, self-paced way for adults to complete high school by demonstrating current competency in basic skills and life experiences. Before being accepted by the program, each person is screened for level of reading, writing, and math. If skill standards are met, the adult is accepted into the program and works on the areas of deficiency. In some states, instruction is offered; in others, students work on their own, with guidance from advisors. These programs are noncompetitive, students get immediate feedback, and they always have the opportunity to correct mistakes.

External Diploma programs were not set up for adults with disabilities in mind, but they have potential for individuals with LD and/or AD/HD who meet the screening criteria. If an interested adult does not pass the screening test, the director of the local or state program may know of community resources, such as tutors or basic skills classes. For information about any of these programs, contact the adult education department in your county or city public school system.

Literacy Groups

Adult education includes a network of literacy groups in communities across the country. These groups are staffed by trained volunteers who give one-on-one tutoring in reading to students, no matter what their level of literacy. People who are totally illiterate are accepted for teaching by Laubach Library International, as well as other groups. Teaching methods are highly structured and individualized.

Although their approaches are not necessarily geared toward learning disabilities, many literacy tutors are aware of the implications of LD and/or AD/HD and adapt teaching to special needs. Before starting a tutorial program, it is important to know if the tutor's methods are appropriate or flexible.

To find out about a local literacy organization, call the toll-free number of the Coalition for Literacy Hotline. (See the Resources at the back of the book.)

Sorting through Your Options

As you can see, there are many options for postsecondary education for individuals with LD or AD/HD. The challenge is to identify the type of programs that best match your career goals and abilities and can provide the support services you need.

Table 6.9 illustrates the systematic way one family went about identifying the most appropriate postsecondary option for Stephen, an 18-year-old with LD and AD/HD.

TABLE 6.9—SELECTING APPROPRIATE POSTSECONDARY OPTIONS: ONE FAMILY'S EXPERIENCE

Stephen and his parents looked at his academic background, the supports he might need in a postsecondary setting, his physical and mental health, his daily living and social skills, his ability to live independently and be self-reliant, and his interests, goals, and wishes. This is what they found:

Academic Assessment

Stephen's SAT® Test scores are low (320 verbal/360 math). His grade average is C+. He gets help with homework in a resource room one hour per day. Stephen's reading comprehension is good. However, his word attack and spelling skills are on a 5th grade level. His math achievement is also low (8th grade). Handwriting is slow, of poor quality, and he has difficulty organizing his thoughts sequentially to write.

Supports Needed for Postsecondary Education

Stephen has the ability to do better work in most areas. His major problem is in writing essays and reports. He will need the most assistance in learning how to organize his thoughts to develop a coherent outline on which to base his essays. He will also need help in building his vocabulary and writing in a clear, organized manner. Stephen understands basic math concepts but would benefit from an algebra/high school math refresher course if he wishes to take higher level math courses. Because of Stephen's poor handwriting, he would benefit from notetaker services or taping lectures. He should word process written assignments. Stephen also needs extra time for exams because of his writing. Oral exams might be another way to solve this problem. Stephen is quick to understand but has short-term memory problems. He could use assistance in developing memory tricks, such as repetitive reviews or use of acronyms. (See Chapters 9, 10, 11 for more information about these types of supports.)

Physical and Mental Health

Stephen is in good health. He needs at least eight hours of sleep every night because without proper rest, he tends to get hyperactive and emotional. He is a sensitive person who covers up his feelings of inadequacy by using his sense of humor and sarcasm to attract friends and admirers. He rarely gets truly de-

To arrive at a decision that is appropriate for you, you will likely have to do the same kind of stocktaking that Stephen and his family did. Whether you are considering working after high school, attending a postsecondary school, or getting

pressed, but his mood swings are frequent—usually a tip-off that things are not going well in school.

Daily Living and Social Skills

Stephen has adequate daily living skills. He can be sloppy and disorganized but no more so than any other adolescent. His social skills are his strength. He is an attractive, young man with good manners.

Independent Living/Self-Reliance

Stephen likes to make his own decisions and wants to be in charge of his life. He gets up on time for jobs and school without parental intervention, but he is generally late for deadlines on bills or papers or for social engagements. Stephen is immature and lacks self-discipline.

Interests, Goals, and Wishes

Stephen wants to be a real estate broker and plans to major in business. He is following the career footsteps of his father (real estate accountant), but he knows he cannot sit at a desk all day and work on figures.

After making this evaluation, Stephen and his family listed possible choices for postsecondary education. They drew up a chart to note the positives and negatives of each option. Together, Stephen and his parents decided that a two-year community college was the best option for him. He felt exhilarated about going to college, especially after his long struggle to build language and math skills. His parents saw this option as the first step in the long-range goal of continuing to increase basic skills while mastering the courses required to acquire the Associate of Arts degree. As much as they wanted him to go away to a four-year college like many of his friends, they knew that this option might lead to failure, given his lack of basic skills and maturity. But they also knew that with a little more time to mature and consolidate his academic achievements, he could transfer to a four-year college.

into a vocational program, the process of assessing the total person and listing all possible options is a valuable way to break through the confusion and fear you and your family may feel about getting ready to go out in the adult world.

Resources

BOOKS

The Armed Forces (and ADD/LD), 1996
Authors: Patricia Latham and Peter S. Latham
Learning Disabilities Association
4156 Library Road
Pittsburgh, PA 15234-1349
Phone: (412) 341-1515
Fax: (412) 344-0224
E-mail: ldanatl@usaor.net
http://www.ldanatl.org

Choosing the Right College: A Step by Step System to Aid the Student with a Learning Disability in Selecting the Most Suitable College Setting for Them
Authors: Henry DeChossis, Lucy Moss, and Elissa Stein
New York University
Henry and Lucy Moses Center for Students with Disabilities
566 La Guardia Place, Suite # 701
New York, NY 10012-1097
Phone: (212) 998-4980
Fax: (212) 995-4114
http://www.nyu.edu/pages/csd/mosesctr.html

College and Career Success for Students with Learning Disabilities, 1996
Author: Roslyn Dolber
VGM Career Horizons
c/o NTC/Contemporary Publishing
4255 West Touhy Avenue
Lincolnwood, IL 60646-1975
Phone: (800) 621-1918, ex. 147
Fax: (800) 998-3103
http://www.ntc-cb.com

College Planning Search Book,
American College Testing Service (ACT)
P.O. Box 168
Iowa City, IA 52243

Phone: (319) 337-1000
http://www.act.org/contacts/index.html

College Time
The College Board
45 Columbus Avenue
New York, NY 10023-6917
http://www.collegeboard.org

**Counseling Secondary Students with Learning Disabilities: A Ready-to-Use
Guide to Help Students Prepare for College and Work**, 1998
Authors: Michael Koehler and Marybeth Kravets
Center for Applied Research in Education
P.O. Box 11071
Des Moines, IA 50336-1071
Phone: (800) 947-7700
Fax: (515) 284-2607
http://www.viacom.com

Dispelling the Myths: College Students and Learning Disabilities, 1990
Authors: Katherine Garnett and Sandra La Porta
Council on Learning Disabilities
P.O. Box 40303
Overland Park, KS 66204
Phone: (913) 492-8755
Fax: (913) 492-2546
http://www1.winthrop.edu/cld

Earn College Credit for What You Know, 1997
Author: Lois S. Lamdin and Susan Simosko
Kendall/Hunt Publishing Company
4050 Westmark Drive
P.O. Box 1840
Dubuque, IA 52004-1840
Phone: (800) 228-0810
Fax: (319) 589-1000
E-mail: orders@kendallhunt.com
http://www.kendallhunt.com

Educational Alternatives for Students with Learning Disabilities, 1992
Author: Susan Vogel

Springer-Verlag New York
P.O. Box 2485
Secaucus, NJ 07096-2485
Phone: (800) 777-4643
Fax: (201) 348-4505
E-mail:orders@springer-ny.com
http://www.springer-ny.com

Falling through the Cracks: Rehabilitation Services for Adults with LD, 1992
Author: J. Osgood Smith
Learning Disabilities Association
4156 Library Road
Pittsburgh, PA 15234-1349
Phone: (412) 341-1515
Fax: (412) 344-0224
E-mail: ldanatl@usaor.net
http://www.ldanatl.org

Financial Aid for the Disabled and Their Families, 1998-2000
Authors: Gail A Schlkackter and R. David Weber
Reference Service Press
5000 Windplay Drive
El Dorado Hills, CA 95762
Phone: (916) 939-9620
Fax: (916) 939-9626
E-mail: findaid@aol.com
http://www.rspfunding.com
gopher://bobcat-ace.nche.edu

Help Yourself: Handbook for College-Bound Students with Learning Disabilities, 1996
Authors: Erica-Lee Lewis and Eric Lewis
Princeton Review/Division of Random House
1 Lake Street
Upper Saddle River, NJ
Phone: (800) 753-3000
Fax: (800) 659-2436
http://www.Randomhouse.com

How Many, What Kind—What Should Be on Your List of Colleges?, 1998
Author: Charlotte Thomas

Peterson's Guides
P.O. Box 2123
Princeton, NJ 08543-2123
Phone: (800) 225-0261
Fax: (609) 243-9150
E-mail: custsvc@pgi.petersons.com
http://www.petersons.com

Independent Study for the World of Work, 1991
Authors: Grandy Kimbrell and Dr. Ben S. Vineyard
Glencoe Division
McGraw-Hill
P.O. Box 543
Blacklick, OH 43004
Phone: (800) 334-7344
Fax: (614) 860-1877
E-mail:customerservice@mcgraw-hill.com
http://www.glencoe.com

The K & W Guide to Colleges for Learning Disabled, 1999
Authors: M. Kravets and I. Wax
Princeton Review/Division of Random House
1 Lake Street
Upper Saddle River, NJ
Phone: (800) 753-3000
Fax: (800) 659-2436
http://www.Randomhouse.com

Learning Disabilities, Graduate School & Careers: The Student's Perspective,
Authors: Adelman and Wren
4156 Library Road
Pittsburgh, PA 15234-1349
Phone: (412) 341-1515
Fax: (412) 344-0224
E-mail: ldanatl@usaor.net
http://www.ldanatl.org

***Learning Support for Young People in Transition: Leaving School for Further
Education and Work,*** 1992
Authors: Jean McGinty and John Fish
Open University Press/

Taylor & Francis Inc.,
47 Runway Road,
Levittown, PA 19057
Phone: (800) 821-8312
Fax: (215) 269-0363
E-mail: enquiries@openup.co.uk
http://www.taylorandfrancis.com/BOOKS

Services for Students with Disabilities in Community Colleges, 1993
Author: Lynn Barnett
U.S. Dept. of Education,
400 Maryland Avenue, SW
Washington, DC 20202-0498
Phone: (800) USA-LEARN
E-mail: CustomerService@inet.ed.gov
http://www.ed.gov

When Looking for a College, Start by Looking at Yourself, 1998
Peterson's Guides
P.O. Box 2123
Princeton, NJ 08543-2123
Phone: (800) 225-0261
Fax: (609) 243-9150
E-mail: custsvc@pgi.petersons.com
http://www.petersons.com

PAMPHLETS
Education for Employment: A Guide to Postsecondary Vocational Education for Students with Disabilities
Authors: Maxine Krulich and Nancy Stout
HEATH Resource Center
One Dupont Circle, Suite 800
Washington, DC 20036-1193
Phone: (800) 544-3284
E-mail: heath@ace.nche.edu
http://www.acenet.edu/About/programs/Access&Equity/HEATH
gopher://bobcat-ace.nche.edu

Education Today Parent Involvement Handbook, second edition, 1996
(ED # 396022)
Author: Susan D. Otterburg

ERIC Document Reproduction Service
74220 Fullerton Road
Suite #110
Springfield, VA 22153
Phone: (800) 443-3742
Fax: (703) 440-1408
E-mail: service@edrs.com
http://www.edrs.com

Financial Aid for Students with Disabilities
HEATH Resource Center
One Dupont Circle, Suite 800
Washington, DC 20036-1193
Phone: (800) 544-3284
E-mail: heath@ace.nche.edu
http://www.acenet.edu/About/programs/Access&Equity/HEATH

Getting Ready for College: Advising Students with LD
See address above.

Guide to the College Admissions Process
National Association of College Admission Counselors (NACAC)
1631 Prince Street
Alexandria, VA 22314

HEATH National Resource Directory on Postsecondary Education and Disability, 1996,
Author: Vicki Barr
HEATH Resource Center
One Dupont Circle, Suite 800
Washington, DC 20036-1193
Phone: (800) 544-3284
E-mail: heath@ace.nche.edu
http://www.acenet.edu/About/programs/Access&Equity/heath/home.html
gopher://bobcat-ace.nche.edu

How to Choose a College: Guide for the Student with a Disability, and
How about College? Guidelines for Students with Disabilities, 1997
Author: Elaine Tarr
HEATH Resource Center
See address above.

List of Colleges/Universities That Accept Students with LD, 1994
Learning Disabilities Association
4156 Library Road
Pittsburgh, PA 15234-1349
Phone: (412) 341-1515
Fax: (412) 344-0224
E-mail: ldanatl@usaor.net
http://www.ldanatl.org

Small Colleges Can Help You Make It Big!, 1998
Council of Independent Colleges
One Dupont Circle, Suite # 320
Washington, DC 20036
Phone: (800) 311-6528
E-mail: cic@cic.nche.edu
http://www.cic.edu

The Student Guide - Five Federal Financial Aid Programs, annual
The Federal Student Aid Programs,
U.S. Department of Education
Phone: (800) 433-3243
http://www.ed.gov/prog_info/SFA/StudentGuide

WEBSITES

Direct Loan Web Page
This site provides counseling and information concerning the federal Direct
Loan Program. They also will help you calculate your repayment costs.
http://www.ed.gov/offices/OPE/DirectLoan

Financial Aid for Students
This site provides information about federal student aid programs, including
Pell Grants, Perkins Loans, PLUS Loans, Federal Work Study.
http://www.ed.gov/offices/OSFAP/Students

Free Application for Federal Student Aid (FAFSA)
This site explains the process and provides forms online for getting financial aid.
http://www.ed.gov/offices/OSFAP/Students

LDOnline

This site includes the article, *College-Bound Students with Learning Disabilities: Assessment of Readiness for Academic Success.*

http://www.ldonline.org/ld_indepth/postsecondary/ldforum_assess.html

Yahoo College Search

http://features.yahoo.com/college/search.html

ORGANIZATIONS

Contact information for the following useful organizations can be found beginning on page 347.

- Academy for Educational Development

- American Association for Adult and Continuing Education (AAACE)

- American Association of State Colleges and Universities

- American Association of University Affiliated Programs for Persons with Developmental Disabilities

- American Council on Education (ACE)

- Association for Career and Technical Education (ACTE), *formerly American Vocational Association (AVA)*

- Association on Higher Education and Disability (AHEAD)

- Center on Education for Training and Employment

- Council for Adult and Experiential Learning (CAEL)

- Educational Testing Service, Inc.

- General Education Development (GED)

- Higher Education and the Handicapped (HEATH Resource Center)

- National Association of Vocational and Education Special Needs Personnel (NAVESNP)

- National Center for Research in Vocational Education

- National Center for the Study of Postsecondary Educational Supports, Rehabilitation Research & Training Center (RRTC),

- National Clearinghouse of Rehabilitation Training Materials (NCHRTM)

- National Institute for Literacy Hotline

- National Institute for Work and Learning

- National Occupational Information Coordinating Committee (NOICC)

- National Transition Alliance for Youth with Disabilities

- NICHCY

7

CHOOSING OPTIONS FOR SUCCESS

A Student's Guide to Admissions, Support, and Counseling

IN THIS CHAPTER:

- Chapter 7-A
  Matchmaking: Finding the Right School

- Chapter 7-B
  Go the Road: Finding the Right Support System

- Chapter 7-C
  Emotional Support

- Chapter 7-D
  Conclusion and Information Gathering Forms

Jordan Knab, Joanne Cashman, & Madeline Sullivan

CHAPTER 7-A—Matchmaking: Finding the Right School

"The Disability Support Services Office (DSS) gave me the help I needed to deal with the frustration of being in a new environment, a new school, and making new friends. All this can be overwhelming for a freshman. DSS helped me and guided me to

*be independent and develop the time management and other
skills necessary to succeed. With this kind of support, the difficult
times were easier and the good times were that much better."*

—Student

*"Change is hard for everyone. Having a learning disability
can make the difficulties of entering college life seem a larger
mountain to climb. It is important for students to know where to
turn if things get overwhelming for them."*

—Disability Support Specialist

Overview

How do you begin looking for the right school? You will want to take time
to think about the strengths, needs, and goals you bring to life after high school.
You also will want to give yourself enough time to collect information about
schools from different sources. There are people who can help you and lots of
information available.

To narrow the choices, you will need to have a good idea of what you are
looking for in a school. As a student with learning challenges, you will need to
decide what type of school interests you. Are you hoping to attend a small college, large university, or a technical-vocational education program? You will also
need to find schools whose admission requirements match your achievements.
Then begins the application and admission stage. After, comes course work. This
chapter will guide you through the selection, application, and admission stages.
Chapter 8 presents information to keep in mind when choosing courses.

Matchmaking

Narrowing the choices among colleges is not easy. But there are steps you
can take to help in this selection and matching process. You can gather information through a number of sources. You can use directories, Internet searches,
and catalogs. Talking with your high school guidance counselor and interviewing
college personnel who work with students with disabilities can also help.

As you begin the selection process, you should organize what you know
about yourself and your family's requirements for a school. We suggest that you
first complete a self-profile listing your strengths and needs, preferred ways of
learning, and special interests and/or concerns. You can also answer the set of

questions below to help you target what to look for in a college or vocational-technical school. This profiling process can help you match what you want with information from different schools. We have included forms at the end of the chapter (pages 173-188) that can further help you do this.

Quarter or Semester System?

An important consideration for students with LD and/or AD/HD is whether the college has a quarter system or a semester system. Colleges with quarter systems have classes that are only ten weeks long. There are three quarters during the academic year (plus summer school). Usually students enroll in no more than three classes or twelve units per quarter for a full courseload.

The work is very intense. This means that there is no "down time" to relax between exams and/or papers. Within two to three weeks of the first class, students are studying for midterms and writing papers. For students who may take longer to read, study, and write papers, a quarter system can be very stressful.

On the positive side, the quarter system allows you to sample more classes within a short amount of time. Some view it as helpful in selecting a major. A quarter system may be workable for you if you practice good time management and keep a balanced courseload. That is, balance classes in which there is a substantial amount of reading or writing, with lab, field, or project-type classes.

In a semester system, classes usually last about sixteen weeks before finals. While students take more classes at one time than in the quarter system, there is

---

QUESTIONS FOR STUDENTS

Q. What size school are you looking for? Do you want to be in an urban or rural environment? Do you want to be on a large or small campus?

Q. Do you want to live at home? Do you need time to be with your family while you are trying out this new academic world?

Q. Do your standardized test scores, grade point average, course history, and class rank match the requirements of the schools you are considering? If not, do you have talents, interests, motivation, and means of compensating that might sway an admissions officer's decision?

Q. Are you comfortable explaining your learning strengths and weaknesses and how you have coped with them?

more time to study for exams, prepare papers and projects, and engage in other school activities. Students with LD and/or ADHD often find the semester system less stressful and more flexible to their needs.

Accreditation

Accreditation means that an institution has been examined by, and met the standards of, a recognized accrediting body. Accrediting organizations are national or regional non-governmental groups, such as the New England Association of Schools and Colleges and the National Association of Trade and Technical Schools.

In addition, specialized accrediting bodies evaluate particular programs within an institution in fields such as allied health, art and design, construction, engineering, law, and medicine. Both "institution-accrediting" and "program-accrediting" bodies are selected by the Council of Postsecondary Accreditation, a non-governmental organization that reviews the quality and performance of accrediting groups on an ongoing basis.

You want to think about accreditation as you select a college, university, or technical or vocational education school. In some fields, students must graduate from an accredited program to be licensed to practice within a profession. Accreditation can also be important if you wish to transfer credits to another school or apply to a graduate program.

Schools usually state in their literature that they are accredited. If there is any question, you or your parents should ask to see the certificate of accreditation or find out if the school is in the process of being accredited.

Selection

Sources of Information

To find out about schools that might be right for you, you can search the Internet, read directories, visit college fairs, or meet with your guidance counselor or a private educational counselor. It is always best to confirm your information with the individual school and/or program. Campus visits and interviews are most useful.

Educational Directories. Looking at directories is a good way to start the selection process. Directories describe the characteristics of the schools and list the entrance requirements, including exams and scores needed, grade point average, class rank, and, in some cases, level of selectivity. There are directories that note services available for students with LD and/or AD/HD, or colleges that have structured postsecondary programs for students with LD and/or AD/HD. Other directories enable you to find which schools offer particular majors. When using directories, be aware that information can be outdated or not based on firsthand knowledge and should be checked against other sources. The Resources section at the end of this chapter lists some popular directories and helpful web sites.

Guidance Counselors. Your high school guidance counselors can help you think about appropriate postsecondary schools. Counselors have directories and catalogues, arrange college nights, and schedule sessions with college representatives. They can also assist you in making arrangements for testing accommodations for the SAT or ACT.

Computerized Guidance Systems. Computerized guidance systems can be helpful resources in making postsecondary decisions. A list of schools that provide support services or offer special programs with students with disabilities can be found on computerized Career Information Delivery Systems, which are commonly referred to as CIDS's. Examples of some commercially developed career information delivery systems include the GIS II (Guidance Information System) or GIS 17, EX-PAN, and DISCOVER. Most high schools and colleges use one of these systems (or similar ones) in their guidance offices or career centers. Information for professionals on locating these can be found by contacting the National Occupational Information Coordinating Council (NOICC).

Private Educational Counselors. Perhaps you are unsure of your career interests or how they relate to your abilities. If so, an educational counselor or consultant may be able to help by providing specialized interest testing and information on schools and careers. To find a counselor in or near your community, you can check the yellow pages (under "Education," "Schools," Counselors"). Your local chapter of Learning Disabilities Association (LDA) or Children and Adults with Attention-Deficit/Hyperactive Disorder (CHADD) may also have this information.

School Visits. Visiting schools is a great way to gather information. You can see the campus, meet students, and have a chance to ask questions on the spot. You may also be able to meet learning specialists, academic counselors, career counselors, and psychological counselors to determine what supports and accommodations are available. The DSS office can be helpful in determining whether your chances for admission are realistic. Informal interviews with support personnel who help make admissions decisions may help your application.

While on campus, you can talk with current students about their experiences at the school. You can also get a sense of the campus. Do students and faculty seem friendly and eager to talk about the school? Is the school isolated?

Are the dorms crowded and noisy? Are there quiet places to study? Does the campus appeal to you?

Shadow a Current Student. A great way to gather information is to arrange a visit where you "shadow" a current student. This way you can experience first-hand what classes, dorm living, and meal time are really like. Many schools have programs for interested students. These include shadowing combined with time for independent visits to the different offices such as admissions, student life, and financial aid.

Internet. The Internet is an excellent source for information on schools that might be a good match for you. Listed in the Resources sections of this book are many organizational websites that have information about, or links to, specialized school programs and services for students with LD and/or AD/HD.

Admissions

After you have gathered information about a school, ask yourself, "Is it a match?" As a student, you need to decide if the school has enough of what you need and want. Consider everything from the school's size, location, range of classes, and services offered to its social atmosphere. If the answer is yes, you should start the admissions process.

Plan to apply to several schools that meet your needs. This gives you options if you don't get into the school of your first choice. An old rule of thumb is to apply to a minimum of three schools, assuming you are able to afford the application fees.

Once you decide to apply somewhere, the Admissions Department becomes a critical source of information. Admissions staff are responsible for selecting students, as well as for working with current and former students. They can advise you about admission requirements, including exams, interviews, application forms, and letters of recommendation.

Interviews

An admissions interview can occur either before or after a formal application is submitted. Some schools require these interviews; others do not. Interviews can take place on the campus or in your community if the school has representatives (usually alumni) who do this.

For some students with LD and/or AD/HD, the interview can make the difference. If you do not meet all the entrance requirements, but believe that your talents, determination, and methods of coping will make you successful, then a strong, positive interview may make the difference. Clearly describing how you work with your learning differences with commitment and confidence can convince an admissions officer to give you a chance.

If you are applying to a special program for students with LD and/or AD/HD, an interview will be an important part of admission. You can expect a personal interview, and at least one parent may be asked to participate. The interview will probably include a developmental history and an evaluation of current assessment information. These programs emphasize not only potential, but student goals and motivation.

Preparing for the Interview

Be Ready. Be prepared to state and describe your positive characteristics as well as successful experiences. Sharing your successes and what made the experience positive can be very persuasive.

Know the School. Although an interview presents a good opportunity to gather information about the school, you should already have a good information base concerning the school, its services, size, programs, etc. You should use this information to discuss why you see yourself as a good match with the school.

Role Play. Many students report that practicing for an interview by role playing helps them feel more confident. They ask a counselor, parent, or friend to "interview" them and practice answering the questions. This approach can help you learn how to dress, how to behave, and how to talk and listen.

Advance Planning. Arrange appointments for interviews as far in advance as possible through the dean of admissions, the DSS office, a university learning specialist, or the director of admissions. With advance planning, residential colleges may be able to arrange for you to sleep in a dorm and attend some classes. Students applying to vocational educational schools or local community colleges may want to spend a day touring the school and asking questions of students and instructors.

Entrance Exams

College entrance exams were developed to predict a student's ability to do college-level work. The two most commonly used exams are the SAT® (Scholastic Assessment Test) exam and the ACT® (American College Testing) exam. A practice version of the SAT is the PSAT/NMSQT (Preliminary SAT®/National Merit Scholarship Qualifying Test). Many high school students take the PSAT/NMSQT in the fall of their sophomore and junior years and the SAT in the spring of the junior year and the fall of the senior year. Colleges consider the best scores only.

Unfortunately, entrance exams are obstacles for many students. To relieve anxiety, some parents and teachers encourage students to take these exams as frequently as possible. (This does not mean that each set of scores must be sent to colleges you are considering.) Taking preparation courses and using software programs are other ways to practice.

Both the SAT and ACT exams can be taken under standard or nonstandard conditions. Nonstandard conditions include:

- extended time,

- use of a cassette or a reader,

- use of an aide to mark the answers, and/or

- a large-type version.

If you take the exam under nonstandard conditions, this will usually be reflected on the report sent to schools. Some accommodations, such as large print and the use of extra breaks, however, are not reported to schools.

Requests to take the exams under nonstandard conditions must be made well in advance of the exam date. Detailed information about special testing arrangements can be obtained from the high school guidance office and testing services (see Resources at the end of the chapter).

Exams for admission to professional and graduate schools (Graduate Record Exams) can also be given under nonstandard conditions. For information, contact the ATP Services (see the organizations listed at the back of the book for contact information).

Application Forms

It is important to fill out application forms accurately and legibly. If you have difficulty with spelling or handwriting, you may want to dictate your responses to someone else to fill in the information. Or see if the schools you are interested in have online applications in which you can type all of the information. It is a good idea to have someone proofread your application before you send it off or submit it online.

SHOULD YOU DISCLOSE YOUR DISABILITY?

Section 504 of the Rehabilitation Act prohibits postsecondary institutions from inquiring whether an applicant has a disability. Application forms *cannot* have questions about disabilities; admissions personnel are trained *not* to ask about or indicate an obvious disability observed in an interview; and secondary schools *cannot* release this information unless authorized by the student.

However, many students with disabilities want and need to know their prospects for admission. A careful reading of recruitment materials and school catalogs can frequently provide some information about services and accommodations. It is more effective, however, to discuss needs, problems, and strengths with the Disability Support Services (DSS) coordinator before applying.

Some students with LD and/or AD/HD advise students who are applying to regular campus programs not to disclose their disability. Others urge students to discuss the disability, but to be very specific about the problem and how it can be accommodated. It is also important to emphasize your strengths, self-insights, and successes. You must decide for yourself whether you need to disclose before admission. After admission, however, you must disclose if you wish to use DSS services.

Many colleges require written/typed essays as part of the formal application process. If you find writing difficult, have your essay proofed and/or critiqued by a parent or teacher. You may also want to investigate whether "alternative" essay formats are permissible for submission. For example, you may want to submit a video or photo essay you made, or a website you designed. If alternative essay formats are not permitted, you may be able to include the other materials as supporting evidence of your talents.

Letters of recommendation are also usually required. It is critical to let the authors of these letters know whether or not you plan to disclose your disability to the college. If you are planning on disclosing, you might recommend that the letter writer address your academic strengths and your ability to accommodate for academic weaknesses. If your past academic history is weak, you might ask your references to focus on your strengths, such as leadership abilities or communication skills.

Applying for Nonstandard Admission

If you do not meet all the requirements for standard admission, you may want to apply for special/provisional or cooperative admission. Under these conditions, you might be admitted if you meet a minimum grade point average (GPA) *or* standardized test score. Both four-year colleges and technical schools often admit a limited number of applicants under this kind of "probationary status." Ordinarily, you will need to maintain a minimum GPA or receive a certain grade on single courses for a given period before you are taken off probation.

Applicants admitted on probation usually have a proven track record of academic achievements or other valuable achievements such as community service or leadership skills. If you are trying for probationary status, your essay, interview, and letters of recommendation should therefore focus on points such as:

- how your true effort and learning is reflected in your grades rather than your test scores (if that is the case);

- academic achievements that might not be reflected in your grades or test scores (material from your portfolio, etc.);

- recognition, honors, or awards you have received outside of school;

- the achievements you have made outside of the academic arena and why you think they prove you can succeed in college.

Getting Your Acceptance/Rejection Letter

In the event you receive a rejection letter from the school(s) you want to attend, what you do next is up to you. You may choose to enroll in your local community college and take courses in your areas of interest. If you do well there and prove that you can handle college-level work, you might reapply to the school(s) that rejected you. Another option would be to begin working while you investigate other school programs that you can apply to in the coming year.

If you receive an acceptance letter from one of your chosen schools, congratulations! Read on to find out about the support services that can help you succeed in a postsecondary program.

CHAPTER 7-B—Go the Road: Finding the Right Support System

Why You Might Need Support

Entering college is both an exciting and stressful experience for most students. It can be a particularly difficult time if you have LD and/or AD/HD. You will need to decide whether you want support services and then how to use them effectively.

Once on the college scene, students often report great pressure to meet new friends, join social groups, and generally to "fit in." You might find this part of the college experience to be especially difficult. You may have feelings of isolation, loneliness, and homesickness, particularly if you have moved to a new location to attend school. You may no longer have regular contact with your family, friends, or other support persons from your home community.

Facing new challenges without a support system can frustrate the most secure individual. Through support programs offered to students in general, as well as through disability support services, colleges provide resources to help students adjust in this new setting. The "menu of supports" offered by colleges can greatly affect the comfort and success you experience. It is important that you understand the supports and use the ones you need.

Investigating Supports during the College Search

If you have LD and/or AD/HD, the search for the right college may involve extra investigation. After narrowing down an area of academic interest and geographic location, you should give close attention to the school's support services. Often, these offices are associated with the counseling center, dean's offices, or student affairs office, or they may exist as independent disabilities support offices.

Once you locate the disabilities support office at the college, investigate whether the office provides direct services. Some disability support offices act only as "clearinghouses" for information about students' learning needs and really do not provide direct student support. Be sure to ask about the number of personnel who serve the office and what kinds of services they arrange or provide for students. Find out about the organization of the office:

- What are the roles of the staff members? Are they involved in service coordination or direct services? Do they advocate for you directly with faculty?

- What is the availability of these staff members?

- What types of services are specially offered to students with LD?

- How are services customized for students with AD/HD?

After narrowing your college choices and visiting campuses, you may want to speak to other students who use disabilities support services. It would be especially helpful to speak to other students with LD and/or AD/HD. If possible, ask about the types of services they have received and their level of satisfaction with those services.

Supports Available to All Students

To some extent, all students benefit from support in making the transition from high school to college. Many colleges now understand this need and provide general programs to assist all students.

Freshman Orientation Programs

Often, colleges offer an orientation program for new students several days before classes begin for the school as a whole. These orientation programs often introduce key faculty and staff (Deans, Department Chairs, etc.) and program personnel (Advisors, Graduate Assistants, Disability Support Staff, etc.). These introductory sessions usually acquaint you with registration procedures, class scheduling, campus social activities and clubs, and college and dorm rules and policies. These orientations are designed to provide good background information about the services provided by the college or university. Be sure to attend orientation sessions.

Freshman Support Series

Increasingly, colleges and universities continue the freshman program beyond the orientation week activities. Many colleges provide a series of workshops throughout the year. During these sessions, student-life staff and academic staff present on many topics and interact with students who may need their services. Topics might include general study skills, time management and organization, counseling services, and test-taking skills. Notices for these workshops are typically posted in the student center, library, etc. Ask a student advisor or check with the counseling office if you do not see any notices posted.

University Counseling Service

Often the university counseling service provides workshops of interest to the student body. These might include topics on career interests, resume building, or specific mental health topics such as dealing with anxiety or depression. Sometimes, under the direction of the counseling service office, informal groups form for support in specific areas of need. Informal study groups or peer support groups are often arranged by this office. Individual counseling and support is generally available through these offices, but the depth and length of treatment may vary from school to school.

Staff within these offices usually include at least one licensed mental health professional. Other staff are often graduate students within related fields who are completing internships or graduate credits. Consequently, the services are typically offered at a reduced rate or may even be free to current students at the university. These offices generally make referrals to outside agencies and private-practice professionals to address more serious problems or concerns you might have.

Orientation Sessions for Libraries and Technical Support Services

At every university, the library staff offer introductory sessions about the organization of their collection and specific reference techniques. These may include instruction on using the library's computer database or overviews of available technology equipment and services. Individual sessions with a research librarian who is skilled in researching specific topics are generally available when scheduled in advance.

Most universities have a technical support service, like a computer center. This office usually handles everything from setting up students with e-mail accounts to supplying adaptive technology in computer hardware and/or software. Often orientation sessions cover the general rules for usage and provide you with the clearance required to use the facility. Beyond these introductory sessions, you may need to schedule individual time with a support technician to work on needed skills.

Study Groups

Once classes have begun, you may find you need academic support. Some professors encourage study groups to form and sometimes students start study groups on their own. Study groups can work in a number of different ways. Students may meet regularly to review class lectures, share class notes, support each other in completing class assignments, and prepare for exams. Sometimes when a project is required, the study group can become the project team.

There are almost always students who want to form study groups, but forming a group does not assure success. The group members must agree to meet regularly and decide on a routine to guide their meetings. The group goals are important in holding a study group together, but students must get their own needs met too! As a result, clear communication among group members becomes very important.

Study groups can be an important way to build academic support. They can also help you get to know other students on a more personal level. If you get involved in a study group, take a good hard look at how helpful the group is to you. If the group meets your needs, continue participation. If not, look for more structured and formal assistance, such as the disabilities support office may provide.

Social Connections and Support

Making new friends is usually a very important part of the college experience. Sometimes, though, it is difficult to establish these new friendships at the beginning of the school year when they are most needed. Many colleges hold events for incoming freshmen during the preceding summer which range from social gatherings to general information sessions concerning the semester to come. These optional events are a wonderful opportunity to meet people, and can make for an easier beginning to the semester. Joining intramural teams and clubs can also be a good way to meet people with similar interests.

At the start of college, you may want to stay in touch with old high school friends or close relatives. You can share your beginning-of-the-year experiences with people you know well and trust.

If you decide to live in a dorm, the Resident Advisor (R.A.) may be able to help you get a social life. The R.A. is typically an upperclassman assigned to your floor. He or she is usually responsible for organizing social activities for students on the floor throughout the semester. The R.A. is also typically responsible for resolving conflicts between the students/roommates on the floor, and for enforcing dormitory rules and regulations. In addition, the R.A. can serve as a great source of information or as a "listening ear" for you.

Supports Available to Students with Disabilities

Many students with LD and/or AD/HD find that they need specialized supports beyond those available to all students. For example, they may need instructors to accommodate their special learning needs in the classroom, assistance in obtaining those accommodations, or tutoring in certain subjects.

How much support is available to you on campus will depend on your school. Ideally, you will have investigated this thoroughly before applying for admission. For some students, the types of support available can make all the difference between success and failure.

There are two basic models for providing disability support services on campus: 1) the contact person model, and 2) the full-service model.

Full-service Disability Support Services Offices

Many colleges, universities, and technical-vocational schools have full service Disability Support Services (DSS) offices. In these schools, there is a staff and a range of organized programs dedicated to helping students with disabilities succeed.

The organization of DSS offices varies greatly among colleges. Most offices provide numerous services: academic support persons, personal mentors, coaching, specific support groups, and referral to other agencies that can help meet students' needs.

Academic support is often provided through readers, note takers, tutors, and coaches. Tutors can be paid or they may be volunteers who have agreed to help students who need assistance in some subjects. These tutors are trained and organized through DSS. They are matched to students based on information the students provided to document their disabilities. Coaches are trained professionals or volunteers who work with students to help them plan and organize their way through academic tasks. Beyond tutoring and coaching, DSS offices can help arrange accommodations for how students are tested and taught. For more information on accommodations, see Chapter 9.

The Contact Person Model

Unfortunately, not all colleges and universities have a *program* for students with disabilities. Instead, they may have a single individual who is responsible for disability accommodation requests. The differences are based in the legal requirements under the Americans with Disabilities Act (ADA) and Section 504 of the Rehabilitation Act (see Chapter 3). Under the law, colleges and universities cannot discriminate based on disability and must make reasonable accommodations for students with disabilities. However, universities are not *required* to provide an office for enabling those services or a staff to support students in using these services.

The minimum responsibility, under the law, can be met by assigning an individual who takes student requests for services, checks appropriate documentation of need, and makes professors aware of the student request. In this relationship, the student and the professor work out the accommodation. The contact person may remain involved if there are ongoing difficulties.

The "contact person model" is a stark contrast to a "full-service model" of a DSS program. Yet, the "contact person model" does meet the minimum requirement of the law. You will want to clearly understand the level of support available through DSS. It is not enough to know that there is a contact person or office. You want to know the amount of direct student support offered and the kinds of assistance given to obtain the accommodations you need to succeed.

Connecting with Other Students with Disabilities

College-age students often feel they benefit from having the friendship and support of other students with disabilities. Some DSS offices have established support groups for students with related disabilities. If the DSS office at your school doesn't have such a group, you may want to inquire about helping to set one up. Some DSS offices can also arrange for a mentor at your school help familiarize you with the campus, facilities, etc. And finally, some colleges have on-campus chapters of national organizations such as the Dyslexia Association of America. These can give you a ready-made source of advocacy and support if you choose to join.

CHAPTER 7-C—Emotional Support

"Part of growing up and becoming an adult includes acknowledging when you need help, and reaching out for it. That is an experience you can't take away from a student; it is a part of the college life."

—DSS Coordinator

"As a student with depression, LD, and AD/HD, I didn't always have the strength to hang out with the other students. When I was feeling really lousy about myself, I would set myself up for failure without realizing it. Lying in bed in my room, I would tell myself that the other students would have already included me if I was really worth it. That would make me feel worse about myself.

"I didn't realize what was going on and didn't know what to do to change the cycle. Feeling bad, I would struggle just to get to class on time. Things that used to come so easily for me all of a sudden became overwhelmingly difficult. I would go to my Algebra class, which used to be my best subject, and now I was lost and couldn't keep up. As hard as it was for me to sit still, I would study twice as hard and twice as much as I did in the past. People around me were keeping up with everything.

"I wasn't able to stay on top of my school work. I wasn't making friends. I felt like I couldn't manage everything. I felt like I wasn't as good as I was in high school. I couldn't sit through the long classes. I got distracted. I blamed myself."

—A student

Students with LD and/or AD/HD often report feeling anxious and frustrated, especially during their early college experiences. In fact, many students without disabilities also feel this way when faced with the increased academic demands and social pressures of college life. For students with LD or AD/HD, however, these feelings may be more intense and lead to depression.

When students with LD and/or AD/HD feel as if the demands of college-level work and the pressures of college are too difficult to handle, they may:

- withdraw socially,

- lose interest in academic pursuits,

- have little appetite,

- sleep later and later, or have difficulty falling and staying asleep,

- skip classes, miss exams, or fail to turn in important assignments,

- begin to abuse alcohol or other substances.

As a student with LD and/or AD/HD, you might find yourself having more and more worries, blaming yourself for things that are out of your control, and having trouble performing routine tasks. Suddenly, you are not able to do the things you know you can and should be able to do. *These are all signals that it is time for you to reach out and talk to someone!*

If you think you may be experiencing significant anxiety or depression, you should talk to someone with whom you feel comfortable. Look for someone with expertise in this area, or someone who knows about counseling resources. Often this may be someone associated with DSS, the school's guidance and counseling office, the R.A., a professor, or a college staff member. Your parents, too, may be able to help you find someone with the right expertise.

Students of your age are usually more likely to underestimate the depth of their anxiety or depression than they are to overplay or dramatize these feelings. You may see symptoms of anxiety, stress, a high activity level, or depression as part of yourself and your personality. It is critical to get support at the first sign of significant anxiety or depression, as these symptoms usually become more intense over time if left untreated.

Counseling can benefit you in many ways. A counselor can help you identify the specific issues that are causing problems for you and can lead you through coping skills and strategies. Through discussions, guidance, and support groups, you can learn better ways to deal with your feelings. A counselor can help you step back from the problem and work to find ways to manage it.

Most colleges have confidential counseling offices on their campuses. The DSS office is usually an excellent referral source for such counseling assistance. Your professors, roommates, family, or friends do not need to know you are seeking help. However, it is a good idea to confide in anyone with whom you would be comfortable, since these folks can be an important part of your support network.

Whatever the situation, don't let your troubles overtake you! Make your appointment and keep it!

"Slowly but surely, I learned to appreciate myself and my disabilities. I first sought out help in college. I started by taking short courses in study skills and time management. This helped some. Then, I began counseling sessions twice a month. This helped more.

"As I continued through college, I would revisit the same issues over and over again. With each attempt at solving my problems, I learned more and more about myself. I learned new ways to interact with my disabilities. I still work on this. The more I learn, the more I try, the easier it becomes and the more joys and successes I have. Most of all, I have learned that it is hard work. BUT, the more I work at it, the more successful I am.

"With the support and guidance of counselors, family, and friends, I am able to get past the bad and develop the good. I now recognize the signs when I'm getting sad. I know what I need to do to keep from getting depressed for a long period of time. I now know why it is hard for me to sit through a long meeting or class. I now have a whole set of strategies that work for me and enable me to be successful. I know what I need to do to remember to pay my bills on time. Best of all, through my support network, I learned that I am not weak for having to learn or act this way. Instead, I am strong for having the knowledge to be successful.

Having AD/HD, among other disabilities, does not have to make me feel bad. I now see that this can be a great asset socially and professionally, if I recognize it as that. At work, they say I have lots of energy and lots of ideas. At parties, now that I am no longer sad all of the time, I enjoy being with people and especially meeting new people. As a student, I have continued to study and to learn. Had someone told me five years ago that I would feel this way and accomplish the things I have, I would never have believed them. Unfortunately, it was at that same time that I would never have considered seeking out guidance in study skills and counseling to receive the support that I so desperately needed.

–A student

CHAPTER 7-D—Conclusion and Information Gathering Forms

Successful individuals share some important qualities: they stay focused on their goals, they are able to express their needs, and they seek assistance when needed. Most importantly, they find more than one way to succeed. There are always options that help people reach their goals. Success in learning and in life is about matching your needs to the available options. At all stages of life, this may require you to explore alternate routes and make adjustments accordingly.

As a student with LD and/or AD/HD, the patterns you establish in dealing effectively with social and academic challenges will sustain you throughout life. Working at exploring, choosing, and evaluating services will prove to be most valuable. In the end, it is your responsibility to find the options that will help you build a life you can live with.

To help you discover and identify your options, a variety of information-gathering forms are included in this section. The beginning forms help you conduct self-assessments. These are followed by forms to help you collect information as you are exploring different schools.

Forms included are as follows:

- Transition Planning for Success: Looking to the Future & *sample*

- Self Profile & *sample*

- How the DSS Office Might Assist Me & *sample*

- School Profile Checklist & *sample*

- Admissions Profile & *sample*

- Disability Support Services Office Profile & *sample*

- Academic Support Center Profile & *sample*

- Counseling Services Profile & *sample*

These following self-assessments were adapted from the *Postsecondary Planning Worksheets,* 1991, by James Alexander and Judy Rolfe and produced by National Association of College Admissions Counselors.

■ Transition Planning for Success: Looking to the Future ■

How can I successfully...	I can do this independently	I can do this with assistance	This person may be able to assist me.	Office location or address, phone number and/or e-mail	Date I completed the task.
1. complete my self-profile?					
2. complete school profiles?					
3. contact various admissions offices?					
4. contact the Disability Support Offices/Academic Support Centers?					
5. contact the Counseling Center?					
6. communicate my disability?					
7. contact a student within the school with a similar disability?					

■ Transition Planning for Success: Looking to the Future ■

How can I successfully...	I can do this independently	I can do this with assistance	This person may be able to assist me.	Office location or address, phone number and/or e-mail	Date I completed the task.
1. complete my self-profile?		X	Ms. Brown, my teacher	Rm. 204: at school brown@school.edu	Oct. 14
2. complete school profiles?		X	Mom	home	Nov. 15
3. contact various admissions offices?	X				Dec. 1
4. contact the Disability Support Offices/Academic Support Centers?		X	Mr. Adams, my guidance counselor	Rm. 108: at school adams@school.edu	Dec. 15
5. contact the Counseling Center?		X	Ms. Brown	Rm. 204: at school brown@school.edu	
6. communicate my disability?	X				
7. contact a student within the school with a similar disability?	X				

■ Self Profile ■

Name: **School:**

Date: **Counselor:**

High School Graduation Date: **Service Coordinator:**

STRENGTHS	WEAKNESSES

HOW I LEARN BEST

SPECIAL INTERESTS

■ Self Profile ■

Name: Jane Doe

Date: November 5, 2000

High School Graduation Date: June 1, 2001

School: Ridgeview High School

Counselor: Mr. Adams

Service Coordinator: Ms. Brown

STRENGTHS	WEAKNESSES
using pictures, notes, papers	writing papers; doing large projects; integrating information from various sources
visual memory	auditory memory
memorizing facts, data, etc.	sitting still in class; paying attention in lectures

HOW I LEARN BEST
note taking; using a computer; drawing pictures in notes; reviewing class notes with a friend or tutor; using advance and post organizers
writing: using a slant board and a pen; editing with a friend's input; brainstorming ideas for a paper/project
using visual aids in class presentations: overheads; drawings; handouts
research papers: summarizing short chapters, reading books before beginning; scheduling progress and due dates; dividing up large projects into short tasks
using calculators, daytimers, and computers to schedule and organize
scheduling myself breaks to move around and release energy; sitting near wall to lean back; bringing snacks and water to class

SPECIAL INTERESTS
music: listening and singing
baseball, football, and soccer
movies, art, and drama

■ How the DSS Office Might Assist Me ■

1. Academically:

2 Scheduling:

3. Socially:

4. Communicating and Problem Solving with Faculty:

5. Self-Advocacy:

6. Emotionally:

■ How the DSS Office Might Assist Me ■

1. Academically:

assist me with coordinating tutoring, classroom note taking, and breaking down large assignments/projects. Provide me with information on available supportive technology.

2 Scheduling:

assist me with coordinating my class schedule, services schedule, and other campus activities schedule. Help me with aligning my courses semester-to-semester.

3. Socially:

help me to identify appropriate peer study groups; get information on social clubs, campus activities.

4. Communicating and Problem Solving with Faculty:

might help me provide information to my professors regarding my disability; educate my professors on different disabilities and their impact in the classroom. They might help me if I have problems with a certain professor.

5. Self-Advocacy:

they might teach me techniques for explaining my disability and need for accommodations to my professors and peers.

6. Emotionally:

they can direct me to appropriate counseling services if I become overwhelmed or can't deal with the pressure of college.

■ School Profile Checklist ■

Name: _____

Where is the school located? City, state: _____

Miles from home: _____

Midwest _____   East _____   West _____   South _____

Rural: _____   Urban: _____   Suburban: _____

What size is this school? Actual size: _____

less than	less than	less than	greater than
1,000 _____	5,000 _____	10,000 _____	10,000 _____

How much does this school cost?

Fall/Spring:

Per credit? _____
per semester? _____

Summer:

Per credit? _____
per semester? _____

Required SAT and/or ACT scores: _____

Do I meet the required scores?   Yes: _____   No: _____

Minimum GPA required: _____

Do I have the minimum GPA required?   Yes: _____   No: _____

What majors that interest me are offered? _____

_____

_____

What extracurricular activities are offered? _____

_____

_____

_____

Other: _____

_____

_____

■ School Profile Checklist ■

Name: Spencer College

Where is the school located? City, state: Spencer, New York

Miles from home: 185 miles

Midwest _____ East X West _____ South _____

Rural: _____ Urban: _____ Suburban: X

What size is this school? Actual size: 2,328

less than 1,000	less than 5,000	less than 10,000	greater than 10,000
_____	X	_____	_____

How much does this school cost?

Fall/Spring:

Per credit? _____
per semester? $12,520 (includes room and board)

Summer:

Per credit? _____
per semester? $12,520 (includes room and board)

Required SAT and/or ACT scores: 950 combined

Do I meet the required scores? Yes: X No: _____

Minimum GPA required: 2.75

Do I have the minimum GPA required? Yes: X No: _____

What majors that interest me are offered? Fine arts/Drama, U.S. History, Women's Studies, Anthropology

What extracurricular activities are offered? Intramural athletics (soccer, basketball, and softball), Art Club, Student Activity Planning Committee, and Campus radio

Other: I like the town. The "downtown" area was small and friendly. There were nice cafes, bookstores, and music stores. There are also great biking trails and a lake near the school. It is a convenient area. I would not need a car.

■ Admissions Profile ■

Name of person contacted: _____

Phone number: _____

What is the deadline for applying? _____

What is needed for a complete application?

Application Form _____   Test Scores _____   Essay(s) _____   Fees _____

Recommendations _____   Transcripts _____   Other: _____

Is an interview required?   Yes: _____   No: _____

Are tours available?   Yes: _____   No: _____

Is there an opportunity to shadow a current freshman for the day?

Yes: _____   No: _____

Is there a freshman orientation program? _____

_____

_____

_____

_____

_____

Name and number of office: _____

Are services provided for students with LD and/or AD/HD? _____

_____

_____

Name and number of office: _____

Are counseling (academic, career, and personal) services provided? _____

_____

_____

Name and number of office: _____

Name and number of office: _____

Name and number of office: _____

■ Admissions Profile ■

Name of person contacted: Ms. Jane McNeal

Phone number: (123) 456-1234

What is the deadline for applying? Feb. 1 (but she recommends I get it in sooner)

What is needed for a complete application?

Application Form **X**   Test Scores **X**   Essay(s) **1**   Fees **X**

Recommendations **2**   Transcripts **X**   Other: documentation of my LD

Is an interview required?   Yes: ____   No: **X**

Are tours available?   Yes: **X**   No: ____

Is there an opportunity to shadow a current freshman for the day?

Yes: **X**   No: ____

Is there a freshman orientation program? Yes. Freshman arrive at school and move into the dorms five days before all of the upper classes. Our days and nights are organized. We are split into groups depending upon our potential majors. We are taught about the school policies, some study strategies. Additionally, there are activities so that we may get to know other freshmen. There are a few extra sessions just for students with disabilities run by the DSS office.

Name and number of office: Student Life Center — (123) 456-3866

Are services provided for students with LD and/or AD/HD? Yes

Name and number of office: Disability Support Services Center — (123) 456-5327

Are counseling (academic, career, and personal) services provided? Yes

Name and number of office: Student Life Center — (123) 456-5433

Name and number of office: Counseling Center — (123) 456-5683

Name and number of office: Career Center — (123) 456-9675

■ Disability Support Services (DSS) Office Profile ■

If there is not a separate DSS office, proceed to the DSS profile and pose those questions to the Academic Support Center.

Name of person contacted: _____

Phone number: _____

What is the current system of support?

_____ **Contact person** supports include: _____

_____

_____

_____ **As needed basis** supports include: _____

_____

_____

_____ **Comprehensive program** providing consistent support includes: _____

_____

_____

What documentation is required and how recent does it need to be? _____

_____

_____

What services are available?

LD Specialist _____   Tutoring _____   Group Study Sessions _____   Computer Labs _____

Peer Support Groups_____   Agency Referrals _____   Other _____

What curricular program modifications are available?

Language Waivers _____   Math Waivers _____   Other: _____

What course accommodations are available?

Untimed tests _____   Oral tests _____   Test readers _____   Extended time for readings _____

Remedial work _____   Note takers _____   Course assignments_____   Books on tape _____

Early access to syllabi _____   Lectures on tape _____   Other: _____

How many service providers are there? _____

■ Disability Support Services (DSS) Office Profile ■

If there is not a separate DSS office, proceed to the DSS profile and pose those questions to the Academic Support Center.

Name of person contacted: John Deer

Phone number: (123) 456-5327

What is the current system of support?

_X_ **Contact person** supports include: monthly or bi-monthly meeting. From there, when needed, they will provide needed supports such as advocacy, speaking with professors, assistance with planning, etc. I can call between meetings if I need.

_X_ **As needed basis** supports include: peer support groups, referrals, assistance with planning, advocacy, study skill tips

_X_ **Comprehensive program** providing consistent support includes: weekly meetings with a learning specialist. In these meetings, progress is charted and guidance is given. There are weekly peer support groups, study skill instruction and remedial work in writing and research.

What documentation is required and how recent does it need to be? weekly meetings with a learning specialist. In these meetings, progress is charted and guidance is given. There are weekly peer support groups, study skill instruction and remedial work in writing and research.

What services are available?

LD Specialist _X_   Tutoring _X_   Group Study Sessions _X_   Computer Labs _X_

Peer Support Groups _X_   Agency Referrals _X_   Other _X_

What curricular program modifications are available?

Language Waivers _X_   Math Waivers _X_   Other: _____

What course accommodations are available?

Untimed tests _X_   Oral tests _X_   Test readers _X_   Extended time for readings _____

Remedial work _X_   Note takers _X_   Course assignments _X_   Books on tape _X_

Early access to syllabi _X_   Lectures on tape _X_   Other: _____

How many service providers are there? 12

■ Academic Support Center Profile ■

This is the academic support office that provides services to all students, not just those with disabilities.

Name of person contacted: _____

Phone number: _____

_____ **As needed basis** supports include: _____

_____

_____

_____ **Comprehensive program** providing consistent support includes: _____

_____

_____

What types of counseling are available?

Academic counseling _____   Study skills instruction _____

Career counseling _____   Tutoring _____

Is there a limit to the number of visits allotted? _____

Does it cost additional money? _____

How many professionals are there? _____

Are there work programs established within the community?

Job placement _____   Internship programs _____   School credit _____

■ Academic Support Center Profile ■

This is the academic support office that provides services to all students, not just those with disabilities.

Name of person contacted: Mary Beth Horton

Phone number: (123) 456-9400

_____ **As needed basis** supports include: Occasional meetings. They send me notification of study skill instruction classes, career discovery forums, and social events.

_____ **Comprehensive program** providing consistent support includes: Weekly meetings. Progress charts, suggestions made and contacts for more specific support if needed.

What types of counseling are available?

Academic counseling X   Study skills instruction X

Career counseling X   Tutoring X

Is there a limit to the number of visits allotted? No

Does it cost additional money? No

How many professionals are there? 18

Are there work programs established within the community? Yes

Job placement X   Internship programs X   School credit X

■ Counseling Services Profile ■

Name of person contacted: _____

Phone number: _____

_____ **As needed basis** supports include: _____

_____

_____

_____ **Comprehensive program** providing consistent support includes: _____

_____

_____

What types of counseling are available?

Academic counseling _____ Career counseling _____ Personal counseling _____

What documentation needs to be provided? _____

_____

_____

Is there group counseling? _____

    Does it cost additional money? _____

Is there individual counseling? _____

    Does it cost additional money? _____

Is there a limit to the number of visits allotted? _____

How many professionals are there? _____

■ Counseling Services Profile ■

Name of person contacted: Elizabeth Hall

Phone number: (123) 456-5683

_____ **As needed basis** supports include: crisis hotline, stand-by appointments with counselors, meetings with counselors by appointment, and literature

_____ **Comprehensive program** providing consistent support includes: weekly counseling sessions, group counseling sessions

What types of counseling are available?

Academic counseling X   Career counseling X   Personal counseling X

What documentation needs to be provided? None

Is there group counseling? Yes

    Does it cost additional money? No

Is there individual counseling? Yes

    Does it cost additional money? No

Is there a limit to the number of visits allotted? 16

How many professionals are there? 9

Congratulations! You've Been Admitted!

Now it is time to compile a folder of the documentation, work samples, and other information you will need to receive needed supports at school. Use the checklist below to help you assemble the information needed to have effective and successful meetings with DSS staff and other professionals.

PLAN FOR SUCCESS FOLDER

_____ Psychological/educational summary and documentation

_____ Samples of work completed with support. Include a description of the type of support provided, as well as the amount required in order to be successful

_____ Letters from teachers, tutors, and friends who have helped you in various ways

_____ The latest IEP (Individualized Educational Program) plan that was used

_____ The latest ITP (Individualized Transition Program) plan that was used

_____ An updated Self Profile

_____ Other requested items

Resources

BOOKS

Accredited Institutions of Postsecondary Education, annual
American Council on Education (ACE)
1 Dupont Circle, NW, #800
Washington, DC 20036
Phone: (202) 939-9300
E-mail: web@ace.nche.edu
http://www.acenet.edu

ADD and the College Student: A Guide for High School and College Students with Attention Deficit Disorder, 1994
Editor: Patricia O. Quinn, MD
Magination Press/American Psychological Association
750 First Street, NE
Washington, DC 20002
Phone: (800) 374-2721, x 5510
Fax: (202) 336-5502
E-mail: books@apa.org
http://www.maginationpress.com

Adventures in Fast Forward: Life, Love, and Work for the ADD Adult, 1996
Author: Kathleen Nadeau
Taylor and Francis/Brunner-Mazel Publishers
47 Runway Road
Levittown, PA 19057
Phone: (800) 821-8312
Fax: (215) 785-5515
http://www.bmpub.com/fager/index.htm

College and Career Success for Students with Learning Disabilities, 1996
Author: Roslyn Dolber
VGM Career Horizons
c/o NTC/Contemporary Publishing
4255 West Touhy Avenue
Lincolnwood, IL 60646-1975
Phone: (800) 621-1918, ex. 147
Fax: (800) 998-3103
http://www.ntc-cb.com

College Planning Search Book,
American College Testing Service (ACT)
P.O. Box 168
Iowa City, IA 52243
Phone: (319) 337-1000
http://www.act.org/contacts/index.html

Coping in College, 1995
Author: Alice Hamachek
Allyn and Bacon

160 Gould Street
Needham Heights, MA 02194-2315
Phone: (800) 852-8024
Fax: (781) 455-8024
E-mail: AandBpub@aol.com
http://www.abacon.com

Coping with College: Successful Strategies, 1984
Author: Luis R. Nieves
Educational Testing Service, Inc.
Rosedale Road
Princeton, NJ 08541
Phone: (609) 921-9000
Fax: (609) 734-5413
E-mail: etsinfo@ets.org
http://www.ets.org

Counseling Secondary Students with Learning Disabilities: A Ready-to-Use Guide to Help Students Prepare for College and Work, 1998
Authors: Michael Koehler, Marybeth Kravets
Center for Applied Research in Education
Phone: (800) 947-7700
Fax: (515) 284-2607
http://www.viacom.com

Help Yourself: Handbook for College-Bound Students with Learning Disabilities (Princeton Review), 1996
Author: Erica-Lee Lewis and Eric Lewis
Princeton Review/Div. of Random House
1 Lake Street
Upper Saddle River, NJ
Phone: (800) 753-3000
Fax: (800) 659-2436
http://www.Randomhouse.com

How Many, What Kind—What Should Be on Your List of Colleges?, 1998
Author: Charlotte Thomas
Peterson's Guides
P.O. Box 2123
Princeton, NJ 08543-2123
Phone: (800) 225-0261

Fax: (609) 243-9150
E-mail: custsvc@pgi.petersons.com
http://www.petersons.com

The K & W Guide to Colleges for Learning Disabled, 1997
Authors: M. Kravets and I. Wax
Princeton Review/Div. of Random House
1 Lake Street
Upper Saddle River, NJ
Phone: (800) 753-3000
Fax: (800) 659-2436
http://www.Randomhouse.com

Services for Students with Disabilities in Community Colleges, 1993
Author: Lynn Barnett
U.S. Dept. of Education,
400 Maryland Avenue, SW
Washington, DC 20202-0498
Phone: (800) USA-LEARN
E-mail: CustomerService@inet.ed.gov
http://www.ed.gov

Succeeding in College with Attention Deficit Disorders: Issues & Strategies for Students, Counselors, & Educators, 1996
Author: Jennifer Bramer
Specialty Press/ADD Warehouse
300 NW 70th Avenue, #102
Plantation, FL 33317
Phone: (800) 233-9273
Fax: (954) 792-8545
E-mail: sales@addwarehouse.com
http://www.addwarehouse.com

Survival Guide for College Students with ADD or LD, 1994
Author: Kathleen Nadeau
Magination Press/American Psychological Association
750 First Street, NE
Washington, DC 20002
Phone: (800) 374-2721, x 5510
Fax: (202) 336-5502
E-mail: Books@apa.org
http://www.maginationpress.com

Swimming Upstream: A Complete Guide to the College Application Process for the Learning Disabled Student, 1994
Author: D. Howard
Learning Disabilities Association
4156 Library Rd
Pittsburgh, PA 15234-1349
Phone: (412) 341-1515
Fax: (412) 344-0224
E-mail: ldanatl@usaor.net
http://www.ldanatl.org

What to Do When Someone You Love Is Depressed, 1998
Authors: Mitch Golant and Susan Golant
Henry Holt Books
16365 James Madison Highway
Gordonsville, VA 22942
Phone: (888) 330-8477
Fax: (800) 672-2054
E-mail: customerservice@vhpsva.com
http://www.vhpsva.com

FACT SHEETS

Linkages/Self-Esteem: Issues for the Adult Learner
National Adult Literacy and Learning Disabilities Center (ALLD)
1875 Connecticut Ave., NW
Washington, DC 20009-1202
Phone: (800) 953-2553
Fax: (202) 884-8422
E-mail: info@nalldc.aed.org
http://www.ld-read.org (go to publications)

What is Mental Illness?
National Alliance for the Mentally Ill
http://www.nami.org/disorder/whatis.html

DIRECTORIES

Accredited Institutions of Postsecondary Education, published annually
American Council on Education (ACE)
1 Dupont Circle, NW
Suite # 800
Washington, DC 20036

Phone: (202) 939-9300
E-mail: web@ace.nche.edu
http://www.acenet.edu

The College Blue Book
Macmillan Publishers
201 West 103rd Street
Indianapolis, IN 46290
Phone: (800) 716-0044
http://www.macmillanusa.com

Colleges in the Middle Atlantic States
Peterson's Guides
P.O. Box 2123
Princeton, NJ 08543-2123
Phone: (800) 225-0261
Fax: (609) 243-9150
E-mail: custsvc@petersons.com
http://www.petersons.com

Colleges in the Midwest
Colleges in the South
Colleges in the West
Peterson's Guides
See address above.

Lovejoy's College Guide
Simon & Schuster
200 Old Tappan Road
Old Tappan, NJ 07675
Phone: (800) 223-2336
Fax: (800) 445-6991
www.simonsays.com

Peterson's Colleges with Programs for
Students with Learning Disabilities or Attention Deficit Disorders, 5th edition, 1997
Editors: Charles T. Mangrum and Stephen S. Strichart
Peterson's Guides
P.O. Box 2123
Princeton, NJ 08543-2123
Phone: (800) 225-0261

Fax: (609) 243-9150
E-mail: custsvc@pgi.petersons.com
http://www.petersons.com

Peterson's Four-Year Colleges
Peterson's Guide to Two-Year Colleges
Peterson's Guides
See address above.

Peterson's Vocational and Technical Schools 2000
Peterson's Guides
See address above.

Vocational and Technical Schools: East
Vocational and Technical Schools: West
Peterson's Guides
See address above.

WEBSITES

CampusTours
From this site, you can link to the webpages or Webcams of hundreds of colleges and universities and also find out about financial aid.
http://www.campustours.com

The College Board
This site helps to get you started investigating and selecting colleges.
http://www.collegeboard.org

CollegeNET
This site has descriptions, homepages, and applications to numerous colleges and universities.
http://www.collegenet.com

Common Application
This site offers an online and downloadable application form that is accepted by about 200 colleges in the U.S. It need only be filled out once if you are applying to more than one of these schools.
http://www.commonapp.org

Embark.com
This site has a variety of articles and tools designed to help students select a college. One feature, the College Matchmaker, allows students to plug in their requirements (including price, location, size, availability of disability assistance) and then displays the names of schools matching those requirements.
http://www.embark.com/ugrad.asp

National Alliance for the Mentally Ill
This site has information, resources, and links on the topic of mental illness.
http://www.nami.org

Online College Applications
This site, hosted by Peterson's, offers you information about schools, as well as the opportunity to send an application.
http://www.applytocollege.com

University Links
This site has numerous links to the home pages of colleges and universities online.
http://www-net.com/univ.html

ORGANIZATIONS
Contact information for the following useful organizations can be found beginning on page 347.

- Academy for Educational Development
- American College Testing
- American Council on Education (ACE)
- American Library Association (ALA)
- American Psychiatric Association
- Association for Career and Technical Education (ACTE), *formerly American Vocational Association (AVA)*
- Association on Higher Education and Disability (AHEAD)
- Association of Specialized and Cooperative Library Agencies (ASCLA)
- Beach Center on Families and Disabilities
- Center for Mental Health Services

- Children and Adults with Attention-Deficit/Hyperactivity Disorder (CHADD)
- Clearinghouse on Adult Education
- Clearinghouse on Disability Information
- Council for Exceptional Children
- Council on Learning Disabilities
- Disability Rights Education and Defense Fund, Inc. (DREDF)
- Division of Adult Education
- Educational Testing Service, Inc.
- ERIC Clearinghouse on Assessment & Evaluation
- General Education Development (GED)
- Higher Education and The Handicapped (HEATH) Resource Center
- The International Dyslexia Association
- Internet Special Education Resources
- The JIST of IT Newsletter
- Job Accommodation Network
- Learning Disabilities Association of America (LDA)
- National Association for Adults with Learning Difficulties (NAALD)
- National Association of School Psychologists
- National Center for Learning Disabilities (NCLD)
- National Network of Learning Disabled Adults (NNLDA)
- National Organization on Disability
- National Parent Network on Disabilities
- NICHCY
- NIMH Public Inquiries
- Office of Consumer, Family, and Public Information
- Office of Special Education and Rehabilitative Services (OSERS)
- U.S. Department of Education

8

CHOOSING COURSES

Arline Halper

Overview

Choosing classes is probably the single most important task that a student is asked to do. Finding the right classes can make the difference between success and disappointment. One path to success is to use all available resources in making these important choices.

During the initial registration period at a college or university, all students go through an academic advisory process to select and sign up for courses needed to fulfill requirements for degrees, majors, or certificates. First-time students at UCLA, for example, meet with academic advisors during the orientation period for assistance planning their programs and help registering for classes. During the following semesters or quarters, students with LD and/or AD/HD are given priority enrollment. This pre-enrollment period allows them to sign up for classes earlier than other students. Staff from the Office for Students with Disabilities is available to assist students with this procedure.

Not all colleges and universities provide students with this level of assistance. Naturally, a very important question to ask colleges before you make your final decision is, "How are students assisted in selecting their classes?"

Getting Help with Class Selection

Some DSS offices have academic advisors on staff. These professionals are trained to help you plan your program, make decisions about majors, and choose specific classes. This service is more likely to be available at community colleges and colleges that have comprehensive programs for students with LD and/or AD/HD. At Santa Monica College, for example, the DSS academic advisor presents a session in "Strategies for Choosing Classes" to each of their learning strategies classes.

At other colleges, the learning specialists work very closely with college academic advisors or counselors. In this situation, the learning specialist, the academic advisor, and you might participate in a three-way telephone conference to assist you in selecting classes for a semester or quarter. Decisions would be made based on:

- your strengths and needs,

- your readiness to take a full or reduced courseload,

- your interest in possible majors,

- the advisor's knowledge of the academic requirements of different majors, and of professors whose teaching style and course requirements are particularly suitable for you.

Following the telephone conference, you would be encouraged to make an appointment to see the academic advisor to develop an overall plan that would lead you to graduation in your major.

While some assistance is available to students in all postsecondary settings, the most successful students are "pro-active" in making their decisions. They think ahead and use the resources on their campus prior to the beginning of the next quarter or semester. Pro-active students with dyslexia, for example, research classes ahead of time so they do not end up in a class with an overwhelming amount of reading and writing.

Strategies for Becoming Informed about Classes

Pro-active students take one or more of the following steps to make informed choices about their prospective classes:

1. Talk to Other Students

Other students are an excellent source of information about classes and professors. You should ask friends and acquaintances whether they took a class you are considering. What were the exams like? How much reading and how many papers were required? How responsive and accommodating was the instructor?

The DSS program at UCLA has a peer-mentor program that matches first-year students with LD and AD/HD with continuing students with LD and AD/HD. The peer-mentors are available to new students to answer their questions about classes, professors, campus life, or accommodations, all from a student's point of view. When you meet with a learning specialist at *your* college, ask to be put in touch with a student in the DSS program who would be willing to answer questions and be a resource or mentor to you.

2. Participate in Orientation Programs

Check to see if the college offers an orientation program for students with LD and/or AD/HD before school starts. These programs provide opportunities to become familiar with campus life and to ask questions of continuing students and advisors about classes, professors, on-campus resources, and services.

3. Audit Classes

An excellent strategy for choosing classes for the following semester or quarter is to observe the class and the professor for a limited period, or even for the entire course. Be sure to check with the department first to determine whether you need a special appointment to visit a class, and what arrangements can be made to audit the class for the entire quarter or semester, if desired.

When you audit a class, you may attend all the sessions, but are not responsible for exams or assignments. Some institutions have procedures to sign up to audit a class on a noncredit basis. In other cases, professors will give permission for visitations for a few sessions. Naturally, you must adhere to the starting and ending times of the class.

During classroom visits, observe the professor's teaching style firsthand. Does he or she involve the students in classroom discussions? What are the assignments like? Does he or she appear to be available to students?

Some students audit classes just before they actually enroll to get a head start on the readings for that class.

4. Check the Net

Most colleges and universities are increasing the amount of information available to students on the Internet. You can view course syllabi, which outline course objectives, textbook(s), readings, and writing assignments. Many professors also have "virtual office hours," offering students and even prospective students an opportunity to interact and ask questions about the course via e-mail.

5. Meet with the Professor

Many professors are happy to meet with prospective students to discuss an upcoming course. Usually, the best time to meet is during the professor's regularly scheduled office hours. This is a perfect opportunity for you to explain your disabilities and any accommodations you will need.

Meeting a professor before the class begins allows you to assess his or her responsiveness, and hopefully impress the professor with your motivation and commitment to learning. Getting the textbooks and the reading list before the class begins also gives you an opportunity to get a "head start" on the reading, and to order books on tape, if indicated.

6. Don't Procrastinate

Don't wait until the last minute to begin gathering information about courses and professors. Most DSS offices offer priority enrollment as an accommodation to students with disabilities. Priority enrollment allows you to register a few days before other students on campus and allows you to get into desired classes.

Full- or Part-time Courseload?

For some students with LD and/or AD/HD, a reduced courseload is essential for success. Some need more time to write papers and study for exams. Others need to balance demanding courses that require a great deal of reading with those that do not. Still others need to hold a part-time job while in school. By taking fewer classes, you have more time to spend on each class.

If you attend part time, you may want to take summer classes so you are able to graduate with your class. Or, you may want to take extra time to complete your program.

Section 504 of the Rehabilitation Act and the Americans with Disabilities Act (ADA) clearly list extended time in which to complete a program as an appropriate accommodation. With a reduced courseload, however, Federal Grants may be reduced, and loans are often pro-rated to the number of units taken each quarter or semester. Colleges or universities may have additional funds to supplement grant monies, however. Check with the DSS office and ask whether they have successfully advocated for students who needed additional financial aid to complete their programs. See Chapter 6 for more information about financial aid.

Before deciding on full- or part-time course work, the following questions should be asked, and the answers weighed carefully:

- How many credit hours per semester or quarter must you earn to maintain full-time status?

- What is the usual timeframe for earning a degree at the institution?

- What is the procedure for making exceptions for students with disabilities?

- What benefits (e.g., student health insurance) would be lost if you do not have enough credit for full-time status? Would financial aid be jeopardized? What about housing?

Whatever your decision, remember that your degree will be well worth your time, no matter how much time it takes to complete.

Learning Strategies Classes

Many colleges and universities have study skills or learning strategies classes to help students improve their reading, writing, time management, and study skills. Credit is sometimes given toward graduation, although you may receive only one or two credits, as compared to three or four for other classes. Also, credits are not usually transferable to other colleges or universities.

Regardless of the credits offered, college level learning strategies and study skills classes may offer you an opportunity to learn essential tools for success.

Strategies classes teach students to develop, use, and maintain a variety of tools for learning. They provide students with sequential, research-based instruction with ample repetition and practice.

Along the same lines as learning strategies classes are remedial classes, designed to help students improve their basic reading, writing, and math skills. Your college counselor or learning specialist should let you know whether remedial classes are available and whether test results indicate that you might benefit from them. Some colleges require that students take basic skills classes as a prerequisite to more advanced classes if they receive low scores on placement exams.

Both learning strategies and remedial classes are usually available at junior and community colleges, and help prepare students for college academic tasks. Some four-year colleges also have specialized learning courses. The learning disabilities program at the University of California, Berkeley, for example, offers an eight-week learning strategies class in math, notetaking skills, textbook strategies, writing, reading, and organization/time management skills, for credit. Other colleges and universities offer a selection of monthly or quarterly workshops as part of the learning disabilities program.

More Tips on Choosing Classes

- Become actively involved in planning your program. This requires you to understand your abilities and needs, your learning style, and your need for specific accommodations and/or special services. Be able to explain these to your academic advisor when needed.

- Prior to entering your college or university, make an appointment with the learning specialist or the appropriate DSS staff person and bring current documentation of your disability. This way you will already be registered with the office, and services will be in place when you request accommodations.

- Find out which professors have more empathy toward students with disabilities, as well as experience in working with them. Ask other students with LD and/or AD/HD to suggest classes that have fewer readings and papers, or take-home exams and oral presentations instead of lengthy papers.

- Variety can motivate you and create more success. Try new courses and take risks. Integrate courses that require intensive daily work (e.g., math) with courses that allow more independent work schedules and timelines.

- Think of daily schedules. Take courses scheduled at times of day when you function at your best (e.g., no early morning classes). Will you be successful with three classes back to back? Arrange courses so that you have free time on campus to participate in activities such as student government, clubs, workshops, and concerts.

- Be sure to consider study time when scheduling classes. For each hour of class, you should plan on two to three hours of homework.

TABLE 8.1—WHAT STUDENTS HAVE TO SAY

What if you don't get the classes that you want?

The best way to get around this is to talk to the professor. Go see him or her and show your interest in the class. Try to make the professor feel very lucky to have such a motivated student in class. The professor may be able to make an exception for you.

Choosing the right class:

Begin by picking out a list of classes that you might take that quarter. Then, begin to eliminate your choices by the following strategies.

- Get opinions about the professors teaching each class from other students, preferably ones who have been at the university for some time.

- Don't take more than three classes each quarter! It will ease the transition to college and will give you more time to study.

- Make sure that the final exams are at least one day apart. Final exams are very important—sometimes it may be more than 50% of your grade. (See the learning specialist if your exams are back to back; some accommodations might be made).

- Do not schedule back to back classes, if possible. There could be quite a long walk between the two classrooms and you may need to see a professor or teaching assistant (TA) before or after the class.

Taken, with permission, from: The Peer-Mentor Newsletter: Surviving Your First Quarter at UCLA—*Contributions of UCLA students with learning disabilities.*

- Stay flexible. If a class is not available this semester or is being taught by a professor who is unsympathetic to students with LD or AD/HD, find out when it is offered next or substitute another class for it.

- Continually evaluate personal goals. Throughout college, your course experiences will contribute to your long-term planning skills. You should be asking yourself questions such as: Why am I attending college? Do I need/want to transfer? Do I want to work toward a transfer? What is my desired major? What do I need to graduate? These responses should be considered prior to selecting courses for individual semesters.

- Read Table 8.1 *(on the previous page)* for students' suggestions about choosing classes.

- Last of all, do not panic. Hang in there. College can be fun; comfort and skill are the result of practice and time.

Don't Forget Your Documentation

Remember: Before receiving services, you must first present current documentation of a disability to the DSS office. The documentation is then reviewed by a learning disabilities specialist to determine whether you are eligible for services and what accommodations can best meet your needs. Refer back to chapter 4 for more information about documenting your disability.

Making the Leap from High School to College

The procedures for selecting college courses from semester to semester and for receiving services and accommodations are very different than in high school. These differences often cause new college students the most difficulty. Students must understand the whole college process in order to be successful from semester to semester and in each course throughout their academic career. Table 8.2 lists important information about college-level support services you should think about as you are choosing courses.

Conclusion

There are many campus resources at colleges and universities to assist students in planning, choosing, and registering for classes. Learning specialists or

TABLE 8.2—College-Level Services

- You are responsible for providing current documentation of your disability to the college.

- Learning specialists or DSS specialists will determine what services are appropriate, based on the documentation, your self-reported learning needs, and requirements of the particular class.

- Even after documentation has been provided and appropriate accommodations have been identified, you must request the accommodation(s) each time they are needed.

- You, with counsel from your advisors, set your own academic goals, considering number of courses per quarter or semester, course requirements for admissions to a major, and grade point average requirements for specific programs.

- Parents are not notified of services you request unless you grant permission for that information to be released.

Adapted with permission from Differences between High School and College *by Ruth Proctor, Coordinator of Support Services for Students with Disabilities, Marymount College Learning Center.*

staff from the DSS office are also available to help you select classes. It is to your advantage to use the resources available as early as possible. With timely academic advice, you can make informed decisions. But remember, no matter how excellent the advisory system, it is up to you to use that advice to your advantage. You are more likely to succeed if you accept responsibility for planning and managing your postsecondary program.

Resources

BOOKS

ADD and the College Student: A Guide for High School and College Students with Attention Deficit Disorder, 1994
Editor: Dr. Patricia Quinn
Magination Press/American Psychological Association

750 First Street, NE
Washington, DC 20002
Phone: (800) 374-2721, ex. 5510
Fax: (202) 336-5502
E-mail: Books@apa.org
http://www.maginationpress.com

Campus Opportunities: For Students with Learning Disabilities
Authors: Judith Crooker and Stephen Crooker
Learning Disabilities Association
4156 Library Road
Pittsburgh, PA 15234-1349
Phone: (412) 341-1515
Fax: (412) 344-0224
E-mail: ldanatl@usaor.net
http://www.ldanatl.org

College Freshmen with Disabilities: A Triennial Statistical Profile, 1995
HEATH Resource Center
One Dupont Circle, Suite 800
Washington, DC 20036-1193
Phone: (800) 544-3284
E-mail: heath@ace.nche.edu
http://www.acenet.edu/About/programs/
Access&Equity/HEATH
gopher://bobcat-ace.nche.edu

The College Student with a Learning Disability: A Handbook, 1997
Author: Susan Vogel
Learning Disabilities Association
See address above.

College Students with Learning Disabilities: A Student's Perspective, 1991
Authors: Wren and Segal
Learning Disabilities Association
4156 Library Road
Pittsburgh, PA 15234-1349
Phone: (412) 341-1515
Fax: (412) 344-0224
E-mail: ldanatl@usaor.net
http://www.ldanatl.org

Rights and Responsibilities of Students with Learning Disabilities in the Postsecondary Setting
Center for Innovations in Special Education (CISE)
Parkade Center, Suite #152
601 Business Loop, 70 West
Columbia, MO 65211
Phone: (573) 884-7275
http://www.tiger.coe.missouri.edu~mocise

Succeeding in College with Attention Deficit Disorders: Issues & Strategies for Students, Counselors, & Educators, 1996
Author: Jennifer Bramer
Specialty Press/ADD Warehouse
300 NW 70th Avenue, #102
Plantation, FL 33317
Phone: (800) 233-9273
Fax: (954) 792-8545
E-mail: sales@addwarehouse.com
http://www.addwarehouse.com

Success for College Students with Learning Disabilities, 1993
Authors: Susan A. Vogel and Pamela B. Adelman
Springer-Verlag New York
P.O. Box 2485
Secaucus, NJ 07096-2485
Phone: (800) 777-4643
Fax: (201) 348-4505
E-mail: orders@springer-ny.com
http://www.springer-ny.com

Survival Guide for College Students with ADD or LD, 1994
Author: Kathleen Nadeau
Magination Press/American Psychological Association
750 First Street, NE
Washington, DC 20002
Phone: (800) 374-2721, ex. 5510
Fax: (202) 336-5502
E-mail: Books@apa.org
http://www.maginationpress.com

Your Plan for Success: A College Preparation Manual for Students with LD, 1995
Author: K.W. Webb
Learning Disabilities Association
4156 Library Road
Pittsburgh, PA 15234-1349
Phone: (412) 341-1515
Fax: (412) 344-0224
E-mail: ldanatl@usaor.net
http://www.ldanatl.org

PAMPHLET

Getting Ready for College: Advising Students with LD
HEATH Resource Center
One Dupont Circle, Suite 800
Washington, DC 20036-1193
Phone: (800) 544-3284
E-mail: heath@ace.nche.edu
http://www.acenet.edu/About/programs/
Access&Equity/HEATH
gopher://bobcat-ace.nche.edu

9

KEYS TO UNLOCKING ABILITY

CHAPTER 9-A—Using Accommodations

Overview

"Having a brain that can't express itself is an incredible frustration."

These words, spoken by an adult who struggled successfully to overcome his LD, tell us why providing accommodations for students with LD and/or AD/HD is necessary. An accommodation is a change that is made to enable you to participate in school or at work in a way that matches your learning strengths. Accommodations are keys to unlocking potential. They make it possible for you to use your natural abilities.

Accommodations can include alternative ways to fulfill course requirements, creative classroom techniques, tutoring, or use of technology. To be of value, accommodations must be tailored to your individual needs. The more complete the information about your specific strengths and weaknesses, the better the chance of choosing the most effective accommodations. The changes suggested in this chapter have been successfully carried out in postsecondary programs throughout the country.

The Question of Equity

Educators use the term *equity* to mean that all students have an equal opportunity to learn. If you have LD or AD/HD, support services and accommodations give you that opportunity. They are *not* giving you an advantage over others but they *are* giving you the chance to overcome your particular learning challenges based on your LD and/or AD/HD.

Accommodations address difficulties in the process for learning—how you receive or demonstrate what you know. Accommodations **do not change** course content or lower academic standards. The federal laws discussed in Chapter 3 ensure that everyone—students, parents, counselors, and educators—must agree at the outset that it is reasonable, fair, and entirely proper to offer accommodations.

Although educators occasionally worry that the quality of education will be lowered by making accommodations, experience has shown that this does not happen. In fact, many techniques for helping students with learning differences use their abilities are also extremely helpful to other students. Instructors who have adapted their classroom approaches have discovered that they have sharpened their teaching skills and that their students' overall performance has improved.

Alternative Ways to Learn

When he was an undergraduate, George, a student with LD, was allowed to submit a written assignment on tape for the first time. He received the first A of his life. The opportunity to do his course work in an alternative way gave him a large dose of self-

confidence, and he went on to excel as a major in architectural technology. Once his self-confidence took hold, he was also able to work methodically on the basic mechanical skills that had overwhelmed him in the past.

The use of alternative ways to fulfill course requirements helps lay the groundwork for academic success. Success leads to motivation, which can in turn lead to further accomplishment. Students who have been filled with self-doubt can now begin to shine. Alternatives are ways to *bypass* obstacles caused by a disability.

Alternatives to Printed Materials

Many students find it helpful to listen to taped textbooks or to have material read aloud by readers. Tapes used in combination with reading strengthen the visual input of print by adding the auditory input of the recorded voice.

Students should begin to learn to use taped books while in high school, as it takes practice to use this alternative successfully. When listening to taped books, take frequent breaks and ask yourself questions about the material. This helps you to focus and sustain your attention. Students with AD/HD may find it helpful to listen to tape recorded lectures while walking or jogging. Some students also benefit from reading important information into a tape recorder and listening to this information to prepare for a test.

Some campuses are developing tape libraries that provide excellent resources. You can contact the DSS office to find out whether your school has such resources and how to access them. Recording for the Blind & Dyslexic and Talking Books, described below, are other sources of books on tape.

You may also occasionally want to use a reader—often a fellow student who volunteers or is paid to read assignments aloud. Readers are helpful when an instructor gives an unscheduled assignment and there is not enough time to tape it. For example, you might be asked to read reprints, materials in the library, and handouts. Some students also need to have exam questions read aloud to them. If you need the services of a reader, you can usually ask the Disability Support Services (DSS) Office to coordinate this for you.

Recording for the Blind and Dyslexic (RFB&D)

Recording for the Blind and Dyslexic, Inc. (RFB&D) is one of the major providers of taped texts and electronic data (E-Text) for students who cannot read general print media. RFB&D is an international organization dedicated to facilitating educational and professional development of individuals with visual, physical, and perceptual disabilities. In addition to numerous E-Texts, the RFB&D library has more than 80,000 texts on tape and its catalog increases yearly.

To use the service, you must complete an application and provide documentation of a disability. Applicants must also submit a registration payment, as well as an annual membership fee. For schools, membership also gains them a discount on equipment and a free catalog of materials. Individuals can find catalog information on the Internet (see Resources).

Recorded texts are lent free of charge to members of RFB&D. Borrowers are permitted to keep texts for up to one year and must submit written requests for extensions. E-Text materials are purchased for a minimal fee and do not need to be returned.

RFB&D's recorded materials require the use of special playback equipment. This equipment is sold by RFB&D or can be borrowed from the National Library Service for the Blind and Physically Handicapped. E-Text materials (reference matter on computer disk) are available for both IBM compatible computers and Macintosh computers. The materials are formatted in ASCII text as well as in BookManager. BookManager is a retrieval software program, developed by IBM, which enables access to the E-Text. This software interfaces well with various assistive technology devices and programs.

As an organization, RFB&D offers numerous other services. They have a scholarship program and a volunteer program. They also can provide students with curriculum ideas, suggested adaptations and modifications, and bibliographical information. In addition, RFB&D sells numerous texts, programs, and types of equipment that may benefit schools, parents, and students alike.

Below are some tips for using the RFB&D service:

- Try to get requests in before peak periods of January-February, June-July, and August-September. See the Resources for contact information.

- Plan on a turnaround time of 5 to 10 business days if you are requesting a text that already exists in the library.

- For new recordings of books not already in the RFB&D tape library, a special request is needed. Also, RFB&D must be supplied with two copies of the printed text to be read. To save time, mail first class or parcel post, *not* Free Matter for the Blind.

- Once RFB&D receives two copies of the requested book, they seek out a volunteer to record it. (Students buy only one copy of textbooks, like all other students. The institution must furnish the other copy.) Additional time for locating a volunteer must be allotted when planning for the first installment. The first installment usually arrives 6 to 8 weeks *after* the volunteer has begun recording the book.

Talking Books

The Talking Books program is supported by the Library of Congress and maintained by the National Library Service (NLS) for the Blind and Physically Handicapped (see Resources). This program lends a wide range of publications in Braille or recorded form to individuals with visual, physical, and perceptual disabilities. The collection includes popular novels, classical literature, poetry, biography, magazines, and music.

To apply for the free service, you must submit documentation by a certified professional stating your need for this alternative format. Usually, a letter written by a "competent authority" stating that you have LD and need taped books is sufficient to qualify for this service.

Although Talking Books is sponsored by the NLS, it is administered by a network of regional and subregional libraries. Application information is available through local libraries, the Library of Congress, and the Internet. Some of the local NLS libraries can arrange to have text materials taped for individual borrowers.

The NLS also publishes a directory, *Volunteers Who Produce Books*. This directory lists, state by state, the names and addresses of volunteer groups and individuals who tape materials. It is available through libraries affiliated with the NLS.

Playback Equipment for Recorded Books

Tapes recorded by RFB&D and NLS cannot be played on standard 2-track cassette machines bought in stores. A special 4-track playback machine is required. The equipment is available on extended loan basis (for eligible borrowers) from regional branches of the Library of Congress. These machines only have the option to play. Equipment with additional features, such as the option to record, may be purchased from a number of sources, including RFB&D or the American Printing House for the Blind (see Resources for additional information).

Alternatives to Notetaking

Some students have trouble taking notes because they cannot quickly comprehend a speaker's words, write legibly, or organize and remember while listening to a lecture. If you have problems in this area that are identified and documented, you can arrange alternative ways to take notes.

Notetakers

A notetaker is usually a fellow classmate who is a good student and a capable notetaker. Occasionally, a notetaker may be someone who is paid specifically to sit in on a class and take notes. Getting the services of a notetaker usually requires that you, the instructor, and, if necessary, the DSS coordinator talk over the problem. In most cases, teachers will ask a classmate to share class notes with you. In some instances, two volunteer notetakers are used. This helps if one is absent.

You might need to photocopy the notetaker's notes. Or the notetaker might use special paper that makes two or three copies as she writes. Carbon paper, as well as a special noncarbon duplicating paper might be used. This paper can be ordered by the college bookstore or the DSS office from the National Institute for the Deaf, Rochester Institute for Technology Bookstore. On most campuses the DSS office will provide paper for notetakers, but you may prefer to provide your own if you are used to a special type of paper.

Taped Lectures

Some students tape lectures and then listen to them in a quiet, non-distracting atmosphere. It is essential to get the instructor's permission before taping a lecture. Sometimes you may need to sign a formal statement that the material will only be used for study purposes. Listening to a tape requires the same skills as listening to a lecture, except that it can be done in private, stopping the machine as needed and taking frequent breaks.

A new method for indexing tapes, developed especially for blind people, can be helpful for students with LD and AD/HD. Using this voice-indexing technique on special taping equipment, you can record headings and subheadings for lectures and other taped materials. You can then skim a recorded text by listening to headings, much the way you skim a book by reading boldface subheadings, italics, original notes, and so forth.

Here are some tips for taping class lectures:

- Use a rechargeable battery-operated tape recorder to eliminate the need to sit next to electrical outlets.

- Use a different tape for each class. To avoid having to change tapes during class, use 120-minute tapes.

- Label the tape with date, class, and lecturer.

- Set the counter at 0 when beginning to record a new class. When an important idea is stated, make a note of the number on the counter to listen to later.

- During class discussions, use the pause button and only tape the essentials.

- Allow sufficient extra study time for listening to tapes.

- Review tapes as soon as possible after a lecture.

- You might try listening for the main ideas on one tape, then repeating these ideas into a second tape. The second tape becomes your class notes.

Using a Laptop

Some students with attention problems or handwriting difficulties prefer to use a laptop computer to take notes. This technique can keep you busy and focused. Some colleges have "loaners" for students, and the department of vocational rehabilitation *may* be able to lend you one too. However, if you find this kind of accommodation helpful, you would probably be wise to purchase your own laptop.

Alternative Ways to Take Exams

Ideally, exams should measure your mastery and understanding of course material, not how well you have learned test-taking strategies. You should also have the opportunity to show what you know without being penalized for your processing or attention problems.

Students with LD and/or AD/HD often ask for accommodations when taking exams. For example, you may have trouble reading or understanding the questions; writing under pressure; organizing thoughts; or remembering mechanics of spelling, punctuation, and syntax. Even the slightest noise, such as the scratching of pencils on paper, may be distracting.

To compensate, you may need additional time to complete exams. Or, you may need to take tests in a separate, quiet room, with a proctor. Some students need to listen to exam questions on tape or give their answers orally. More rarely, a test might be shortened for a student.

Other accommodations individual students have worked out with individual instructors:

- writing papers instead of taking tests;

- outlining the answers to the test in abbreviated form, then meeting with the professor to give oral answers;

- writing tests in the classroom, then later typing the answers on a word processor in the DSS office to compensate for handwriting issues;

- taking the exam on a laptop (when using this option, the instructor may need to check the computer to see that there is no access to test information on the hard drive or disk).

Typical Test Modifications

- Having material read.

- Listening to taped tests.

- Dictating answers to a scribe.

- Having extended time to take a test.

- Being allowed to ask for clarification of questions (this modification is not used frequently).

- Dictating answers onto a tape and then word processing them.

- Getting help in proofreading answers for spelling and syntax errors.

- Taking oral rather than written exams.

- Taking large print tests.

- Using calculators and spelling dictionaries.

- Using scratch paper for outlining and drafting answers.

Readers and Scribes

On many campuses, readers and scribes are available to help with test taking. A reader reads test questions aloud, while a scribe (also called clerk, secretary, or exam writer) writes down answers dictated by a student. Both readers and scribes are oriented to student needs and trained not to give assistance in answering questions. Their services are usually available through the DSS office.

When rapport between DSS and faculty is good, readers or scribes can also administer exams. In some cases, college departments prefer to have their own proctors present in the room as well.

Arranging Test-Taking Alternatives

Alternative test-taking procedures must be arranged in advance, preferably soon after a course begins. Readers and proctors need to be lined up and test-taking rooms or offices reserved. You are expected to take responsibility for informing the faculty and DSS coordinator or learning specialist that you need special test-taking services. Students must usually bring a copy of the course syllabus to the DSS office to verify testing dates.

Alternatives to Written Composition

Written assignments can be difficult for many students. Despite your intelligence, you may have trouble putting ideas together, using correct grammar and spelling, and writing legibly. Strategies that can help include using word processors with spelling and grammar checkers, or using dictating and editing services. Editing services are not available on all campuses, but some have writing labs where staff can help you write and edit your papers.

Students with AD/HD and/or LD often have trouble with long assignments such as research papers. In these cases, breaking the assignment down into manageable parts seems to help. For example, make a deadline to finish your library research, another deadline to complete note taking, another deadline to have a rough draft done, a deadline for using editing services, if available, and a deadline for polishing the paper in time to turn it in by the due date.

Using Special Talents

Some students persuade their instructors to allow them to substitute another project for traditional research or writing assignments. They then draw on their special talents to express the ideas called for in an assignment.

One student presented a beautiful photographic essay on rural life instead of a written report for a sociology course. Another student presented a fine oil painting to illustrate an oral report on dreams. An education student observed and reported orally on techniques of teaching in four different classrooms to fulfill a research assignment on teaching methodology. A student in a class on criminology spent many hours in court learning about the justice system and was given extended time to write an essay.

Both reading and writing difficulties were overcome through these nontraditional ways of doing assignments. Yet in each case, the objective of the course was met. Actually, more time may be spent in completing alternative assignments than in doing the work in a traditional way.

A Few General Guidelines for Success

You may benefit from one or more of the following strategies:

■ Sit in the front of the class. This can help you pay attention to the lecture/professor and lessen distractions.

■ Avoid lecture classes that last more than one hour.

■ Ask professors if you can sit in the back of the class so you can get up and walk the hallways for a few minutes when needed (without disturbing others).

■ Use effective study skills. Take a class in this area if you are uncertain about your skills.

■ Use time management skills. Develop a daily "to-do" list, use a personal planner or checklists, set deadlines for projects, divide each day into hours and plan your schedule for each hour.

■ Ask the DSS office about a support group on campus so you can meet with other students to discuss strategies and perhaps form study groups.

Waivers

A waiver gives you permission to modify degree requirements. It might allow you to substitute one course for another, or release you from the requirement to pass a particular course to graduate.

As more students with disabilities go to college, faculty members are increasingly confronted with requests to grant waivers in courses that are particularly difficult for students (e.g., foreign languages, statistics, and English composition). This issue touches the core of the academic world. The legal obligation to make college accessible to all who are qualified, regardless of disability, can conflict with the ideals of administrators and faculty. The concern is that changing requirements by substituting courses or bypassing certain requirements will dilute the meaning of a diploma. These are very difficult questions that will be debated for a long time.

You should be cautious in requesting waivers, and make sure you understand the consequences. For example, if you get a foreign language waiver, you may not qualify for some graduate or professional programs that require foreign language skills.

In determining whether there are grounds to grant you a waiver, your school should focus on what you can or cannot do because of your disability. A deaf

Foreign Language Waivers

Foreign languages create severe problems for many students with LD. Consequently, some colleges and universities permit some form of modification, including:

- dropping the requirement,

- substituting courses on literature, history, and culture for the language of the country,

- modifying the instructional approach by eliminating reading, writing, or oral/aural components,

- providing taped texts and/or extensive tutoring,

- allowing the foreign language requirement to be fulfilled by courses in sign language.

student would not be expected to take a music appreciation course that depended on listening. The grounds for revising specific requirements for students with LD and/or AD/HD are similar. In other words, is there something about the nature of your documented disability that makes it impossible or nearly impossible for you to pass a specific course?

Substitution of Courses

To recommend substitute courses for required courses, a DSS specialist might look at the purpose of including those required courses in the curriculum. For example, if the purpose of studying foreign languages is to experience a foreign culture, then courses in that country's history or literature might be appropriate substitutes. For like reasons a history major with dyscalculia (inability to do math) was permitted to substitute a class in oral interviewing techniques for a statistics class. The rationale: The statistics class was required as a research tool, not as a math requirement.

College Policies for Granting Waivers

How eligibility for waivers or substitutions is determined differs from college to college. Some colleges allow students who are diagnosed as having LD to petition a dean or committee for waivers. Others allow students to petition for a waiver or other modification only after unsuccessfully trying the course. Another strategy is to permit retroactive withdrawal from a failed course. Some colleges recommend that students take difficult courses at another school, such as a community college, during the summer and transfer the credits.

The following are a few examples of how some campuses have resolved the waiver issue:

- **The school offers a general studies degree in which some of the courses in the core curriculum can be audited.** A general studies degree is a program of study put together by a student and his advisor so the student can study what is of interest to him. A degree in general studies can have an emphasis on a major field of study (e.g., business). In addition, a course may be waived if a student has attempted several times to pass it.

- **An advisory committee reviews requests for curriculum modifications.** This committee makes recommendations after the director of DSS presents different students' cases. Results of diagnostic testing must document reasons for requests for waivers or substitutions. The academic unit or department involved participates in making a final decision based on the committee's recommendation.

- **A list of courses that fulfill the same purpose as foreign languages is developed.** These courses may consist of additional English credits. To arrange to take them as a substitute for foreign language courses, students must document their disabilities.

- **Professional, Technical, or Vocational Schools.** In these schools, students must meet all licensing requirements for technical programs. Generally, however, waivers or substitutions can be arranged for courses that are not required for licensing.

Conclusion

Each of the alternative methods for fulfilling degree requirements, including waivers, has the same purpose. Each provides learning opportunities for students who cannot acquire or express knowledge in traditional formats. Each makes it possible for learning to take place in a different way.

The key to using accommodations is to be able to match your learning strengths and needs to your program, courses, and instructors. There are many accommodations and supports available. The challenge is to discover which ones are most useful to you and then learn how to use those accommodations to your maximum benefit.

CHAPTER 9-B—My Tutors Deserve Roses

Overview

Working with a tutor can help you shine. A tutor can patiently review and clarify difficult assignments or offer proofreading and editing suggestions. Tutors can also give more specific help, such as working with you to find the main ideas in a complex reading passage, or helping you graphically represent complex concepts. A tutor who is willing to take the time to understand how you learn can play a key role in your success. One student expressed his gratitude by saying, "My tutors deserve roses and champagne. They are my mainstay."

It may be necessary for the tutor to prod and push. It may be necessary, as one tutor put it, to act as "the student's ego" until you can go on alone. But the tutor is not there to do your work. Whatever your learning strengths and needs may be, the goal of tutoring is to make it possible for you to work independently.

What Tutoring Services Are Available?

Many campuses offer some form of tutoring service. These services are usually provided by peer tutors, who are graduate students or upper-level students with strong academic records. Arrangements for a peer tutor can usually be made through an instructor, department head, or the DSS Office. Peer tutors may be paid by the institution, through a work-study arrangement with the financial aid office, or directly by you.

Peer tutoring works well for many students with LD and/or AD/HD. Some students find it especially easy to explain their particular problems to a peer tutor. Together, they are able to develop practical strategies for doing the work.

If peer tutoring doesn't work for you or is not available, you may have other options. A part-time instructor or retired teacher may be willing and able to tutor in specific subject areas. Reading centers or graduate departments of special education may have instructors who can work with you on an individual basis. High school special education teachers or remedial teachers in reading or math may be available to tutor after school hours. These professionals have experience and expertise that can make a difference in a tutoring relationship.

Professional tutors, specializing in working with adolescents and adults with LD and/or AD/HD, offer a higher level of skill. These educational specialists are not always easy to find, although their ranks are growing. They often have advanced degrees in special education, with a specialty in LD and/or AD/HD.

If you are looking for a professional tutor, check with your DSS office. Local chapters of the Learning Disabilities Association (LDA), the International Dyslexia Association, or Children and Adults with Attention-Deficit/Hyperactivity Disorder (CHADD) can also be helpful. Private agencies that offer tutoring services may be listed in the yellow pages under "Education," "Schools," or "Tutoring." Be sure to check on the qualifications and recommendations of private tutors by asking for names of previous clients.

Supervision and Training of Tutors

Schools vary greatly in how they orient, train, and assist tutors in their work. Without the backup of training or supervision, many tutors find they do not have the skills to be effective. You want to find out how your DSS office prepares and supports tutors.

On some campuses, there are formal training programs to prepare tutors. On others, orientation and preparation of tutors are loosely organized. Learning specialists or other professionals may work informally with a network of tutors.

A trained cadre of tutors is a great asset to a campus program. Most training programs work with peer tutors and frequently seek students who are special education majors. Training programs might include seminars, workshops, or mini courses on LD and AD/HD for tutors, conducted before each semester. These are followed by regular meetings or individual conferences between tutors and coordinators.

Regardless of how tutors are trained on your campus, ongoing supervision and communication are keys to success. Your tutor needs to have access to someone (a DSS coordinator, a professor, a reading specialist, or a counselor) who can discuss ideas for teaching, and can help resolve any problems that arise.

The Tutoring Session

For tutoring to succeed, both you and your tutor must make a commitment to the goals of tutoring. Before tutoring starts, you must agree about time, place, and frequency of sessions. The choice of a site for tutoring must weigh convenience, atmosphere that supports studying, and other factors. Some tutoring programs draw up a simple contract signed by each participant. Typically, you will be asked to agree to basic responsibilities, including arriving promptly, contacting one another if it is necessary to cancel, and being prepared for each tutoring session. The number of sessions each week varies.

Tutoring sessions have to be focused. The tutor needs a firm idea of what the course covers and what assignments are due. Giving him or her a copy of the syllabus, with a detailed course outline, is a must.

You and your tutor need to have a clear idea of what will be worked on at each session. To conduct the session, your tutor should know what was covered by the instructor in the last class or classes and what reading has been required.

Your tutor may want to spend time finding out how well you grasp the content and what kinds of help you will need to learn the required content.

Depending on your needs, sessions can include work on skills in listening, organizing notes, managing time and assignments, reading for main ideas, outlining and concept mapping, revising memory techniques, and studying for and taking exams. The tutor may also help you with learning strategies. For instance, if you decide to tape lectures, the tutor can give you tips for listening to tapes for main and subordinate ideas.

Dealing with the Whole Person

Besides helping you with academics, your tutor might help you with interpersonal skills. For example, your tutor may give you feedback on your communication skills or take time to discuss social issues with you. Your tutor's perspective can also be helpful when you are trying to figure out difficult interpersonal situations with instructors or friends.

One tutor described himself as a "catalyst, stabilizer, and expediter— with a little of counselor added." He believed that he should give the students he tutored a sense of their own competence and capacity to succeed. But remember that tutors are not counselors. If you feel a strong need for social and emotional support, you should probably find out about support groups or counseling. (See Chapter 7.)

Sometimes students want friends or family members to be their tutors. This is quite often *not* a good idea. A tutor must sometimes push, prod, and demand. A friend or family member may not have the "heart" to help you reach your full potential in this role. A tutor needs to maintain an objective role when working with you.

When Problems Arise with a Tutor

For you and your tutor to have a successful relationship, you need to have mutual respect. Your tutor should be friendly, know how to put you at ease, and be relaxed and accepting. For your part, you need to be honest about your learning strengths and needs and know what you want from a tutoring session.

If one of these elements is missing, conflicts can arise between you and your tutor. You may also begin to feel negative about the relationship if either one of you feels that you are not making progress.

If problems arise, ask for help at the DSS office. The DSS office often can facilitate a conference with you and the tutor to iron out problems. A learning specialist may want to observe the tutoring session to ensure your tutor is using effective strategies and that you are following through with the strategies given in the tutoring session. In the event a relationship just does not work out, the DSS office should assist with finding another tutor.

Conclusion

Tutoring can be a helpful support service for any student who finds a course particularly challenging. Since tutoring *is* a support service, however, it is not

Tips for Tutoring Sessions

- The tutor should give undivided and sincere attention at every session.

- At the first meeting, some time should be spent setting up a positive, friendly relationship.

- There should be goals for each tutoring session.

- Patience is important. An important part of tutoring is finding alternative ways to explain ideas and concepts. Tutoring sessions should help break down ideas and processes into understandable parts.

- Tutors don't always have all the answers. Tutors should be honest and students should be understanding.

- Simpler materials can be helpful but they should be age-appropriate.

- Tutoring should promote a multisensory approach. Visualizing, hearing, touching, and moving around can help in the learning of a new idea or concept.

- Sometimes brief breaks are needed.

- Sessions should be positive and honest. Celebrate successes and target what still needs to be learned.

- Keep logs of appointments. Keep track of progress.

Note to students: Tutors work hard. A sincere "thank you" is worth a dozen roses.

something you will necessarily always need. You may outgrow the need for a tutor after several semesters, or may need tutoring only during semesters when you must take especially difficult classes. Whatever the case, don't hesitate to ask for assistance if you need it. It is far wiser to get the help that will enable you to learn on your own than to struggle on your own and possibly fail.

CHAPTER 9-C—Keys to Unlocking Ability: AD/HD Coaching

What Is AD/HD Coaching?

AD/HD coaching is a term coined by Edward Hallowell and John Ratey to describe the process of systematically guiding someone with AD/HD to better manage his day to day life.

If you have AD/HD, AD/HD coaching can help you identify and stay on the path to success. It can help you discover ways to maximize your strengths and talents, compensate for your weaknesses, and be accountable—for actions taken and lack of action, too. Coaching helps you become a better self-manager because it is about performance—forging the link between what you know and what you do. And last but definitely not least, AD/HD coaching can provide you with structure, support, skills, and strategies.

You may know *what* changes you want to make in your life, but you may not know *how* to make those changes. Or you might get distracted from your goals. A coach can help get you started on an on-going process of defining long-range goals and short-term objectives, and keep you on the defined path once it becomes clear.

Is Coaching the Same As Tutoring?

Coaching and tutoring are different but complementary. The primary focus of tutoring is generally on subject matter content, on offering assistance with *academic* skills such as math, reading, or studying. Coaching is about *life* skills and helps with things like time management, organization, and how to motivate yourself, be persistent, and develop routines and rituals to help you succeed.

However, there *are* some similarities between coaching and tutoring. Both look at the whole person and have the goal of enabling you to function independently. Both a tutor and a coach should be an emotionally neutral person in your life. And both coaching and tutoring see you as inherently capable of achieving whatever you set your mind, energy, and persistence to do.

Is Coaching the Same As Psychotherapy?

No! Coaching is different from psychotherapy. Psychotherapy is generally long-term and deals with problems you have relating to others or coping with your own feelings. Coaching acknowledges these issues but is more interactive and directive. The AD/HD coach assists and encourages you in learning new strategies and techniques for handling your particular functional difficulties, helping to break tasks down into manageable-sized pieces, and to translate thought into action.

How Does Coaching Work?

You and the coach work as a team, identifying areas of difficulty and agreeing on strategies to use to try to overcome these difficulties. You agree to become accountable for your time and actions, and the coach agrees to hold you accountable. The coach is flexible and can work with you in person, by telephone, fax, or e-mail. Depending on the coach's availability and your preference, you might meet together once a week for a half hour to an hour, or several times a week for a brief "check in." You will probably be asked to leave e-mail or phone messages for your coach about the progress you're making on your various goals.

Generally, you will work on two areas with your coach:

1. skill areas that are hard for you, such as time management and organization;

2. lifestyle issues such as diet, sleep habits, exercise programs, and other aspects of self-nurturing.

Often students with AD/HD think that skill areas are their primary concern. They may not realize, however, that paying attention to lifestyle issues can help promote overall well-being. For example, your AD/HD symptoms may become more frequent or severe during times of stress and fatigue. Examining lifestyle issues and making changes can lead to less stress and make it easier to learn new skills.

Coaches can also help you with feelings of being overwhelmed. When you are super-saturated by stimuli, you may tend to "shut down." Coaches can help you learn to select target areas to concentrate on—leaving everything else outside the area of focus for that moment.

How Long Does Coaching Last and What Does It Cost?

There are as many answers to this question as there are coaches and clients. Depending on your needs, a coaching relationship may last a few weeks, several months, or become an on-going professional relationship. An average client might expect to spend at least several months in a coaching relationship.

To receive coaching services, you may need to pay your college or a private coach out of your pocket. On the other hand, your college may not charge a fee for coaching or you may be working with a peer coach at no charge. If you are paying a fee you should know that the price for AD/HD coaching depends on various factors, including your geographic region and the qualifications of the coach. Fees generally fall somewhere between the fees charged by a professional organizer and psychotherapist in your area.

Finding a Coach

Currently there is no industry standard for AD/HD coaches training. This means that you have to interview prospective coaches carefully. You can use the following questions to help you learn more about a coach's training, experience, and background.

- What percentage of your practice is devoted to individuals with AD/HD?

- How long have you been doing AD/HD coaching?

- I have identified the following as one of my coaching needs. . . . What is your experience in this area?

- How do you prefer to work (only in face-to-face meetings, by telephone, or through e-mail)?

- How often do you think we might need to meet/speak?

- What are your fees?

- How and when is payment due?

- Can you provide me with the names of references? (These may be either previous clients who have given the coach permission to use their names as a reference or professional colleagues who are familiar with the coach's work.)

- When would you be available for an initial interview?

To find an AD/HD coach in your geographic area, you can go to the web site at www.americoach.com

The 4 S's to Success in Coaching

Structure

Structure, planning, and organization are important factors in everyone's lives. Perhaps they are even more important in the lives of students with AD/HD, many of whom have difficulties in these critical areas. Without structure, you are at the mercy of the winds and are blown about like a rudderless ship: you are reactive. With structure, you can craft your days and your destinies, your own course on life's seas: you are pro-active.

Support

Support is important for everyone. It is crucial for individuals with AD/HD, who too often have spent years feeling blamed, criticized, and misunderstood. People seeking coaching are frequently working on several levels simultaneously. On the one hand, you want to work on improving skills. On the other hand, you need an opportunity to tell your story, to feel that the coach *understands* you, and has empathy for where you have been and where you want to go.

Skills

Individuals with AD/HD are inconsistent. One day, one hour you can do something (perform); the next you can't. One day, one hour you perceive a situation one way; the next it all looks different. Your world may not be entirely predictable. Both events and relationships may be experienced as being somewhat random, with effects not always tied to specific, understandable causes. Therefore, it is necessary for you to work on skill building. When you *do,* your world becomes more predictable.

Strategies

Strategies are the tools coaches use to help you learn new ways to achieve. Strategies are the methods you learn to help yourself more efficiently navigate your life day by day. Learning new strategies for handling old difficulties is fun, interesting, challenging, rewarding! Developing new ways of thinking and coping challenges you deeply and requires a willingness and commitment to go from "automatic pilot" to the thoughtful, reasoned approach used by seasoned navigators.

Conclusion

For coaching to work, you have to be willing to be accountable for your time and actions. You have to want to change inside—not point a finger at your parent, school, or boss. Coaching requires a commitment and day-by-day, hour-by-hour work. Although coaching is also fun, exciting, and challenging, the old adage "no pain, no gain" fits too.

Coaching isn't magic. It isn't "the answer" to all of your problems. But it is a forum for learning, a way to develop new, helpful behaviors. It is a system that offers structure, support, skills, and strategies. And perhaps most importantly, as Edward Hallowell and John Ratey point out in their book *Driven to Distraction,* coaching can offer hope.

CHAPTER 9-D—Understanding and Using Technology

Overview

Computers and related technologies benefit all our lives in many ways. Some ways are obvious—for example, when we use computers to figure our taxes or use the Internet to send e-mail. Some ways are less obvious—for example, when computers improve the accuracy of weather forecasts or when computerized traffic signals ease traffic congestion.

How do we prepare for the increasingly computerized and technological world of tomorrow? Are these new technologies going to produce new barriers? Fortunately, the answer seems to be "No." New technologies are more likely to create bridges than barriers.

Computers and related technologies are actually expanding opportunities and increasing access for anyone with LD and/or AD/HD in school and post-school life. They provide us with tools to help us overcome problems in remembering, writing, reading, spelling, and math.

Instructional and Assistive Technology

The terms "instructional technology" and "assistive technology" are used in different ways. In this discussion, we will use them to describe two basic ways that technology can benefit you in school and post-school life.

Instructional technologies, as the name implies, are technologies such as computers, tape recorders, videos, etc. that are used in instruction. Some instructional technology products are specifically developed for students with disabilities, but such products are relatively rare. Much more common are instructional technology products that are designed and used with all students. Schools also use as instructional technologies many products designed for more general uses, such as word processors and calculators.

Assistive technologies are used by individuals with disabilities to overcome specific aspects of disabilities. Several federal laws define an "assistive technology device" as:

> "any item, piece of equipment, or product system, whether acquired commercially off the shelf, modified, or customized, that is used to increase, maintain, or improve functional capabilities of individuals with disabilities."

Assistive technology devices are often associated with physical and sensory impairments. Examples of such devices include hearing aids, motorized wheelchairs, communication boards, etc. However, individuals with LD and/or AD/HD can benefit from assistive technology devices as well. For example, if your LD affects your spelling, you may use an electronic dictionary, or if you have poor organizational skills, you may use an electronic organizer.

Instructional and assistive technologies sometimes overlap. For example, schools frequently use word processors as instructional technologies for writing instruction, but word processors can also have assistive technology benefits for students with handwriting or spelling problems. Calculators provide another example. In a typical math class, most students may be using calculators to allow them to focus on math concepts rather than computations. A few students in the same classroom may be using calculators as assistive devices to overcome difficulties in adding, subtracting, multiplying, or dividing.

Technology Research and Issues

Research on instructional technologies shows that computers and related technologies (multimedia, the Internet, etc.) can improve learning. It is often difficult, however, for schools to use these tools to full advantage. Schools can't simply purchase the technology and watch the test scores shoot up. Teachers must be educated; the curriculum must often be adapted; the technology must be integrated into the curriculum and matched to the students; and access must be ensured for all students, including those with disabilities.

Few instructional technology products are specifically designed for students with LD and/or AD/HD or other special needs. This means that you and your advisors may need to figure out ways to make general purpose instructional technologies appropriate and accessible for you.

Research on assistive technologies shows that they too can be extremely beneficial, but much depends on the specific technology, the individual student, and the situation. Assistive technology can be underused, misused, or abandoned, and may even be harmful if the conditions are not right. For example, if students and teachers are not appropriately prepared, assistive devices like computers can actually impede student learning and performance by introducing distractions and demands (e.g., keyboarding, software operation, equipment maintenance).

An important issue in selecting assistive technology is whether it will be used to "work around" the disability, to "remedy" the disability, or both. For example, a student with dyslexia may be given a tape recording of a textbook chapter so that he can work around his reading problem and learn the information in the chapter. However, this approach does little to remedy the reading problem. To remedy the disability, computer software might be used to improve reading skills. In some cases, assistive technology may be used both to work around and remedy a disability. For example, a student with dyslexia might listen to the tape recording and follow along in the textbook, noting unfamiliar words for later practice.

Whenever assistive technology is used only to "work around" the disability, it is important to consider whether you are developing a dependency on the technology that might not be in your best long-term interests. Sometimes such a dependency is unavoidable. In fact, most people these days are dependent on various technologies. How many of us could function without a calculator? It's why some educators advocate using the minimum assistance possible.

Obtaining the Benefits of Technology

Technology is not magic. Obtaining the benefits of instructional or assistive technology requires careful attention not just to the technology, but also to:

- how well the technology matches your needs in the situation;

- how well your school and home can support the use of the technology; and

- the ultimate goals and purposes for the technology.

Gaining access to technology sometimes requires that you advocate for yourself, making it clear that a specific type of technology is a needed accommodation.

Since instructional technologies are used by all students, your instructors should be familiar with them. You may, however, have to make sure that you have the access you need to these technologies, and that they are appropriate and useable for you. For example, you may need to adjust schedules or pull strings so that you have the time you need in the computer lab. Also, you may need to talk to the instructor to make sure that the instructional technologies used in a class will be of benefit to you.

In contrast, assistive technologies are used only to overcome aspects of disabilities, so your instructors will probably be less familiar with them. To help instructors understand your need for assistive technology such as books on tape, you may need to enlist the assistance of the DSS office, a Vocational Rehabilitation counselor, an assistive technology specialist, or similar professional. Chapter 9-E offers more information about advocating for accommodations.

Funding Technology

Federal laws such as the Individuals with Disabilities Education Act (IDEA), the Americans with Disabilities Act, and Section 504 of the Rehabilitation Act can help ensure that students with disabilities have the assistive technologies they need. (See Chapter 3 for information on these laws.) In addition, funding for assistive technology is available from public and private sources, such as Vocational Rehabilitation, Social Security, and private insurance.

Assistance in exploring funding options may be available from a DSS office or a Vocational Rehabilitation counselor, as discussed in Chapter 5. Your state technology assistance project might also be able to help. Each state and territory has such a project funded under the Technology Related Assistance for Individuals with Disabilities Act, also known as the "Tech Act." Your Tech Act project may also have assistive technology you can try out, or be able to suggest appropriate technology for your needs.

The National Institute on Disability and Rehabilitation Research (NIDRR) is the federal office that administers the Tech Act. You can obtain contact information for the various state Tech Act projects from the NIDRR's website, by phone, or by mail:

> National Institute on Disability and Rehabilitation Research
> Office of Special Education and Rehabilitative Services
> U.S. Dept. of Education
> 400 Maryland Ave., S.W.
> Washington, DC 20202
> Phone: (202) 205-8134
> http://www.ed.gov/offices/OSERS/NIDRR/index.html

NIDRR also funds a number of resources that can help you learn more about assistive technology devices. One such resource is a website called ABLEDATA at http://www.abledata.com/. Look at NIDRR's website, or contact them by phone or mail, for information about other helpful resources.

Computer Hardware

Computer hardware is often classified according to what it sits on top of. There are desktop computers, laptop computers, and palmtop computers. Portability can be an advantage, but there are trade-offs in size, cost, and power (meaning the speed and capabilities of the computer). It can all be boiled down to the statement, "Small, cheap, powerful—pick any two." A laptop computer, although small, will cost more than a desktop computer of equal power. Palmtop computers are small and relatively cheap, but generally less powerful than larger computers.

Computer hardware can also be classified according to the range of purposes it serves. General purpose computers can perform an almost unlimited range of functions depending on the software that is used. In contrast, special purpose computers have a limited range of functions. General and special purpose computers have their relative advantages and disadvantages. For example, you can get word processing capabilities by purchasing a general purpose computer and word processing software. Or, you can purchase a special purpose word processing computer more cheaply, often with built-in software, specially marked keys, and a built-in printer. The cheaper computer has fewer functions and fewer options for upgrading, however.

Some software, such as basic word processing and e-mail software, places minimal demands on computer hardware. A relatively inexpensive computer can handle such software, even a computer that is obsolete for other purposes (and sometimes available at little or no cost). In contrast, some software places great demands on hardware, and a computer must be carefully selected to make sure that it has sufficient memory, speed, and storage capacity. Examples of such demanding software include advanced, full-featured word processing programs; some multi-media and graphics software; some World Wide Web browsers; and software that converts speech into written text.

Word Processing Software

Words and numbers are the raw materials of education. And not surprisingly, the two most commonly used and indispensable technologies in schools are calculators and word processors.

Word processors can function as both assistive and instructional technologies. However, for word processors to have these benefits, you will usually need at least minimal skill with the keyboard. (Word prediction and speech recognition are two ways around this requirement, as explained below.) Several programs are available to help you develop typing skills. (Ultrakey by Bytes of Learning is a good one.) Your school can also be a good source of advice for selecting a specific typing program.

Word processing software varies widely in capabilities, ease of use, and demands on the hardware. A basic word processing program allows you to type and edit a document, format the text, save the document on a disk, and print the document. Most current word processors also provide spell checking, and some even provide grammar checking.

Other word processor features that may be especially useful for students with LD and/or AD/HD include:

- **Text-to-speech Capability.** This allows the computer to read a document aloud. This feature can allow you to confirm that you typed the words you thought you typed and that your syntax is correct. Currently, the quality of computerized speech can leave something to be desired. You should try out a text-to-speech program before buying one.

■ **Outlining Capability.** This allows you to develop a document in an outline structure, expanding and collapsing text under the outline headings, and rearranging topical sections of text. This capability can help you organize your writing and learn about text structures. However, such benefits are rarely automatic. Generally, you will need training in the use of the outlining features, and also need to learn organizational strategies based on the outlining features.

Spotlight on Kurzweil 3000

An example of software that can be extremely helpful for students with reading disabilities is the Kurzweil 3000 reading software, by Lernout & Hauspie. This software can scan practically all typed text, then highlight and read it, silently or aloud. It can also read and highlight text from the Internet, such as public transportation schedules, menus, or community events. Users tailor the software to match their own unique strengths and needs: select speed, highlighting preferences (syllable, word, phrase, line, sentence, paragraph), sound or mute, and magnification of words or entire text.

As a student, you could have it read your tests to you without teacher assistance. Its highlighting features could enable you to extract information so as to quickly and easily create notes and study guides. When writing, its word prediction component can help you with spelling, and it can also offer synonyms to improve your writing. Its spellchecker can read aloud, further helping you select the correct word. When combined with voice recognition software for dictation purposes, the software can alleviate many of the burdensome writing problems people with LD face.

The Kurzweil 3000 software interfaces with many assistive technology devices such as joysticks.

For further information:

> Kurzweil 3000
> Lernout & Hauspie
> 52 Third Avenue
> Burlington, MA 01803
> Phone: (781) 203-5000
> Fax: (781) 238-0986
> E-mail: education.info@lhsl.com
> http://www.lhsl.com/education

- **Word Prediction Capability.** Word prediction works as follows. As you type the letters of a word, the computer displays a list of words that begin with the letters you have typed. Eventually, the intended word appears on the list, and you select it by typing a number rather that continuing to type the word. This feature reduces the number of keystrokes required to produce text, and can be useful to anyone who has difficulty with the process of keying in text.

- **Speech Recognition.** It is easier for computers to produce speech than to understand it—they are better talkers than listeners. However, inexpensive and innovative speech recognition programs by companies such as IBM and Dragon Systems are available. Each year they become more accurate and better able to understand different speakers and normal speech. Computers are already capable of translating speech into written text and responding to predefined spoken commands (such as "Start word processor" or "Shut down"). It will be a number of years before computers are really able to understand speech (such as "What are all these colored lights, Hal?"). But as speech recognition progresses, it greatly expands the computer's usefulness, particularly as an assistive device. Again, before buying such a program, it is best to try it out and see how well the computer is able to translate your speech into text.

Beyond the Word Processor

Many students use their computers strictly for word processing. However, computers can provide many other useful benefits for students with LD and/or AD/HD. Some uses worth investigating are described below.

Organization Tools

Computers can help you store and organize information in a number of ways that support learning. Databases and outlines are two familiar types of software to serve this function.

"Concept mapping" software is a less familiar, but useful organization tool. This type of software allows you to store information and then display and manipulate it in graphic structures or concept maps. Figure 1 displays an outline of some of the information of this chapter produced using a type of concept mapping software called *Inspiration.* Figure 2 displays the same outline converted by

---

Technology can benefit students with LD

1. Two types of technology
Instructional technology
 Computers etc. used in instruction
 Mostly developed for general student populations
Assistive technology
 Used to overcome disabilities
 Not just for physical or sensory impairments

2. Research and issues
Instructional technology
 Implementation factors are important
 Appropriate and accessible for students with LD?
Assistive technology
 Benefits depend on student, tech and situation
 "Work around" or "remedy" the disability?

3. Obtaining the benefits of technology
No "magic bullet"
May require "advocacy"
 Federal laws like IDEA, ADA, 504 can help ensure rights
 Funding available under voc rehab, SSI, private insurance

4. Computer hardware
Classified by size: Desktop, laptop, palmtop
Classified by range of purpose--general or specific
Different software places different demands on hardware

5. Word processing software
Can be instructional and assistive
Special features
 Text-to-speech
 Outlining
 Word prediction
 Speech recognition

6. Beyond the word processor
Organizing tools
Multimedia
World wide web

fig. 1

---

software into a concept. Figures 3 and 4 show how you can display different levels or portions of the concept map.

In addition to concept mapping software, some instructional software can provide a structured basis for students to collect information from various

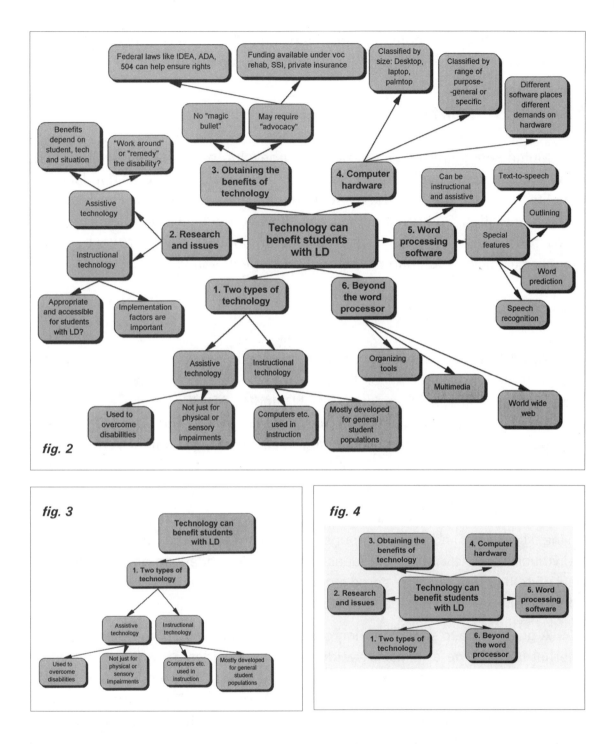

fig. 2

fig. 3

fig. 4

sources and complete projects. One example is *Search Organizer* by Education Development Center.

As discussed in Chapter 11, there are a variety of technology products to help people organize their time and activities. For example, there are small devices such as the *Palm Pilot* and software programs such as *Microsoft Outlook* that include calendars, task lists, address books, etc. These products may be useful, but you should try them out to see how they work for you. In some cases, they complicate things more than they help. It may be that an old-fashioned "low-tech" approach such as a planning notebook may be the answer for you.

Multimedia Software

Multimedia software can allow you to develop products that include text, graphics, sound, and video. Such software may have motivational and learning benefits for you. It may also be useful if you have learning disabilities related to reading or writing. Some instructors may allow you to develop projects in multimedia form instead of written form as an accommodation. *Hyperstudio* by Roger Wagner Publishers is a good example of this type of software.

The World Wide Web

The World Wide Web is an important information resource in education and everyday life, and skills in searching and retrieving information are becoming more critical. Sometimes students with LD and/or AD/HD may have difficulties with the vast, disorganized nature of the World Wide Web, and may need to learn specific techniques and strategies for negotiating this environment. A media specialist, librarian, or tutor on your campus may be able to provide instruction in these techniques and strategies.

The Web is also a terrific resource for connecting with others. There are online discussions and support groups on about any topic you can imagine. Some individuals use the Web to get ideas about accommodations and strategies to deal with their disability. For some students, it is easier to ask questions or share information over the Web than face to face.

A good place to start exploring options for connecting with others over the Internet is *LDOnline* at http://www.ldonline.org/. Besides providing informative articles and links to other useful sites, *LDOnline* offers electronic bulletin boards on a variety of topics, including postsecondary education. The International Dyslexia Association's website also has a bulletin board where you can post and answer questions at http://www.interdys.org/.

Conclusion

Technology is like any other tool. The challenge is to find the technology applications that work best for you and learn how to use them. This takes an investment of time and money, but the payoff can be increased productivity and creativity.

CHAPTER 9-E—The Art of Coordination

"I felt like a thousand pounds had been taken off my back. I finally had someone who was there for me."

This is how one student described the help he received from the coordinator of DSS on his campus. Others have described coordinators as a lifeline—the first person to give them the support they needed to discover how to use their strengths.

We use the word *coordinator* to refer to the person on campus who is designated to work with students in obtaining accommodations and dealing with related problems. This chapter explains what to expect from your coordinator and how to work with him or her in order to ensure your accommodations work.

The Role of the Coordinator

Coordinators act as liaisons with faculty and administrators to:

- raise awareness of learning differences,
- explain accommodations,
- intervene on behalf of specific students, and
- win institutional support for services.

They also assess individual students' needs and help to develop and implement plans to accommodate their needs. In addition, they respond to questions about campus services from prospective applicants and advise parents before and after admissions.

At colleges with special programs for students with LD and/or AD/HD, coordinators also discuss admission of qualified applicants with admissions counselors. To do these many tasks, coordinators need a combination of tact, empathy, knowledge of learning differences, interpersonal skills, and administrative ability.

Who has the role of coordinator depends on the institution. On most postsecondary campuses, it is the DSS director or a DSS staff member. It may be a learning specialist, the director of a separate program for students with LD and/or AD/HD, a counselor at a learning center, a faculty member, or an administrator.

Contacting the Coordinator

Students find their way to the coordinator's office by different routes. Some students assess available services as part of the college application and selection process. In other cases, a faculty member or counselor may recommend that a student contact the DSS Office; an admissions officer may refer the student to the coordinator during the admissions process; or a student may initiate the contact upon arrival at the school.

Sometimes students knock on the coordinator's door only after a period of feeling overwhelmed. They may be unable to admit defeat or may fear the stigma of being labeled *LD or AD/HD* . Some may only just have realized that they have LD and/or AD/HD. They may be grieving at the thought that something is wrong with them, hoping for a cure, and fearful that somehow the disability will hurt their jobs or their relationships.

The coordinator must be able to see past the defensiveness and anger that may be present, acknowledge the pain, understand the fear of experiencing repeated failure and rejection, and perceive feelings of self-worthlessness. Starting with the first meeting, the coordinator must communicate respect for the student's worth and belief in the student's capacity to manage his life.

Developing a Plan for Success

Once diagnostic results are in, the coordinator's job is to help students understand the information in clear, non-technical terms. At this point, students need to be reassured that having LD or AD/HD is not the end of the world and that there are ways to cope with their problems.

This might also be the time for you as a student to ask for help reassessing goals and choices. Do you need more remedial work? Is your current program the right one? Is the level of support sufficient? If you decide to continue in this setting, then the DSS coordinator should help you make plans for needed support services and/or accommodations.

Use of Resources

To help you implement your plan, the coordinator will suggest you make use of resources on and off campus. These include:

- academic support services (math labs, writing workshops, study skills seminars, developmental reading courses, computer labs);

- courses in the regular curriculum that can strengthen a student's social skills and personal development (communications, assertiveness training, psychology and human development); and

- tutoring, counseling and self-help programs.

Often, coordinators themselves work intensively with students in building academic and social strengths. They may teach you study skills strategies, counsel you on career goals and interpersonal problems, and supervise tutors. A coordinator may sit in on a lab or a class to help you figure out how to get around a problem.

Obtaining Accommodations

To obtain course work accommodations, students must be able to explain their needs to instructors. The coordinator's sensitive leadership can help students learn to communicate information about their learning needs in a positive way and to discuss their needs with clarity and confidence.

Many coordinators set the stage for communication between students and instructors by writing letters to instructors—with the student's consent. Letters usually include the fact that the student has a documented disability and that specific accommodations will be needed for the course. This letter must come from the DSS office, as faculty know that any letter from that office has documentation of a disability behind it. On some campuses, the DSS coordinator and the student create the letter together.

Sometimes the coordinator and the student may meet jointly with an instructor. In that way, a student who is not ready to be a self-advocate can learn to negotiate accommodations and then do it alone next time. Frequently, coordinators use role playing to prepare students to talk to instructors, and reduce their tension and uncertainty.

The Coordinator's Relationship with Faculty

Many faculty members do not understand hidden disabilities such as AD/HD and LD. Some may even believe that people with learning challenges do not belong in a postsecondary program. They may think that accommodations are cheating—a way of getting away with doing less work.

On campuses throughout the country, coordinators are working to overcome misconceptions and are enlisting the cooperation of faculty members. Many of them have developed excellent fact sheets and brochures for distribution to faculty, describing LD and AD/HD in clear, plain terms. In addition, coordinators hold workshops, in-service training, and informal meetings with faculty. There they may simulate LD and AD/HD so faculty can understand what it feels like to have a disability, and discuss how various accommodations work.

Gradually, coordinators build a network of supportive faculty members, who, in turn, use the coordinators for help with students in their classes. Ongoing dialogue creates an environment of trust and cooperation in which referrals can be made, problems resolved, and appropriate accommodations implemented. As faculty members get involved in working out accommodations for students in their own classrooms, myths disappear and empathic understanding can grow.

The Coordinator's Relationship with Parents

Parents frequently need support when their son or daughter enters a postsecondary program. On some campuses, coordinators are available to counsel parents during this transition period. Parents may feel apprehensive about their son or daughter being away from home for the first time. Parents must also realize that their son or daughter has reached the age of majority, and will be treated as an adult by the campus. Primarily, this means that parents have no rights to information about their child unless he signs a release of information. Parents often feel that if they are paying for their child's education, then they have the right to check on his progress, grades, and lifestyle. In the public school, K-12 setting, this information was available to parents; but not anymore!

The Role of the Student

To facilitate a student's success, coordinators must know how to work with many people. However, the ultimate goal is to enable students to take responsibility for resolving their own problems, getting accommodations, and becoming active participants in their education.

No matter how many accommodations or services are available on a campus, it is the student's responsibility to obtain and use them. Some students know their academic strengths as well as their stumbling blocks and they know what accommodations to ask for. Other students must go through a crisis before they begin to understand and resolve their problems. For many who do not know why they are failing, the shame, the confusion, and the panic can be immobilizing. For others, the fear of disclosing their disability or the lack of information about where to turn for help can also keep them from taking action.

There are solutions. But the search for them must start with you, the student, assuming responsibility. This involves understanding your own problems, being able to explain them in a simple and clear way, and becoming a self-advocate. None of these are easy tasks, but for some, the most difficult one is self-advocacy.

Self-Advocacy

To be a self-advocate means to be able to articulate needs and negotiate for assistance. It means being assertive in a diplomatic way. It means choosing words that accurately describe what accommodations are needed and why. It means expressing confidence in one's ability.

Some students find the task comfortable. Their instructors are easy to talk with and may already be sensitive to problems of students with LD and/or AD/HD. Other instructors simply need reassurance that students will fulfill the course requirements.

For many students, negotiation can be scary and unnerving. It can be learned, however, from DSS coordinators, counselors, or other students who have been through the mill. As discussed earlier, coordinators have developed instructional material and techniques to help students work out their individual situations. Form letters, checklists, documentation, role playing, support groups, and modeling are all in the coordinator's tool box.

As in any negotiating, attitude is important. If you are angry or bitter, you will be less likely to convince an instructor of the need for alternatives than if your are self-assured and cooperative. Successful negotiating depends on: 1) you knowledge of your learning profile, and 2) your ability to assure instructors that granting accommodations does not mean granting special advantages. Re-read Chapter 5 for more information about advocating for yourself.

Working with the Coordinator

Obviously, the coordinator does not work in a vacuum in developing a plan to help you succeed at school. You, as the student, need to work together with the coordinator to make sure your needs are met.

Early on, you can help the DSS coordinator understand how your disability affects you—in writing, speaking, thinking, listening, etc. You are, after all, the expert on your needs. You and the coordinator can then jointly determine what accommodations might be needed for any given class. The coordinator can explain the demands of the class (lecture-based, extensive notetaking, heavy reading assignments, etc.), and you tell him or her where you might need assistance.

You can also help the coordinator do the best job for you by requesting his or her assistance in a timely manner. Your coordinator might serve hundreds of students with disabilities and obviously cannot help them all at once. If you need a reader, a notetaker, or some other accommodation, contact the coordinator several weeks *before* classes begin. Don't wait until the first week of class when the coordinator is deluged with requests for accommodations.

If, for some reason, you cannot establish a good relationship with the DSS coordinator, talk to a teacher, counselor, advisor, or R.A. with whom you do have a good relationship. This person may be able to help you see a better way of interacting with the coordinator, or be willing to act as an intermediary. Or your counselor might be willing to sit down with you and the coordinator to help develop your accommodation plan. If all else fails, find out who the coordinator's supervisor is and make an appointment to discuss your difficulties with the supervisor.

What If There Is No DSS Coordinator?

If you do not have access to structured services on your campus, learning to advocate for yourself is more difficult. But even so, the more self-knowledge you have, the better the possibility of explaining your disability. And the more information about LD or AD/HD you can bring to the instructor, the better the chance for starting a dialogue. (This book, and, in particular, Chapter 9 might help your instructors understand your problems.)

If you are willing to share your problems with other students, you might discover ways to work out some of your difficulties. Examples include forming study groups or finding students who are willing to tutor you or check your notes and papers for correct spelling.

Under the law, students with disabilities have the right to accommodations whether there is a DSS coordinator or not. However, there are very few, if any, campuses that have not assigned this role to someone within the institution. The Counseling Center or Admissions Office should have the name of the Disability Services Coordinator for the campus.

Conclusion

As adults with LD and/or AD/HD move through postsecondary education, their role is constantly challenged by new courses and new tasks. As David, a college graduate, put it, "We LD people are always navigating new waters." David's undergraduate years were tightly scheduled to allow time to work with readers, to write and rewrite notes and outlines, to dictate to scribes, to manage a part-time job, and to keep up with other demands of college life. By putting in tremendously hard work and long hours of study, however, he succeeded. He and other students with LD and/or AD/HD need to become skilled at finding creative solutions to problems, in taking risks, and in testing their resolve. Their greatest accommodation is to keep trying, despite the odds . . . whenever they trip, to get up and try again.

Resources

BOOKS

ADD and the College Student: A Guide for High School and College Students with Attention Deficit Disorder, 1994
Editor: Patricia O. Quinn, MD
Magination Press/American Psychological Association
750 First Street, NE
Washington, DC 20002
Phone: (800) 374-2721, x 5510
Fax: (202) 336-5502
E-mail: books@apa.org
http://www.maginationpress.com

Computer-Assisted Instruction for Students at Risk for ADHD, Mild Disabilities or Academic Problems, 1996
Authors: Renet L. Bender and William N. Bender
Allyn & Bacon
160 Gould Street
Needham Heights, MA 02194-2315
Phone: (800) 852-8024
Fax: (781) 455-8024
E-mail: AandBpub@aol.com
http://www.abacon.com

Educational Technology & Learning Disabilities: A Resource Directory of Software and Hardware Products, no date
Learning Disabilities Association
4156 Library Road
Pittsburgh, PA 15234-1349
Phone: (412) 341-1515
Fax: (412) 344-0224
E-mail: ldanatl@usaor.net
http://www.ldanatl.org

Effective Microcomputer-Assisted Instruction for the Vocational Education of Special Needs Students, no date
Authors: Lloyd Tindall and John Gugerty
The Vocational Study Center,
University of Wisconsin-Madison
Publications Unit
Educational Sciences Building
1025 West Johnson Street
Madison, Wisconsin 53706

Hyperstudio
Roger Wagner Publishers
Phone: (800) 497-3778
E-mail: care@hyperstudio.com

Innotek Software Resource Guide: For Selecting Software for Children with Special Needs
Author: Lekotek
Learning Disabilities Association
4156 Library Road
Pittsburgh, PA 15234-1349
Phone: (412) 341-1515
Fax: (412) 344-0224
E-mail: ldanatl@usaor.net
http://www.ldanatl.org

Inspiration
Developers: Donald Helfgott, Mona Helfgott, and Bruce Hoof
Inspiration Software, Inc.
2920 SW Dolph Court, Suite 3
Portland, OR 97219

Phone: (503) 245-9011
Fax: (503) 246-4292
http://www.inspiration.com

***Promoting Postsecondary Education for Students with Learning Disabilities:
A Handbook for Practitioners***,1993
Authors: Loren Brenkeroff Stanshaw and J.M. McGuire
Pro-Ed
8700 Shoal Creek Blvd.
Austin, TX 78757-6897
Phone: (800) 897-3202
Fax: (800) 397-7633
E-mail: info@proedinc.com
http://www.proedinc.com

**Succeeding in College with Attention Deficit Disorder: Issues and Strategies
for Students, Counselors and Educators**, 1996
Author: Jennifer S. Bramer
Specialty Press
300 NW 70th Avenue, Suite 102
Plantation, FL 33319
Phone: 800-233-9273

Tutor Resource Manual: Tutoring Students in the Community College
Author: Violet Cain Roberts
EASE Project
Office of Special Education and Rehabilitative Services (OSERS)
U.S. Dept. of Education
400 Maryland Avenue, SW
Washington, DC 20202-0498
Phone: (800) USA-LEARN
E-mail: CustomerService@inet.ed.gov
http://www.ed.gov

Tutoring High School and College Students with LD: A Training Manual, 1993
Authors: Gallik and Kirby
Learning Disabilities Association
4156 Library Road
Pittsburgh, PA 15234-1349
Phone: (412) 341-1515
Fax: (412) 344-0224

E-mail: ldanatl@usaor.net

http://www.ldanatl.org

Ultrakey

Bytes of Learning

908 Niagara Falls Blvd., #240

North Tonawanda, NY 14120-2060

Phone: (800) 465-6428

Fax: (905)475-8650

E-mail: custserv@bytesoflearning.com

http://www.bytesoflearning.com

PAMPHLETS

Adults with Disabilities and Distance Learning

HEATH Resource Center

One Dupont Circle, Suite 800

Washington, DC 20036-1193

Phone: (800) 544-3284

Fax: (202) 833-4760

E-mail: heath@ace.nche.edu

http://www.acenet.edu/Abut/programs/Access&Equity/HEATH

Assisting College Students with Learning Disabilities: A Tutor's Manual, 1986

Authors: Pamela Adelman and Debbie Oelufs

AHEAD

P.O. Box 21192

Columbus, OH 43221-0192

Phone: (614) 488-4972

Fax: (614) 488-1174

E-mail: ahead@postbox.acs.ohio-state.edu

http://www.ahead.org

Assistive Technology: Meeting the Needs of Adults with Learning Disabilities, 1996

Author: Adrienne Riviere

National Adult Literacy and Learning Disabilities Center (ALLD)

1875 Connecticut Ave., NW

Washington, DC 20009-1202

Phone: (800) 953-2553

Fax: (202) 884-8422

E-mail: info@nalldc.aed.org

http://www.ld-read.org/ALLDassistive.html

**Assistive Technology for Postsecondary Students with Learning Disabilities:
An Overview**, 1998
Authors: Marshall H. Raskind and Eleanor L. Higgins
http://www.ldonline.org/ld_indepth/adult/index.html

College Students with Disabilities and Assistive Technology: A Desk Reference Guide, 1997
Authors: Anne R. Thompson, Leslie L. Behtea, Harry F. Rizer, and Melanie D. Hutto
Miss. Dept. of Rehabilitation Services/Project PAACS
1281 Highway 51 North
Madison, MS 39110
Jackson, MS 39215-1698
Phone: (800) 443-1000
http://www.mdrs.state.ms.us

Computers, Technology and People with Disabilities, no date
American Council on Education (ACE)
1 Dupont Circle, NW
Suite #800
Washington, DC 20036
Phone: (202) 939-9300
E-mail: web@ace.nche.edu
http://www.acenet.edu

Educational Software for Students with LD
HEATH Resource Center
One Dupont Circle, Suite 800
Washington, DC 20036-1193
Phone: (800) 544-3284
Fax: (202) 833-4760
E-mail: heath@ace.nche.edu
http://www.acenet.edu/About/programs/Access&Equity/HEATH

Facts: Books for Blind and Physically Handicapped Individuals, 1997
National Library Service for the Blind and Physically Handicapped
1291 Taylor Street, NW
Washington, DC 20542
Phone: (800) 424-8567
Fax: (202) 707-0712
E-mail: nls@loc.gov
http://www.loc.gov/nls

How to Evaluate and Select Assistive Technology Devices
The Arc of the United States
500 East Border Street, Suite 300
Arlington, TX 76010
Phone: (817) 261-6003
Fax: (817) 277-3491
E-mail: thearc@metronet.com
http://www.thearc.org

WEBSITES
ABLEDATA
This page has assistive technology and rehabilitation information for consumers, as well as links and databases.
http://www.abledata.com

Closing the Gap
Closing the Gap is an organization that focuses on computer technology for people with special needs. The website offers access to a Resource Directory—a database of hardware and software that can be searched online and includes ordering information. Ads for jobs and equipment are listed in the Classified section.
http://www.closingthegap.com

LD Online: Examples of Accommodations from State Assessment Policies
An informative site with effective models of accommodations for all students.
http://www.ldonline.org/ld_indepth/special_education/
peer_accommodations.html

BUSINESSES, ORGANIZATIONS, AND GOVERNMENT OFFICES
Contact information for the following useful organizations can be found beginning on page 347.

- American Association for Adult and Continuing Education (AAACE)

- American Coaching Association

- American Council on Education (ACE)

- American Printing House for the Blind

- Americans with Disabilities Act Technical Assistance Line

- Apple Computer, Inc.

- Association for the Advancement of Rehabilitation Technology (RESNA)

- Association of Specialized and Cooperative Library Agencies (ASCLA)

- Association on Higher Education and Disability (AHEAD)

- Attention Deficit Information Network (Ad-IN)

- Bytes of Learning

- Center for Applied Special Technology (CAST)

- Children and Adults with Attention-Deficit/Hyperactivity Disorder (CHADD)

- Closing the Gap

- Coalition for Literacy Hotline

- Council for Exceptional Children

- Council of Administrators of Special Education, Inc.

- Council on Learning Disabilities

- Dragon Systems, Inc.

- Education Development Center, Inc.

- ERIC Clearinghouse on Adult Career and Vocational Education

- Higher Education And The Handicapped (HEATH) Resource Center

- IBM

- The International Dyslexia Association

- International Society for Technology in Education (ISTE)

- Internet Special Education Resources

- Learning Disabilities Association of America (LDA)

- National Adult Literacy and Learning Disabilities Center (ALLD)

- National Association for Adults with Learning Difficulties (NAALD)

- National Center for Learning Disabilities (NCLD)

- National Library Service for the Blind and Physically Handicapped (NLS)

- National Network of Learning Disabled Adults (NNLDA)

- National Organization on Disability

- National Rehabilitation Information Center (NARIC)

- NICHCY (National Information Center for Children and Youth with Disabilities)

- Recording For the Blind and Dyslexic (RFB&D)

- Rehabilitation and Disability Services/ABLE DATA

- Roger Wagner Publishers

10

How to Keep the Glare Off the Chalkboard

IN THIS CHAPTER:

- Overview

- Classroom Strategies that Work

- Identifying Students Who Need Help

- Expectations

Juliana Taymans & Arden Boyer-Stephens

Overview

The teaching environment can make a big difference in a student's ability to participate and keep up with course work. Seemingly little things can prevent students from picking up important information, following the flow of a course, carrying out assignments, or even knowing what is expected.

The sun may glare on the chalkboard, making it hard for students with visual perception problems to distinguish letters. Or, instructors may speak too softly or too rapidly, making it difficult for students with auditory perception problems to comprehend a point or catch the announcement of a quiz. Students with learning disabilities may struggle hard to listen, take notes, remember, and pay attention for an entire lecture, and still fail to "get" the main ideas of a lecture. Tension mounts, intensifying the impact of the disability and the likelihood of mistakes.

Fortunately, there are a range of techniques that can prevent or minimize this type of confusing scenario. These are techniques that any classroom instructor can use to make it easier for *all* students to participate in class. We have included this information for you to use in two ways. One, you can use it as a guide to help you decide whether to take a course from a particular instructor. You could sit in on a class or two or talk to other students about the course and use this information to assess the match between your learning style and the instructor's teaching style. Two, you can give this chapter to an instructor to read before you discuss your learning profile and desired accommodations.

A range of techniques can foster full participation not only by students with LD and AD/HD, but by other students as well. These techniques are not complex. They include course work organization, clear expression of ideas, selection of appropriate materials, and opportunities for students to demonstrate knowledge in alternative ways. Most importantly, these techniques must reflect the instructor's high expectations for student achievement as well as dedication to student success.

Most of these classroom techniques are tried-and-true approaches for effective teaching. They have the power to create accessible classrooms in which expectations are clear, students' questions and problems are respected, and communication is informal, relaxed, and often mixed with humor. These techniques increase the effectiveness of the teaching-learning process.

Classroom Strategies that Work

Instructors play a critical role in the success of students with LD or AD/HD. Some of the instructional practices that help students with learning challenges are discussed below. These same strategies often benefit other students in the class as well.

Course Work Organization

Detailed Syllabus. A well-organized, detailed syllabus can serve as a powerful organizer for students. A helpful syllabus includes:

- course themes,
- objectives,
- weekly topics,
- classroom activities,
- required reading and writing assignments, and
- dates of tests, quizzes, and vacations.

A complete course calendar of this type increases a student's ability to understand the sequence of topics and the relationship of assignments to main themes. Having the syllabus available by pre-registration helps students plan. Posting course materials on websites is another good way to give students ready access to important course materials before, during, and after the course.

Clear Course Expectations. Rules should be clarified in advance: how students will be graded, whether makeup or rewrites of papers are allowed, and what the conditions are for withdrawing from a course or getting an incomplete. These rules should be listed in the syllabus.

Classroom Communication

Invite Students to Self-disclose. Students can feel unsure about disclosing their disabilities. Open and honest communication can best be accomplished at the beginning of the course and is more effective than during or after a problem has occurred. It is a good idea to make written and oral announcements to the entire class at the beginning of each semester, stating that help is available for students with disabilities. At this time, the instructor can encourage students to use the Disability Support Services (DSS) Office. If instructors have questions or concerns, this is a good time for them to contact the DSS learning specialist.

One instructor uses the following message.

> "Please let me know right away if you have a documented disability that requires special arrangements to be made, such as seating adjustments in testing situations, providing copies of notes, or other accommodations. Talk to me as soon as possible, after class or during my office hours."

Clarity of Expression. An instructor who speaks at an even speed, emphasizing important points with pauses, gestures, and other body language, helps students follow classroom presentations. These gestures and behaviors may be developed so as to serve as cues for specific student behaviors. For example, some instructors stop speaking for a few seconds, cueing students that what they just said was important enough to write down. Instructors can discuss what they do to emphasize points. Making eye contact can be important in maintaining student attention and encouraging participation. In addition, giving clear guidelines for student presentations can help students learn better from each other.

Availability. The more available an instructor is to students, the more chances there are for students to discuss difficulties they are having and for instructors to share concerns. It is important for instructors to set office hours that meet the needs of students in a class, as well as to be available just before and after class. Many instructors give their e-mail address on their syllabus so students can contact them at any time with questions.

A Two-Way Street. Classroom communication is not a one-way street. It is not up to the instructor alone to understand how a student's disability interferes with learning. Students themselves must take the initiative in giving their instructors a clear idea of the kinds of compensatory strategies they need. Students also need to remember that it is not necessarily easy for the instructor to make accommodations. An instructor does not necessarily have to agree to a specific accommodation that a student requests if another accommodation would do the job as well or better.

Instructional Strategies

Technical Vocabulary. All students benefit when the most important new vocabulary is highlighted and explained. Simple drawings and large print can clarify definitions in handouts. Students also need to know how to spell terms that are used. New vocabulary used in context explicitly shows students how the terms are correctly pronounced and used.

Multisensory Teaching. All students, especially students with LD and/or AD/HD, learn more readily if material is presented in as many modalities as possible (seeing, hearing, speaking, touching). Can a concept be explained in more than one way? Can it be demonstrated? Giving assignments both orally and in written form can avoid confusion.

Reviews, Previews, and Outlines. Students can greatly benefit throughout the learning process if the instructor briefly presents numerous reviews. A teacher should review the major points of the previous class and highlight main points to be covered that day. A strong reinforcement is to end class with a post review and a preview of the following class. When possible, key information should be outlined and presented in more than one form, such as written on the board or flip chart, presented orally, and/or outlined in a handout.

Interactive Class Sessions. Student learning can be enhanced when instructors provide opportunities for questions and answers, including during review sessions before quizzes and tests.

Advance Notice of Reading Assignments. Some students are slow readers and others comprehend most effectively when they read in short sessions with breaks. These students may need additional time to complete reading assignments. For students who are using books on tape, lead time is crucial in order for them to obtain a taped copy (which can take a month or more to secure).

Aids to Capturing Lecture and Discussion Points. Some students have difficulty with the act of writing, difficulty listening and writing at the same time, or trouble taking notes in an organized manner. Students facing such learning challenges may ask to tape class sessions or to receive copies of other students' notes. Teachers may also provide students with outlines of notes expected to be taken during each class.

Cues for Reading Comprehension. Students with LD and/or AD/HD may need help finding the main ideas and supporting details in difficult reading passages. Some instructors prepare handouts that outline a chapter and show students how to identify the author's key points. Study guides with questions for students to answer can help students practice unlocking the meaning of difficult reading assignments.

Quiz, Test, and Exam Preparation. Test taking is a skill that some students may still be developing. When teachers provide study questions similar to those used in course tests, it can help students learn both the important content and how to demonstrate mastery of that content. Examples of good answers give students a clear model of what is expected of them.

Assessment Accommodations. Some students may ask for accommodations in the assessment process. This can range from extended time on an exam, to alternate exam formats, to flexible assignment formats. Students should present a clear rationale for the request. The DSS learning specialist can assist faculty in understanding the request and negotiating appropriate ways to meet course requirements.

Accessibility of Course Materials

Students with LD and/or AD/HD may need help using printed course materials, due to their problems with reading, organization, and/or attention. Instructors can use several strategies to translate text materials into the student's best channel for learning or to compensate for difficulties paying attention while reading.

Advance Copies of Textbooks. There are several ways teachers can help students who *must* get printed materials taped. First, professors can have the bookstore order texts sufficiently ahead of time (two to four months before a class starts) to allow taping before the semester begins. Second, providing publisher website information can help students find supporting materials produced by the publisher or authors. Some publishers offer books in alternate or customized formats such as audio tapes or computer disks

Well-Organized Texts. If professors are selecting a new text for a course, and several are under consideration, it helps to be aware that some texts are better organized than others. Students benefit from texts that include final chapter summaries, subheadings, effective use of graphics, glossaries explaining technical language in plain English, and good indexes. Texts with accompanying study guides help some students focus on key concepts.

Other Tips

- Teach students memory tricks and acronyms as study aids. Use examples from current course work, and encourage students to create and share their own tricks.

- Encourage students who have self-disclosed disabilities to sit in the front of the classroom where distractions are fewer and it is easier to hear and see well.

- Give students the chance to repeat verbally what they have learned— as a check for accuracy. This can take place during class discussion time or after class.

- Be aware that some students are particularly self-conscious about talking in front of groups. Ask these students questions with short answers, or start the answer, trying not to interrupt once the student begins to respond.

- Give feedback. Errors need to be corrected as quickly as possible. If the student does well, praise is equally important for self-awareness and to build confidence.

- Be discreet. Don't call attention to a student's disability or accommodations in front of the class.

Special Tips for Vocational Instructors

- Label machinery, equipment, tools, and other workplace materials to help students read technical terms. Also label sizes, such as a two-quart pan or a size five drill bit.

- Use clearly labeled containers (i.e., pint, liter, etc.) to develop understanding of volume measurements.

- Have students use devices such as pedometers, optical tape measures, or other remote measuring devices, which can help develop their concept of, and skill in, measurement.

Identifying Students Who Need Help

No matter how much instructors prepare to make their classrooms accessible, there are often students in need of additional help. Some are reluctant to identify themselves, while others do not know they have LD and/or AD/HD. An instructor who can spot a struggling student may be able to avert a crisis for all involved in the teaching-learning process.

Characteristics of Postsecondary Students with LD and/or AD/HD

Many college students with LD and/or AD/HD are intelligent, talented, and capable. Many have developed a variety of strategies for compensating for their learning challenges. However, the degree of severity of the disability varies from individual to individual. Individuals also vary in their willingness to disclose their disability. A note of caution, students who come from divergent cultural and language backgrounds may exhibit some of the language-related behaviors cited below. It should not be assumed that these individuals have disabilities.

The checklist on pages 264-265 lists some common indicators of LD and/or AD/HD. When using this checklist, remember that it is not a complete list of characteristics, nor does it necessarily indicate the presence of a learning disability or attention deficit disorder.

In addition to having some of the learning needs on this checklist, a student with LD or AD/HD may also lack interpersonal skills due to perceptual problems. For example, a student may be unable to discriminate between sincere and sarcastic comments or to recognize other subtle social cues such as distancing body language, facial expressions, and voice tones. These difficulties can hinder social interactions and result in social isolation.

Referring a Student for Help

Whether faced by a crisis or a chronic problem, many instructors find it uncomfortable to bring up a suspected disability with an individual student. If an instructor needs advice regarding a student's academic problems or wants to refer a student for extra help, he or she can contact the office for Disability Support Services (DSS) or other academic support services. DSS can offer advice and sug-

TABLE 10.1—LEARNING NEEDS CHECKLIST

A. Reading Skills

___ Slow reading rate and/or difficulty in modifying reading rate in accordance with the material's level of difficulty

___ Uneven comprehension and retention of materials read

___ Difficulty identifying important points and themes

___ Incomplete mastery of phonics, confusion of similar words, difficulty integrating new vocabulary

___ Skips words or lines of printed material

___ Difficulty reading for long periods of time

B. Written Language Skills

___ Difficulty planning a topic and organizing thoughts on paper

___ Difficulty with sentence structure (e.g., incomplete sentences, run-ons, poor use of grammar, missing inflectional endings)

___ Frequent spelling errors (e.g., omissions, substitutions, transpositions), especially in specialized and foreign vocabulary

___ Difficulty proofreading written work and making revisions

___ Compositions are often limited in length

___ Slow written production

___ Poor penmanship (e.g., poorly formed letters, incorrect use of capitalization, trouble with spacing, overly large handwriting)

___ Inability to copy correctly from a book or the blackboard

C. Oral Language Skills

___ Inability to concentrate on and to comprehend spoken language when presented rapidly

___ Difficulty in orally expressing concepts that they seem to understand

___ Difficulty following or having a conversation about an unfamiliar idea

___ Trouble telling a story in the proper sequence

___ Difficulty following oral or written directions

D. Mathematical Skills

___ Incomplete mastery of basic facts (e.g., mathematical tables)

___ Reverses numbers (e.g., 123 or 321 or 231)

___ Confuses operational symbols, especially + and x

___ Copies problems incorrectly from one line to another

___ Difficulty comprehending word problems

___ Difficulty understanding key concepts and applications to aid problem solving

E. Organizational and Study Skills

___ Difficulty with organization skills

___ Time management difficulties

___ Slow to start and to complete tasks

___ Repeated inability, on a day to day basis, to recall what has been taught

___ Lack of overall organization in taking notes

___ Difficulty interpreting charts and graphs

___ Inefficient use of library and reference materials

___ Difficulty preparing for and taking tests

F. Attention and Concentration

___ Trouble focusing and sustaining attention on academic tasks

___ Fluctuating attention span during lectures

___ Easily distractible by outside stimuli

___ Has difficulty juggling multiple task demands and overloads quickly

___ Hyperactivity and excessive movements may accompany the inability to focus attention

___ Trouble meeting people or working cooperatively with others

---

This checklist was developed from "College Students with Learning Disabilities," published by AHEAD: Association on Higher Education and Disability, 1998.

gestions about dealing with a student's academic difficulties. Diagnostic information can be shared either by the student or by DSS, with the student's consent.

If a student is not aware that he or she might have LD and/or AD/HD, the instructor should not suggest this as a possibility. However, he or she can suggest that the student visit the DSS office for assistance with academic problems. If the student follows up with a visit to DSS, the office may then refer the student for testing or evaluation. The DSS office would generally *not* contact the student first. This is due to confidentiality issues and because students in postsecondary programs must self-disclose their disabilities before assistance can be offered.

As instructors become familiar with individual strengths and needs, they can reach an agreement with the student on the best way to deal with classroom difficulties.

Expectations

It is important that instructors set realistic and high expectations for both themselves and their students. Instructors must truly believe that all students in their class can learn and master the concepts. They must also believe that they can teach all students in their class.

Nothing impedes the teaching-learning process more than low expectations. Low expectations are the start of a self-fulfilling prophecy that is detrimental to the success of the student. The goal instead should be to appropriately challenge students, so they succeed about 80 percent of the time. When students are appropriately challenged, they are more likely to maintain motivation throughout the course and deal effectively with any challenges or problems that may arise.

Conclusion

The most productive learning environment is one in which students and instructors form honest and respectful relationships aimed at meeting course goals. Student success should be the basis of satisfaction for all involved. Instructors can benefit from teaching students with LD and/or AD/HD when they broaden their instructional repertoire, allowing more students, with and without disabilities, to achieve.

Resources

BOOKS

Attention-Deficit/Hyperactivity Disorder in the Classroom: A Practical Guide for Teachers, 1997
Authors: Carol A. Dowdy, James R. Patton, Tom E. C. Smith, Edward Polloway
Pro-Ed
8700 Shoal Creek Blvd.
Austin, TX 78757-6897
Phone: (800) 897-3202
Fax: (800) 397-7633
E-mail: info@proedinc.com
http://www.proedinc.com

Classroom Assessment Editions, 2nd edition, 1993
Authors: Thomas A. Angelo and K. Patricia Cross
Jossey-Bass, Inc.
350 Sansome Street, Fifth Floor
San Francisco, CA 94104
Phone: (800)956-7739
Fax: (800) 605-2665
E-mail: webperson@jbp.com
http://www.jbp.com/genorder.html

Complete Reading Disabilities Handbook: Ready-to-Use Techniques for Teaching Reading Disabled Students, 1997
Author: William H. Miller
Center for Applied Research in Education
P.O. Box 11071
Des Moines, IA 50336-1071
Phone: (800) 947-7700
Fax: (515) 284-2607
http://www.viacom.com

Curriculum Adaptations for Students with Learning and Behavior Problems: Principles and Practices, 1997
Authors: John J. Hoover and James R. Patton
Pro-Ed
8700 Shoal Creek Blvd.

Austin, TX 78757-6897
Phone: (800) 897-3202
Fax: (800) 397-7633
E-mail: info@proedinc.com
http://www.proedinc.com

Educating Students with Mild Disabilities: Strategies and Methods, 2nd edition, 1998
Editors: Edward Meyen, Glenn Vergason, and Richard Whelan
Love Publishing Company
4925 East Pacific Place
Denver, CO 80222-4822
Phone: (303) 757-2579
Fax: (303) 782-5683

Faculty Inservice Education Kit
AHEAD
P.O. Box 21192
Columbus, OH 43221-0192
Phone: (614) 488-4972
Fax: (614) 488-1174
E-mail: ahead@postbox.acs.ohio-state.edu
http://www.ahead.org

Helping Students Become Strategic Learners: Guidelines for Teaching
Author: Karen Scheid
Brookline Books/Lumen Editions
P.O. Box 1047
Cambridge, MA 02238
Phone: (800) 666-2665
Fax: (617) 868-1772
E-mail: BROOKLINEBKS@delphi.com
http://people.delphi.com/brooklinebks/index.html

Learning Disabilities: Characteristics, Identification, and Teaching Strategies,
3rd edition, 1997
William N. Bender
Allyn and Bacon
160 Gould Street
Needham Heights, MA 02194-2315
Phone: (800) 852-8024
Fax: (781) 455-8024

E-mail: AandBpub@aol.com
http://www.abacon.com

Learning Disabilities: Theories, Diagnosis, and Teaching Strategies, 7th edition, 1998
Author: Janet Lerner
Houghton Mifflin Company
1900 S. Batavia Ave
Geneva, IL 60134
Phone: (800) 733-2828
Fax: (800) 733-2098
E-mail: storemanager@hmco.com
http://www.schooldirect.com

Promoting Postsecondary Education for Students with Learning Disabilities: A Handbook for Practitioners, 1993
Authors: Loring C. Brinkerhoff, Stan F. Shaw, and Joan M. McGuire
Pro-Ed
8700 Shoal Creek Blvd.
Austin, TX 78757-6897
Phone: (800) 897-3202
Fax: (800) 397-7633
E-mail: info@proedinc.com
http://www.proedinc.com

Reading, Writing and Spelling: Multisensory Structured Language Approach
Authors: Helaine Schupack and Barbara Wilson
International Dyslexia Association
8600 LaSalle Road
Chester Building, Suite 382
Baltimore, MD 21286-2044
Phone: (410) 296-0232
Fax: (410) 321-5069
E-mail:info@interdys.org
http://www.interdys.org

Rights and Responsibilities of Faculty Concerning Students with Disabilities, 1994
Center for Innovations in Special Education
Parkade Center, Suite # 152
601 Business Loop, 70 West
Columbia, MO 65211
Phone: (573) 884-7275

Scaffolding Student Learning: Instructional Approaches and Issues, 1997
Editors: Kathleen Hogan and Michael Pressley
Brookline Books/Lumen Editions
P.O. Box 1047
Cambridge, MA 02238
Phone: (800) 666-2665
Fax: (617) 868-1772
E-mail: BROOKLINEBKS@delphi.com
http://people.delphi.com/brooklinebks/index.html

Strategies for Teaching Students with Learning and Behavior Problems
Authors: Candace S. Bos and Sharon Vaughn
Allyn and Bacon
160 Gould Street
Needham Heights, MA 02194-2315
Phone: (800) 852-8024
Fax: (781) 455-8024
E-mail: AandBpub@aol.com
http://www.abacon.com

Succeeding in College with Attention Deficit Disorders: Issues & Strategies for Students, Counselors, & Educators, 1996
Author: Jennifer Bramer
Specialty Press/ADD Warehouse
300 NW 70th Avenue, #102
Plantation, FL 33317
Phone: (800) 233-9273
Fax: (954) 792-8545
E-mail: sales@addwarehouse.com
http://www.addwarehouse.com

Teaching Students with Learning Problems to Use Study Skills, 1998
Authors: John J. Hoover and James Patton
Pro-Ed
8700 Shoal Creek Blvd.
Austin, TX 78757-6897
Phone: (800) 897-3202
Fax: (800) 397-7633
E-mail: info@proedinc.com
http://www.proedinc.com

Textbooks and the Students Who Can't Read Them: A Guide for the Teaching of Content, 1993
Author: Jean Ciborowski
Brookline Books/Lumen Editions
P.O. Box 1047
Cambridge, MA 02238
Phone: (800) 666-2665
Fax: (617) 868-1772
E-mail: BROOKLINEBKS@delphi.com
http://people.delphi.com/brooklinebks/index.html

PAMPHLETS

Attention Deficit Disorder in the Classroom
(CHADD Fact Sheet # 6)
CHADD
8181 Professional Place, Suite 201
Landover, MD 20785
Phone: (800) 233-4050
Fax: (301) 306-7090
E-mail: national@chadd.org
www.chadd.org/facts/add_facts06.htm

Feedback: Enhancing the Performance of Adult Learners with Learning Disabilities, 1997
Author: Adrienne Riviere
National Adult Literacy and Learning Disabilities Center (ALLD)
1875 Connecticut Ave., NW
Washington, DC 20009-1202
Phone: (800) 953-2553
Fax: (202) 884-8422
E-mail: info@nalldc.aed.org
http://www.ld-read.org
http://www.ld-read/alldfeedback.html

Improving Quality of Student Notes, 1993
Author: Bonnie Potts
ERIC Clearinghouse on Assessment & Evaluation
College of Library and Information Services
University of Maryland-College Park
1129 Shriver Laboratory
College Park, MD 20742

Phone: (800) 464-3742

Fax: (301) 405-7449

http://www.ericae.net

BUSINESSES, ORGANIZATIONS, AND GOVERNMENT OFFICES

Contact information for the following useful organizations can be found beginning on page 347.

- American Association for Adult and Continuing Education (AAACE)
- American Association of State Colleges and Universities
- American Council on Education (ACE)
- Association on Higher Education and Disability (AHEAD)
- Children and Adults with Attention-Deficit/Hyperactivity Disorder (CHADD)
- Clearinghouse on Adult Education
- Clearinghouse on Disability Information
- Council for Adult and Experiential Learning (CAEL)
- Council for Exceptional Children (CEC)
- Council on Learning Disabilities
- Disabilities Studies and Resource Center
- ERIC Clearinghouse on Disability & Gifted Education,
- Higher Education And The Handicapped (HEATH) Resource Center
- Internet Special Education Resources
- Learning Disabilities Association of America (LDA)
- National Association for Adults with Learning Difficulties (NAALD)
- National Attention Deficit Disorder Association (National ADDA)
- National Center for Learning Disabilities (NCLD)
- NICHCY (National Information Center for Children and Youth with Disabilities)
- Roads To Learning

A BAG OF TRICKS
Study Skills and Strategies for Learning

Stefanie Coale Silvers & Juliana M. Taymans

CHAPTER 11-A—Overview

Arnold has great difficulty sitting down to study, especially when he has to write papers. He meets with a learning specialist once a week to go over his schedule for the week. However, that does not always guarantee he accomplishes everything that he is supposed to get done.

Arnold's strength is his memory, which fortunately enables him to do well on exams if he just skims class materials the night before. He has also found that having a "study buddy" is very helpful. When studying for exams, he helps his study buddy with memory strategies as his study buddy helps him go over his notes and "talk out" the material. This helps Arnold tremendously for several reasons. First, Arnold often misses information in class, because his mind "wanders off" at times. His study buddy fills him in on information he has missed. Second, meeting with a study buddy forces him to review his notes as well as the book. Third, "talking out" the material and putting it into his own words reinforces the learning process. For Arnold, the key is to use his strengths to learn the material, finding a way that works for him to compensate for his weaknesses.

Lisa is an extremely hard working student who meets with a learning specialist once a week to go over her courses and concerns. Together, she and the learning specialist problem-solve and come up with some other options when she runs into difficulty. For example, one semester, she received a 'D' on her first exam in Women's Studies. Lisa and the learning specialist went over the exam to see what areas caused her difficulty and what types of questions she got wrong.

Lisa has trouble with memory and found she had either focused too much or too little on the details. The learning specialist also pointed out that Lisa missed more questions that were based on lectures rather than on the book. Lisa was already receiving extra copies of notes, but at times she found the professor's style of lecturing difficult to follow. She was able to get all the information down (because she had an extra copy of notes) but she had trouble seeing the connections between the information. Lisa's solution was to highlight the areas she did not understand and then set up a standing appointment with the professor each week to discuss the areas in which she had questions. Lisa received a better grade on her next exam and for *the course. Like Arnold, Lisa worked with several people to grasp the material and to do well on the tests.*

Mike has great difficulty with reading comprehension and writing papers. He receives a second copy of notes from fellow students in all his lecture classes. He meets with a learning specialist to work on outlining papers, reading strategies, and setting up a weekly schedule for studying and getting papers done. Also, he works with the Writing Center and a Writing Specialist to edit his papers. His greatest area of difficulty in writing is taking material he has read and expressing these ideas in his own words on paper to get his points across clearly. Many times the learning specialist reads his paper out loud to see if he can hear the mistakes. Next she asks what he is trying to say and then writes down what he has said. Lastly, they work together to create coherent sentences and paragraphs from what they wrote down.

Mike is learning to use a computer program that reads aloud what is on the computer (such as a paper) so he can hear the mistakes or lack of coherent writing. Like the previous students, Mike works with several people and services to succeed in college.

Study Skills and Strategies for Learning

Like Arnold, Lisa, and Mike, most students with LD and/or AD/HD are bright students who are quite capable of mastering the content of college-level courses. To succeed, however, they may need to fine-tune the strategies they use for learning, and they may need some assistance in learning how to show what they have learned.

One method of learning how to learn that has proven successful with adolescents and adults with LD and/or AD/HD is called the "learning strategies approach." Learning strategies are step-by-step ways for students to learn how to complete important academic and daily living tasks. They help students learn how to think and act when reading, writing, studying, and taking tests. The resource section on page 337 provides information on specific learning strategies and how to learn more about this way of teaching and learning. Anyone who is teaching, tutoring, or advising students with learning challenges will find this section useful.

Study Skills Courses

Many colleges now have study skills courses that are available to all students. Study skills can mean strategies to improve reading comprehension, writing, test taking, notetaking, and listening skills. Study skills can also mean learning to manage time, to set priorities, and to improve daily living and social skills. The content might be given as part of one course, such as English Composition. It might also be presented in a separate course or workshop, or taught in tutorial sessions.

Study Skills programs can usually be found in English and Psychology Departments, learning centers, or the Disability Support Services (DSS) office. Students are frequently referred to these programs if no special courses exist for them. But, too often, this is not enough for students like Arnold, Lisa, and Mike, who need more specialized help.

How and where students with LD and/or AD/HD can get Study Skills instruction depends on the campus and the student. On many campuses, teachers, advisors, DSS coordinators, or learning specialists are working very hard to devise ways to help these students.

Helpful Suggestions

The skill areas covered in this chapter are time management, organization, listening and notetaking, test taking, reading comprehension, writing, memory, and other personal strategies for success. This information is a compilation from interviews with students, insights from individuals who offer postsecondary services, and printed resources. Remember, there is no one right way to study. Most of us learn effective study skills through trial and error. You need to experiment and use and adapt techniques until you find the approach or approaches that are appropriate—your own bag of tricks!

CHAPTER 11-B—Time Management

"Over organize, always be willing to work 31 percent harder, start your papers early in the semester, and give yourself plenty of time to prepare for exams and assignments."

This advice from an adult with LD who made it through college underscores the value of learning how to manage time.

Managing time is often the hardest thing students with LD and/or AD/HD have to do, especially since college requires more skills in this area than high school. Some students may have never used a calendar. Others may not know how long it takes to complete an assignment. Many get involved in too many activities, or are unable to set priorities effectively. In addition, students with LD and/or AD/HD must allow extra time to read, to listen to taped notes, or to complete written assignments. Faced with conflicting demands and distractions, students can end up with impossible deadlines and too many commitments.

Learning a system for managing time can be the single most important step a student can take. However, for some students with LD and/or AD/HD, the pressure of creating and sticking to a schedule can in itself be extremely stressful or not fully possible. It may take much effort, help, and practice before a student finds a system that works.

How to Schedule Time

The more observant you are about yourself, the easier it will be to work out a realistic schedule. Paying careful attention to lifestyle, learning style, and academic obligations is an important starting point. Important questions to ask yourself are:

- How long does it take me to get ready in the morning?

- What time of day am I most alert?

- How long can I study at a time?

- What types of things distract me the most?

- What rewards can I give myself to keep motivation up?

- How long do my different commitments really take me?

Use Calendars for Planning

You need to develop a system that will enable you to keep track of:

- important dates in the future (such as due dates for term papers);

- recurring obligations (such as classes or tutoring sessions that occur at the same time every week);

- specific things you need to accomplish each day (such as homework assignments).

For some students, the solution is to get three separate calendars or day planners to keep track of monthly, weekly, and daily activities. Others are able to use one calendar to record all their obligations. Which system you choose will depend on your preferences. For example, if you cannot remember to look at three separate calendars, having one master calendar might be the best option. Or if the amount of detail on one master calendar is too overwhelming or confusing for you, keeping three different calendars might work better. Or if you have a software program for time management with a variety of options, you may need to explore different ways of using those options before you discover what works best for you.

If you decide to use just one calendar, it may help to color code different types of events (e.g., red for due dates of major projects, blue for classes, and black for daily activities). If you use three different calendars, it will be important to develop a routine of checking them at a certain time each day, or to post them in a location you can't miss.

Step One

Get a planning system and learn how to use it. The beginning of the semester is the time to make up your schedule. Get a calendar or calendars with plenty of space for writing in monthly, weekly, and/or daily obligations. Or, if you enjoy using technology, get a software program, electronic calendar, or watch with a planning system.

Step Two

Record important academic and social obligations for the semester. Look at every course syllabus to check for deadlines throughout the semester. Then, add all due dates for assignments, papers, and exams to your calendar. Include dates of sports events, concerts, plays, etc. if you are on an athletic team or participate in performing arts. Also plug in holidays and personal obligations, such as an anniversary party or your cousin's wedding.

Step Three

Make out a sample weekly calendar. Use one with slots for each hour. Fill in the times of all classes, lectures, labs, and other things that will not change during the semester (jobs, clubs, tutoring sessions, appointments, chores). Don't forget to fill in the times for sleeping, meals, social life, sports, and recreation. After entering all the activities on the calendar look at the slots that are empty. These are the hours each day that can be used for studying.

Step Four

Plan what you will do each day. Use a daily planner, notebook, or computer program to make up a list of things to do each day. In the evening, take a few minutes before bed to write down study needs for the next day—and a schedule to do it. Check syllabi for reading assignments and the monthly calendar for due dates of exams, quizzes, and papers. Is it time to start studying for an exam or to do a first draft of a paper? Leave enough time—even more than enough time—to meet deadlines.

This is the time to make decisions about how to use those empty slots. Be honest. Is enough time planned to complete reading assignments listed in each syllabus for that week, to go over lecture notes, to work in the biology lab? How long does it really take you to read a history chapter with breaks? Don't try to get too much done at once. Write down your planned accomplishments for each available slot. Is the plan working? If it isn't, make a new plan.

Other Tips for Time Management

- Study in tolerable doses, and plan a reward after completing a certain amount of reading, writing, or reviewing. Take lots of breaks and note progress made.

- Try to maintain a regular time and place to study. Most importantly, find an environment that works. This might mean trial and error during the first semester, but it should pay off later. For example, try an empty classroom one week, the library the next, or a study hall in a dorm for upperclassmen.

- Try different methods of reminding yourself what you need to do. For example, try jotting tasks on an index card or Post-It note. Then carry it in your wallet or put it where you will see it when you wake up in the morning. Or try a watch with a programmable calendar or a software program that uses graphics or sound to remind you of obligations.

- A large monthly wall calendar that can be easily seen each day can help keep you aware of the big picture.

- To figure out how much time to set aside for long-term projects, count backward from the due date and estimate how much time will be needed. Always allow more time than you think you need, since you may not be aware of all the steps that will be needed or you may need to do some problem solving. If uncertain, speak to the professor, teacher assistant, or learning specialist about how many steps are involved and what each step entails. This can give a better sense of how much time the project will require, and usually helps with the anxiety of the "unknown," especially when tackling a new project.

- Make sure that the due dates are clear for each assignment.

- Consider asking to turn in rough drafts ahead of schedule to get feedback early in the process. Or ask the professor if you can set up due dates to turn in parts of the assignment to make sure you get each step done in a timely manner.

- Keep the syllabus for each course in a place where it won't get lost. Make an extra copy just in case. Some students paste the syllabus inside the front cover of a course notebook or give an extra copy to their tutor, learning specialist, or even a study buddy to hold.

Strive for Balance

The goal of time management should be to enable you to balance academic demands with social activities. If you are spending every waking moment going to class or studying, something is wrong. It may be that you are taking too many classes or too many difficult classes, or that you are not receiving the right accommodations. Or you may not be scheduling your time efficiently. If you find yourself in this situation, you may want to ask DSS staff to help you figure out how to reschedule or lessen your workload.

CHAPTER 11-C—Organizing All Those Things

Organizing All Those Things

"Don't stuff all of your papers in your backpack" is a comment that one learning specialist is always making to her students. She says, "So many of my students just gather up their papers, handouts, syllabi, and notes that they have either taken themselves or had taken by a notetaker and shove them all together into their backpacks or notebooks. The result is that they can never put their finger on what they need without having to go through every piece of paper."

Disorganization for anyone is uncomfortable; for a student with LD and/or AD/HD, it can mean disaster. Misplacing an assignment or a syllabus, losing handouts, and having notes from many subjects jumbled together make it impossible to function effectively.

The tips below have come from successful students and adults with LD and/or AD/HD. Modify the ideas, depending on your need. Some students like to have a notebook for each subject (each in a different color); others use a large notebook for all their subjects. Some students keep everything in a backpack; others take only what they need for the day. Ultimately, you will need to develop your own individualized way of organizing things.

Tips for Getting Organized

- Some students re-type all their notes into a computer and save all notes on disks, which are marked with dates and courses.

- Some students place different colored Post-It notes around their room, on notebooks, or even by their bedside to remind them of things they are afraid of forgetting.

- It is important to separate course materials. Put handouts or assignments in separate folders, notebooks, or sections of a large notebook. Be sure to use dividers, preferably different colors for each subject.

- Create a helpful system for keeping papers, books, and other possessions. One student got a cardboard box that was large enough for file folders. She then made a folder for each subject, and every time she got a handout that could not fit into her notebook, she put it in the appropriate file. When she had to get all of the material together for an exam or a paper, she could easily find what she needed.

- Be sure to put the notes notetakers have taken and the tape recordings of lectures with the other material for that course. Date all your notes and tapes immediately.

- Always have a place for each thing. Keep calculators and planners in one place and return them to that place. Organize your clothes, books, and school supplies. Make sure you have sufficient shelf or other storage space so you don't end up with big piles of papers, books, etc. from different classes all jumbled together. It may even be helpful to include extra time for organizing your things in your schedule.

- Going through your backpack or attache case on a regular basis helps. You can put papers you need to save in notebooks or folders and discard the rest.

- Keep keys on a big ring to find more easily. Or, use a bright colored key chain. Also, many athletic stores and hardware stores sell key chains that can be worn around your neck, attached to pants, or even to a bag.

- Keep extra coins for laundry machines, parking meters, buses, and vending machines in a specific place.

- Every evening or morning make a list of everything needed for classes, labs, or meetings. Include reminders for money, transportation, and food. Check the list in the morning before leaving your room, so nothing is forgotten.

CHAPTER 11-D—Listening and Notetaking

One of the biggest differences between high school and college is the greater emphasis on notetaking in college classes. In high school, most teachers test from the reading materials. In college, most professors test at least 30 percent from lectures. Also, notetaking is a strategic process. Successful students take care to learn how professors differ on what they emphasize on their tests.

Notetaking is hard work for all students. For students with LD and/or AD/HD, it can be overwhelming and extremely frustrating. Students with AD/HD may find they miss some information because of the challenge of staying focused during lectures lasting 50 minutes or more. Others find it challenging to keep up with the pace of listening to the lecture and taking notes at the same time.

To make sure that their notes are complete, students with learning challenges must usually spend much more time than other students in rewriting, consolidating, listening to tapes of lectures, and seeking help from advisors and classmates. They also must be creative and imaginative in figuring out ways to emphasize major points. The rewards come when material is recalled more easily and when exam preparation is not a last-minute scramble. This section covers strategies that may help you reap those rewards.

Improving Listening Skills

One way to improve notetaking skills is to learn to be a more effective listener.

Prelistening: Getting Set to Listen

- Before going to class, review your lecture notes from the last class and your reading notes on the topics that will be covered. Preview (in the syllabus) any assignments relating to the class.

- Be familiar with the spelling and meaning of key terms likely to be used in class. Keep a list of all new words for easy reference.

Listening: Being There

- Sit in the front of the room to increase concentration on the instructor and lessen distractions from peers.

- Write down any brief outlines that are on the board. If using a notetaker, be sure he makes a copy of the outline.

- Date notes, record the course name, and number each page.

- Use regular loose-leaf notepaper. The left-hand margin is a good place to write down key words and phrases.

- Use only one side of the paper.

- Listen for organizational clues, such as "following are three major topics," or "these are the steps," or "in summary."

- Put main thoughts in your own words.

- Jot down essential points. Listen critically and be discriminating about what to include in notes.

- Use short phrases and key words and leave plenty of white space on each page.

- Put large question marks in the margin if something is confusing or does not make sense. Schedule a time to get clarification.

- Develop and use a personalized shorthand method (see Table 11.1). For example, write only the beginning of words, such as ref for reference or def for definition.

- Make doodles in the margin to emphasize major points.

- Use highlighters to draw boxes around key ideas.

- Color code notes; for example, red for facts to memorize, yellow for theory, and so forth.

- Use any other visual techniques that help make ideas stand out. One student uses purple ink for outlines and draws pink stars for major points.

Post Listening

- Review your own notes or notes taken by a notetaker no later than eight hours after the class.

- Fill in any information from other sources such as study groups about the topic discussed in class.

- Clarify with the instructor anything that is confusing or difficult to understand.

- Cluster and categorize points in the lecture. If necessary, or if it is helpful, rewrite notes in any format that makes the information clearer.

- Ask another student, counselor, or learning specialist if you can go over your notes to talk the information out with someone. In some study skills classes, this review is part of the curriculum.

- Keep your own notes and the notetaker's notes with all of the other material about that course.

- Keep notes in chronological order.

TABLE 11.1—Notetaking Symbols and Abbreviations

This list is not intended to be exhaustive but will give you some ideas upon which you can build your own list. Be creative!

P.	page	∼	about
#	number	>	greater than
b/c	because	<	less than
b/4	before	∴	therefore
wd	word	→	means
w/	with	X, □	important passage, word
w/o	without		
2	to, too, two	T	information that could be used as a test question
ie.	that is		
eg.	for example	✓	check later
re.	concerning	S	summary
etc.	in addition	cont'd	continued
vs.	versus	—	dashes for words if the speaker is too fast (come back later and use the context to fill in the missing words)

Write only the beginning of a word. Examples:

ref	reference	comp	compare, comparison
diff	difference, different	ex	example
def	definition		

Write only consonants and omit vowels. Examples:

impt.	important	lk	like

Use **g** to indicate "ing" Examples:

writg   meetg   answerg

Don't erase or blank out a mistake; draw a thin line instead.

(reprinted from Barbara Scheiber and Jeanne Talpers, *Unlocking Potential*, Washington, DC: Adler & Adler, 1987.)

Improving Notetaking Skills

Chapter 9 discussed some accommodations that may make notetaking easier for you. For example, you might benefit from a notetaker or from asking for an extra copy of notes from peers, teaching assistants, or even the professor. You might also find it easier to use a laptop computer to take notes.

There are also a number of notetaking techniques that benefit all students that might improve your notetaking skills. Some of the most useful are discussed below.

The AWARE Strategy

The AWARE Strategy was developed specifically to help college students take notes. Learning specialists can help students learn how to use this system

The AWARE Strategy

Step 1: Arrange to take notes

    Arrive early
    Take seat near front/center
    Obtain pen/notebook
    Make note of date

Step 2: Write quickly

    Indent minor points
    Record some words without vowels
    Use common abbreviations
    Note personal examples—connections you are able to make with
    the material from what you already know

Step 3: Apply cues

    Attend to what the instructor verbally stresses and other
    organizational verbal cues
    Record stressed lecture ideas
    Make a check mark before these ideas

Step 4: Review notes as soon as possible

Step 5: Edit notes

    Add information you forgot to record
    Add personal details—your ideas about what you heard

by having them first practice with audio taped lectures and then apply the steps in real lecture situations. The box on the left outlines this strategy.

Diagrams, Flow Charts, and Graphic Organizers

Diagrams and flow charts are highly effective, visual ways of graphically summarizing notes. Some students use these techniques for reviewing or consolidating textbook and/or lecture notes for exams. One example of a graphic organizer is in Chapter 9-D on Technology. The following is another example.

Although this diagram was created by a software program, many students draw their own with pencil and paper.

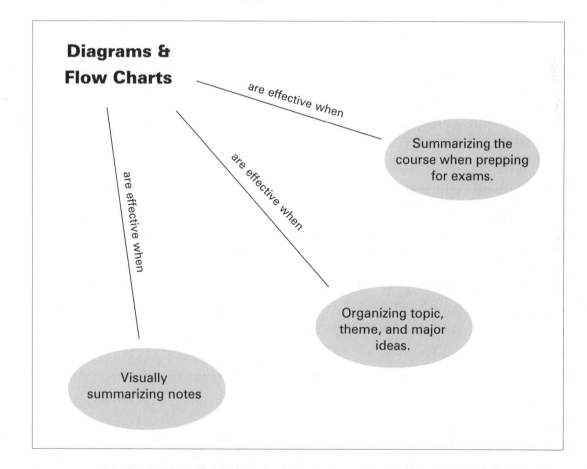

The Cornell Notetaking System

The Cornell Notetaking System makes it easier to highlight and recall major ideas from lectures or textbooks. To use this method, you divide the paper into two columns:

1. **the left column** (the recall column margin) is for key words and phrases;

2. the right column is for the bulk of the information.

In reviewing for exams, cover the right column—the bulk of the material—and use the left column words to recall the content. The following is an example based on information in this chapter.

■ Notetaking ■	
Notetaking	Difficult for ALL, especially for those with LD and/or AD/HD.
	College professors typically test more from notes than readings.
	It takes creativity and practice to find effective ways to emphasize important points.
3 Steps	Prelistening
	Listening
	Post listening
Prelistening	Getting ready to listen
Listening	Being there and taking notes
Post listening	Reviewing and editing for better understanding and memory
Tips and Strategies	AWARE
	Cornell Notetaking System
	Diagrams, flowcharts, and graphic organizers

Finding a Notetaking System That Works

To find out more about these and other notetaking strategies, check to see whether your school offers study skills classes that cover notetaking skills. Having one or more study buddies can also give you the opportunity to learn about notetaking systems that work for others and may work for you. Experiment with different types of strategies to determine whether one type is easier for you in all situations, or whether it makes sense to use different strategies in different situations.

CHAPTER 11-E—Test Taking Skills

*"How will I ever get through next week? I have three final
exams and a paper due, and I haven't even started on my paper."*

Anyone who has ever gone to college knows the anxiety in those words. But semesters do not have to end this way. Students who have learned effective study skills, including time management, reading, writing, and notetaking, find that they can get through exam time with minimal frustration. Many colleges are giving guidance to students who need help in studying for exams. Learning centers, DSS offices, counseling and guidance services, as well as some academic departments, are good places to check for handouts and other materials on test taking. Some strategies are obvious; others can be acquired.

This section outlines ways to prepare for exams and quizzes and gives suggestions for taking different types of exams. Students who need further help should check with learning specialists, faculty advisors, and instructors.

Preparing for Exams

Gather Information

Find out what the test will cover and what types of questions will be asked (essay, objective multiple choice, or true/false). There are strategies for taking each of these kinds of tests. (See pages 292-295.)

Talk to the instructor, especially if you need to clarify some aspect of the course. Find out what the instructor is looking for. For example, in a History course does the instructor want specific dates or the time period? Specific facts about an event or what led to the event and the significance of the event? Are there themes that have been stressed throughout the course?

Try to locate previous years' exams only if this is an acceptable practice at your college or university. This varies from school to school and professor to professor. Check with individual professors before doing this. Sometimes, student organizations such as sororities or fraternities have test banks, or professors keep old exams on reserve at the library or post them on the Internet. Possibly, the instructor might simply share a back copy.

Especially if you cannot examine an old copy of the test, talk to students who have taken the course in the past.

Request Accommodations Early

As discussed in Chapter 9, a variety of testing accommodations are available to students with documented disabilities. They include: taking exams in private, quiet rooms, extended time, having questions read aloud, and using a laptop for essay exams. Make sure you understand how to request accommodations through the DSS office and speak to professors in the beginning of the semester about needed testing accommodations.

Review throughout the Semester

Remembering is easier when reviews are done throughout the semester rather than cramming the night before.

Read the textbook and lecture notes systematically. Make summaries on cards or tapes to review when doing other things, such as traveling to and from school. Pretend to be the instructor and after each chapter come up with at least three questions that could be asked on a test. Think about an essay to write about or answer some sample true/false or multiple choice questions.

For students with AD/HD, reviewing throughout the semester might be a real struggle. Meet with other students, your tutor, or a learning specialist once a week to go over material. This creates a structured study schedule and makes it less likely that you will need to relearn material the night before the exam.

Summarize Lecture and Textbook Notes

Consolidate lecture and textbook notes into summary sheets and recite them. Paul, a student with LD, thinks that this is the most effective strategy for test preparation. By summarizing lecture and textbook notes, he achieves three things:

1. Review notes and add other information;

2. Pull material together by category, which makes it easier to recall during an exam;

3. Create a concise summary (approximately ten pages) to study just before the exam.

To do this summarizing, Paul recommends using the Cornell Notetaking System. This technique was described on page 287.

Memorize Terms

For some students, memorizing can be a real struggle. For students with AD/HD, the greatest challenge can be just sitting down and concentrating long enough to memorize the information. One helpful strategy is to set up a weekly schedule to study/ review material with a fellow student from that class or even a tutor. Students with LD and/or AD/HD might also benefit from learning to use mnemonics (see page 308) or to make visual representations of important events. These techniques can be learned through counseling centers, learning centers, the DSS office, or tutors.

Study with Others

Talk about the exam with other students, especially students who are knowledgeable about the course content. Organize study groups, or study with a group of successful students. For example, you might ask a "study buddy" to talk out the material that is likely to be covered by the exam.

Prepare Your Body

It is very important to get a good night's sleep prior to the exam. This will help you think more clearly, so you can express yourself in the precise manner you want. Equally important is to eat well the day of the exam. It is added pressure to go to an exam with a growling stomach.

Do What Works for You

As Chapter 9-I explains below, there is no one right way to study. Whether you need loud background noise or complete quiet, a neatly organized desk to sit at or a comfortable bed to sprawl out on, you should do whatever keeps your mind alert and engaged.

Taking the Exam

Before You Begin

Arrive Early. Select a seat where the light is good, the blackboard is easy to see, and distractions are minimal. If needed, use relaxation techniques before the exam starts. Don't sit next to worriers or anxiety carriers.

Understand the Directions. Read and listen to all instructions before beginning. If in doubt, raise your hand and ask the proctor.

Skim the Exam. Look at each question to determine how many points each is worth. This helps you plan how much time and effort to give each section. Figure out what is required for each question. Is the question asking for comparison, summarizing, listening, reviewing, justifying? Are you supposed to answer objectively or subjectively? Objective tests look for facts derived from readings and class lectures, not personal opinion. Usually if a professor wants your opinion, he or she will give essay exams or assign a paper.

Be sure to wait until the professor has finished previewing the test and/or giving additional information and instructions not already typed up in the exam.

During the Exam

Answer Easy Questions First. Skip questions that seem impossible to answer. Start at the end of the exam and work backwards, if the types of questions at the end seem easier. Go back to the difficult questions at the end. A little credit is better than no credit.

Look for Relevant Information. Often test questions include relevant information and important clues that may be valuable throughout the exam. Underline or highlight potentially helpful information.

Use the Full Time. Use any extra time to check your work.

Trust Your Instinct. Some students go back and change their answers. Most of the time the first response was correct.

Tips for Taking Different Types of Exams

This section offers some basic information about taking different types of exams. For more detailed information, consider taking campus study skills courses or consulting study skills books. They often give excellent ideas on how to prepare for each of these kinds of questions.

Essay Exams

After reading the essay question, write a "rough" outline, making sure to write down the main points that need to be addressed. Use this outline as a guide in writing the essay. When you are finished, check to make sure you included all important main points before turning in the exam.

Use the essay question to create the first sentence. This helps make the first sentence a clear, strong statement about the topic. It announces what the essay is about and makes it easier to organize facts, ideas, and details. For example, the essay question is: "Describe the primary reasons the southern states seceded from the U.S., beginning the Civil War." Begin your essay by stating: "There are several reasons why the southern states seceded from the U.S., beginning the Civil War. "

Use transition words such as *for example, accordingly, nevertheless, following are, similarly, finally.* These will help you draw connections from sentence to sentence and paragraph to paragraph. This will result in a logically reasoned essay.

True/False Exams

Watch for words that overstate, such as *all* or *always,* as well as words that understate, such as *some* or *most.* Be careful! For the statement to be true, all parts must be accurate and correct. For example:

Q. All colleges give guidance to students who need help in studying for exams. True or False?

A. False

Other words to watch for are: *none, usually, sometimes, never, good, bad, more, equal, less.*

Multiple Choice Exams

Multiple choice questions can test different types of information. These types range from straight definitions or theories to application of information (which require different skills).

- In taking a multiple choice exam, read all of the answers. Then eliminate those that are foolish or clearly not correct, as well as those that seem to overstate/understate. If one answer stands out as right, then that is the one to mark. Still not sure? Circle the best one and come back to the question later.

- Sometimes the answer is elsewhere in the test, or a word in another question may trigger a response. Still not sure?

- Read the prefixes (*hyper-, under-, sub-,* etc.) and suffixes (*-able, -ology, -ish,* etc.) to assist with meaning.

- Look for subject and verb agreement between the question and possible answers. Check also to see whether the teacher has left clues such as ending a question with *an,* indicating that the answer will start with a vowel. (e.g., "An animal that eats both meat and plants is an _____?)

Try this multiple choice question:

Q: In preparing for exams,

      (a) Wait until the night before to study.

      (b) Get as much information as possible about the exam, including types of questions.

      (c) Read the book from cover to cover.

A: (b) Get as much information as possible about the exam, including types of questions.

Did any of these answers seem foolish? Did the more detailed answer seem appropriate?

Mark Your Answers Carefully

Watch *where* you write, as well as what you write—especially when taking exams with separate answer sheets or that require you to fill in boxes or circles to indicate your answer. Use a ruler, file card, or the edge of a sheet of paper to help you keep your place on the answer sheet. As you take the exam, periodically check that you have not accidentally skipped a line on the answer sheet—or all answers below that point will be wrong. If using this type of answer sheet is especially hard for you, you might consider asking whether you can write your answers directly on the exam paper or booklet as an accommodation.

Sentence-Completion and Short-Answer Exams

Read sentences carefully and pull out what the examiner is asking. This should help give a context for each question. As in all other tests, go through the exam and answer questions on familiar information first. Then go back to the other questions and again focus on the context, and see if other parts of the exam give any clues in answering the question. If all fails, jot down anything that comes to mind about the question.

Q: Name the major parts of the nervous system and what each one consists of.

Pull out what the examiner is asking: name the parts—nervous system— what it is made of.

A: The nervous system is divided into **two** major parts. The **first** is the *central nervous system* which is comprised of *brain and spinal cord*. The **second** is the *peripheral nervous system* which consists of *all other nerve connections that are not in the brain and spinal cord*.

Reviewing Exams

Spend some time going over exams when they are returned. A careful review can be very helpful in preparing for future exams. Look to see what kinds of questions you missed. This can help you study more effectively next time. Also, be sure to find out the correct answers. This will be helpful when preparing for midterms and finals since these questions are often taken from previous exams.

Ask yourself the following questions:

- What kinds of questions did I miss? Were they based on the book? or more from class notes?

- Did I spend too much time on one question or section?

- Did I overlook main points and get sidetracked by details?

- Did I misread any questions?

Your tutor or a learning specialist at the DSS office may be able to help you learn ways to avoid repeating your mistakes on the next exam.

Conclusion

Exam time is tense for all students. Fortunately, there are many techniques and strategies for studying and taking exams. Become an expert in test taking strategies. Don't be afraid to seek help from counselors, instructors, and other students.

CHAPTER 11-F—Reading Comprehension

Understanding course content is crucial to succeeding in a postsecondary setting. To read with understanding requires many skills: recognizing letters and words, knowing the meaning of words by themselves and in the context in which they are used, and spotting and identifying the author's purpose and structure. What is the author's message? How is the author presenting the material? Does it confirm your previously held opinions, or does it relate to other ideas and concepts? How can this information be used in work, studies, and daily life?

This section presents a few strategies that often help students with LD and/ or AD/HD improve their reading comprehension. Study skills classes can also help you learn techniques and strategies for increasing your reading comprehension. In addition, there are many books that can help you overcome barriers to comprehension. Some of the most helpful are listed on pages 312-316.

Multipass

One strategy that can boost reading comprehension is named Multipass. This is one of the many strategies developed by the University of Kansas, Center for Research on Learning.

Multipass is a strategy that leads the student through a chapter in order to:

- increase his comprehension;

- ensure he is meeting the desired goals of the assignment;

- reduce the information that needs to be sorted;

- structure the new knowledge in the reader's mind;

- increase the likelihood that a student will be able to maintain and retrieve the information for longer periods of time.

This process systematically guides the student through the reading passage three times:

1. Survey Pass,

2. Size-up Pass, and

3. Sort-out Pass.

This guided process is used instead of reading a chapter from start to finish.

Stage 1: Survey Pass

The survey pass helps the reader get oriented. While gathering the main ideas, themes, and the organization of the chapter, the reader also learns their relationship to other chapters in the book.

To begin, you read the title and the introductory paragraph. Next, you read the table of contents in order to learn its relationship to the entire text and/or course. From there, you look through the chapter in an orderly fashion, reading the section titles and subtitles. You also examine any pictures, captions, or graphics included in the chapter. This step gives clues to the passage's organization. Next, you read the summary, if provided. At this point, you paraphrase what you have learned so far. Now, you have orientation, some knowledge, organization, and questions to consider during your second pass.

Stage 2: Size-Up Pass

This stage allows a reader to find the most crucial information. In this stage, you will be able to gather the relevant details required to fulfill the goals of the assigned reading.

Initially, you read the questions at the end of the book. Are there any questions you can already answer from your work during the survey pass? From here, you must go through the chapter looking for clues—bold faced or italicized words, subheadings, etc. As you come to each clue, you create a question from it. Then read the preceding and following information around the clue to find the answer. Afterwards, you must paraphrase the answer. This will help you to better understand the information, retain it throughout the semester, and retrieve it during a test.

Stage 3: Sort-Out Pass

In the sort-out pass, the reader tests himself on what he has learned so far. Now, you note those questions you were not able to answer from the size-up pass. You must guess which section the answer would be located in. If the answer is not found, you repeat this pass until you are able to answer all the questions.

This strategy can strengthen your comprehension if you are determined. Also, once you have pinpointed all the main ideas and important points in the chapter, it may make it easier for you to organize your notes from the chapter.

Learning to Read Like a Writer

All good writing has a similar structure. Strong readers look for this structure much as a writer builds from it. The building blocks of writing include:

- **Main Idea:** Make sure you know what the paragraph is about. The main idea is often given in the first sentence. Sometimes the main idea is stated at the end. Other times, the main idea is not stated outright, but you see repeated words or ideas throughout the paragraph that allow you to figure out what the main idea is.

- **Topic Sentence:** The topic sentence may be anywhere in the paragraph. It is usually a reinforcement to the main idea of the paragraph. It may also describe the manner in which the major points will be presented.

- **Major Points:** A paragraph has at least two major points. Major points serve as explanations or defenses for the main idea and topic sentence. For example, a topic sentence explaining a process will be supported by sentences and words describing order such as *first*, *second,* and *third*, or *after*, *before*, and *then*. Each step will serve as a major point within the paragraph. As another example, a main idea describing cause and effect may be surrounded by transition words such as *because*, *despite*, and *therefore,* which develop into major points.

More Tips for Reading

- Go back to the paragraphs that are difficult to understand. Find the topic sentence and see if this helps to identify the main ideas, or look for the subject of the supporting sentences.

- Professors or teaching assistants are wonderful resources to help guide reading. Tell them that reading comprehension is a challenge for you. Ask for guidance on what to focus on in reading. Ask for some questions to help you focus on a reading assignment.

- Work with a "study buddy" to recite and review the reading. Talking about a reading assignment can be a wonderful way to reinforce and better understand the content.

- A content tutor can be another great resource, especially if getting the reading done is the greatest challenge. See Chapter 9B.

- **Minor Points:** These expand upon the major points and are webbed into the paragraph using transition sentences. For example, minor points might explain additional details in a process.

- **Transitions:** Transitions function much like road signs (e.g., Exit 1 mile, or Merge Left). They help us find our way within a written passage—to see connections between sentences, either within a paragraph, or between paragraphs. Some of the words and phrases used in transition sentences include:

  - Addition words, to help build an idea: *and, also, in addition.*

  - Time words to tell sequence: *first, next, then, last*

  - Contrast words to show how ideas are different: *however, but, on the other hand*

  - Illustration words to signal that an example is coming: *for example, for instance*

The structural elements found in good writing smoothly translate in and out of outlines. The main idea becomes roman numeral *(I.)*, and is naturally supported by at least two major ideas, which are named *(A.)* and *(B.)*. If applicable, minor points then become the next indentations, *(1.)* and *(2.)*. Transition sentences do not appear in the outline, but they work to connect the different points within the outline. Table 11.2 gives an example of translating the various types of sentences in a paragraph into an outline.

TABLE 11.2—The Building Blocks of Writing

Sample paragraph:

Presidential primaries play an important role in our democratic process. First, they promote more direct contact between presidential candidates and voters. In states with primaries, candidates spend time meeting voters and debating each other. Second, candidates have to be able to explain their stand on issues over a period of time and answer difficult questions. Finally, the primary process gives voters an opportunity to formally express their opinions of candidates before the national election in November.

Paragraph translated into an outline:
I. Importance of presidential primaries to democratic process
    A. promote contact between candidates and voters
        1. candidates meet voters and debate each other
    B. require candidates to explain their stands and answer questions
    C. give voters opportunity to express opinions before national election

These same structural elements may be easily translated into a concept map. For example, the main idea would be at the top of the map, with supporting ideas connected underneath. Chapter 9-D provides an example of the same information in both outline and concept map form.

Whether you are reading or writing, knowing these structural elements can greatly improve your proficiency, comprehension, and expression. As you read, you can ask yourself, "What is the main idea? What are the major points supporting it?" This will help increase your comprehension level as well as your ability to express the information in your own words or style. Additionally, such questions can be used to structure your notes, or as strong starting points for any papers you need to write about the reading.

CHAPTER 11-G—Writing

"Fear of writing is my biggest obstacle."

"Getting the thought out—that's the hardest part."

"I can say it, but I can't write it."

Writing is a complex task. Ideas that float in the brain must be translated onto paper. Points must be selected, organized, and put into logical order. Sentences must be woven together with correct grammar, punctuation, capitalization, syntax, and spelling. This task requires integration of many skills— including memory, sequencing, organizing, language structure, motor skills, and visual-motor integration.

For many students with LD and/or AD/HD, writing is painful. Problems with mechanics constantly get in the way. Spelling errors nag, thoughts get stuck, and content may be limited. Handwriting or word processing may be difficult and time consuming. Frustrated by the entire process, students frequently have what they call "writing phobia." They fear that any writing they do will make them look stupid.

The Importance of Writing

If writing is difficult for you, getting help is critical. Writing papers and exams is essential for mastery of most postsecondary courses. And in the working world, written communication takes place every day. Writing is the face of literacy one shows the world.

Writing is one way to learn from our reading, listening, speaking, and daily living. Writing is also a process. Each of us brings strengths and challenges to the writing process. The key is to recognize them and then build on your strengths and develop strategies to improve areas of need. The good news is that writing is a skill and like any skill, practice with feedback is the key to improving. There are tools to help with each step of the writing process. With the proper support, students entering postsecondary education as unsure writers can improve their writing greatly.

This section focuses on techniques that can help you become a better writer. Many of the ideas are basic tips for writing and can be used by all students. For students with LD and/or AD/HD, it is essential to learn these or similar approaches for overcoming writing blocks. Students, their instructors, and support service providers at the DSS office can use the ideas as a beginning and explore further on their own.

Practice, Practice, Practice

The best way to learn to write is by doing it. Improvement comes by tackling the task. Without practice, it gets harder and harder to overcome mental blocks about writing.

Whatever you are writing, it is important to avoid self-criticism. Students who are unsure about writing frequently think that everyone else writes easily. They feel that a first draft should be perfect, and they edit every word as they write. Self-criticism can keep the process from even getting started.

It helps to realize that good writers throw many drafts into the wastebasket. Replacing negative thoughts with positive ones can also be helpful. For example, instead of thinking, "This will be terrible," try thinking something more positive like, "I can do this.

Below are some strategies to help you get the words flowing from your pen or word processor.

Write without Stopping

Try to write steadily for about ten minutes every day, without stopping, correcting, or worrying about quality. Any everyday subject like "what I had for breakfast" could start this kind of activity. If it's easier, say it into a tape recorder. Or try a speech recognition program, as discussed in Chapter 9-D. If you're using a word processor, you may want to turn off the automatic spell check or grammar check so you don't get bogged down fixing small errors.

Keeping a daily journal helps many people get into a writing habit. Again, it is important to write without worrying about mistakes. Whatever gets put down is part of the act of capturing thoughts in written form.

Use Personal Experiences

Adults who have struggled through the writing process stress the importance of using one's own experiences in developing ideas. Personal experiences with family, jobs, schools, friends—all the big and little things in life—are powerful sources for writing.

Online Correspondence

Using a computer with an Internet connection is a good way to loosen up your writing. Sending E-mail can be a great way to write on a daily basis. E-mails can be short and informal and nobody expects perfect grammar.

Participating in online discussion groups or sending others "instant messages" can force you to write more quickly. In these kinds of written conversations, you have to type the first thing that comes into your mind to keep up with the conversation.

Break Writing into Tasks

Whatever the writing assignment is, it helps to divide it into tasks. One way of dividing the work is to tackle it in four stages:

1. prewriting,

2. drafting,

3. reviewing and revising, and

4. sharing with an audience.

Stage 1: Prewriting

Prewriting is a time to gather ideas and to ask questions that can bring ideas into focus. English teachers have found that during this period students benefit greatly from talking over their topics with peers, instructors, and others. Here are some questions that can get the process started.

Guiding Questions for the Prewriting Stage

Topic: Think about the content and purpose of the assignment.

What topic/s do I already know something about?

What topics/s am I most interested in?

What resources can help me with different topics?

Point of View: Think about personal connections with the topic.

What ideas and information do I bring to this topic?

What is the purpose of this assignment?

Am I persuading, explaining, describing, proving?

Audience: Picture the people who would read the final product.

Who is my audience? Students? Instructors? The community?

What do my readers want to know about the topic?

Form: Be clear about the writing style for the assignment.

Is this an essay? A research paper? Creative writing?

How long should it be?

Do I write in first person (I), second person (you), or third person (he, she, it, they)?

Talk to other students about the assignment and be sure to check out their advice with the instructor. The clearer the answers, the easier writing will be.

Gathering Ideas

Instead of staring in panic at a blank page, try techniques such as brainstorming, interviewing, and mapping to help to identify main ideas.

Brainstorming

Brainstorming can be done in a large group, in small groups of two or three, or by individuals working alone. The first step is to list ideas, whether they come out as single words or phrases. Let them flow. Don't try to organize or be selective at this point. If possible, put up a large sheet of paper and list ideas with a colored marking pen.

The second step is to cluster ideas into categories. On a new sheet of paper, write headings that describe each category. List the ideas that fit. The result is a loose outline of main and supporting ideas.

Interviewing

Find out what other people on campus or in the community think about the topic. What do they see as most important? Why? You can also use the Internet to interview people. Some websites have experts who can answer questions on different topics, or you can get feedback from online bulletin boards or discussion groups.

How many people you interview will depend on how much time you have and the usefulness of the information you are receiving. Be sure to get the correct spelling of names. Keep notes of ideas or use a tape recorder. However, remember the goal of this step is to generate more ideas on the topic and to gain a better understanding of the topic and/or the assignment. This information will not necessarily be reported in your paper.

Mapping & Graphic Organizers

Mapping is a way to organize information. Instead of starting with a sequential outline in an orderly one-two-three approach, mapping allows personal associations. That is, it lets you make connections between ideas that make

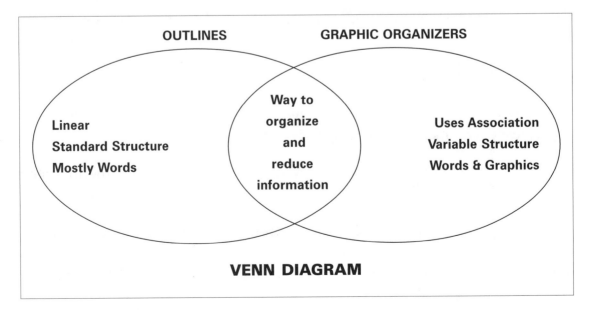

OUTLINES   **GRAPHIC ORGANIZERS**

Linear
Standard Structure
Mostly Words

Way to
organize
and
reduce
information

Uses Association
Variable Structure
Words & Graphics

VENN DIAGRAM

sense to you. Many students find that mapping allows them to see the most important ideas. Also called webbing, clustering, or drawing a mind map, mapping is especially helpful for visual learners and for students who have difficulty with sequential outlining. The Postsecondary Options web diagram below is an example of mapping.

Graphic organizers can offer a structure for organizing ideas. For example, a compare-contrast organizer will have a different structure than a sequence organizer such as a traditional outline. A good example of a compare-contrast organizer is a Venn Diagram. You use two or more circles to represent two or more sets. Where the circles overlap, you list common details. The independent areas of the two circles list the unique details.

Once the important information you have gathered is placed in the organizer, the structure for writing a first draft is in place.

There is no one way to map and cluster thoughts. The key is for each person to find a way that helps him best think about, organize, and remember important ideas.

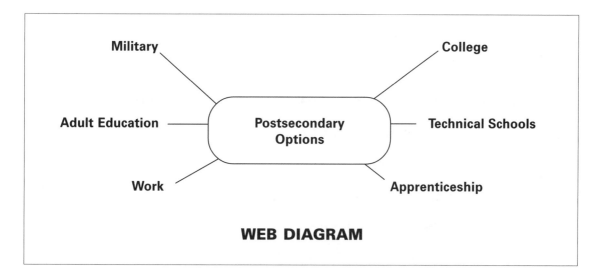

WEB DIAGRAM

Stage 2: Drafting

After gathering and organizing information and ideas, it is time to write a first draft. The purpose is to get down on paper the important ideas you want to present. At this point, the mechanics of grammar and spelling are not important. You are thinking and writing and trying to put prewriting ideas into sentences and paragraphs. It is easy to feel confused or overwhelmed with ideas. What is important is getting the ideas into a written format.

While writing a first draft, ask yourself questions to make sure that you are doing as the assignment asks:

- What is the purpose of the paper?

- Who is my audience?

- What are my main ideas?

- How can I make the main idea clear?

- Have I supported my main idea?

- How am I structuring my paper?

Stage 3: Reviewing and Revising

This is the feedback stage. You ask others to read your paper and tell you what is clear and what, specifically, needs to be revised. You can ask peers, instructors, and learning/writing specialists for suggestions for improvement. Some questions to ask are:

- Is the organization clear?

- What points are clearest?

- Does the introduction give the reader a clear picture of the subject?

- Does the ending match the rest of the paper?

- Is the point of view clear?

- Does the draft match the assignment guidelines?

- Are paragraphs well developed?

- Are sentences too long or too short?

- Can the vocabulary be improved?

- How are the mechanics (spelling, grammar, and punctuation)?

A final draft often is the result of many revisions. Be sure to plan ahead for enough time to complete the assignment. Focusing on content and organization at one time and mechanics at another helps some writers. Allowing time between drafts can also help you read with a fresher view.

Stage 4: Sharing with an Audience

The last step in writing is to share the final product and receive feedback. Sometimes this means handing in the paper and getting back comments and a grade. Other times it can mean making an oral presentation and getting peer feedback.

Producing a final product that looks good makes a statement about an author's investment. Think about including the 'little things' that make a good impression such as: using high quality paper, laying out the title page neatly, using graphics if appropriate, changing print fonts for section headings, etc. Word processing "know-how" can be a big help during this final stage.

Individual Assistance

Some students need individualized assistance with all or some steps of writing. The person who provides the assistance may be a classroom instructor, a tutor, an individual at the writing center, a learning specialist, a graduate assistant, or a peer. If you usually need assistance, you must plan appropriately. Consider the schedule of the person who is assisting you, your own schedule, and the timeframe of the assignment. Don't wait until a couple days before the due date to find someone to help.

One talented and intelligent student with LD spoke of freezing when a writing assignment was due. She was unable to "get thoughts unstuck." With the help of a learning specialist, she finally overcame her writing block. The specialist listened to her talk and took down the ideas as they came out. Then together, they began to put them in order. They went over the final draft carefully, looking at flow of sentences, vocabulary, and grammar. Working in this way, the student's panic about writing lessened. Her anxiety went down and her skills went up.

Extra time spent focusing on individual strengths and needs can help remove blocks and set the stage for effective expression of ideas.

CHAPTER 11-H—Memory

Memory can be a nagging challenge for many students with LD and/or AD/HD. Here are some basic rules and tricks that can help.

- **Decide to remember.** Memory experts say that if a person doesn't remember something, it's probably because he didn't try to remember it in the first place. Perhaps the person was daydreaming while listening to a speech or reading a chapter. Deciding to remember takes extra concentration, motivation, and interest.

- **Understand material to be memorized.** If material is complicated or technical, ask questions until it's clear. When reading or taking notes, paraphrase important information.

- **Don't try to remember everything.** Key ideas or main points are what's important. The cues for reading (Multipass), notetaking, and exam preparation provide good background for remembering.

- **Organize in clusters.** Cluster information into categories; use a graphic organizer if that helps. Categories for causes of the American Revolution might be issues, people, events—with major facts under each one. Keep categories to a manageable number, and don't overstuff each one with too much detail.

- **Say it aloud.** After reading and thinking about information that is important to remember, look away or cover the page and say it out loud in a conversational tone. Writing it down will help, too.

- **Visualize.** Make a picture. It is practically a surefire way to store and recall information. Drawing a timeline, a simple diagram, or a silly cartoon helps to fix ideas in the mind and bring them back when you want them.

- **Make up mnemonics.** Mnemonics are verbal aids to helping you organize and remember information. Mnemonics often use first letters of key words, terms, or names to form a word or phrase. For example, "HOMES" stands for the names of the Great Lakes: **Hu**ron, **O**ntario, **M**ichigan, **E**rie, **S**uperior. Likewise, "**F**at **C**ats **G**et **D**izzy **A**lways **E**ating **B**utter" stands for the order of sharps in musical notation. Another type of mnemonic involves thinking of a <u>pie</u>ce of <u>pie</u> to remember how to spell "piece." Many students with LD find that making lists of their own mnemonic tricks and reviewing them frequently boosts their confidence and reduces errors.

- **Use associations.** Association, making meaningful connections, is a powerful tool for memorizing, especially if the association is visual. To be even more effective, the experts say, the association should be to something absurd and exaggerated. One way to do this is to create a humorous mnemonic. For example, TEENS can stand for the five sense organs (tongue, eyes, ears, nose, skin). The visual association could be a mental picture of five teenagers, each with an exaggerated sense organ. Associations to other senses can strengthen memory too. Some people put key words to the tune of a familiar song. Others remember by using their hands. Putting a machine together, step by step, combines tactile associations with visual memory.

■ **Trade techniques with a friend.** Share your memorization techniques with a study buddy and find out what other memory techniques he uses—either general or specific to the exam.

■ **Practice.** Make opportunities for success. Practice using the memorized information before you need to use it.

CHAPTER 11-I—Chewing Apples and Other Quirks

Many people need to go through a process of trial and error to discover the strategies that will enable them to successfully complete school or work-related tasks. Mistakes can be worth the time and pain involved, if the result is self-insight that leads to a positive plan. As you mature, your personal strategies will become part of your self-knowledge and can then be used whenever needed.

This section highlights a range of factors to consider when trying to determine how you learn best. The study skills guides at the end of this chapter can guide you to other techniques that may be helpful.

Environmental Factors

Your physical surroundings can have a big effect on your ability to concentrate and retain information.

Quiet vs. Noise. Although a quiet, non-distracting place to study is helpful to most students, others study best while listening to music or even watching TV. Background music can block out other distracting noises and thoughts, and help a student to relax and concentrate. By all means, use headphones if your roommate does not share your preference for background music.

Color. Color can be a great stimulus for learning and an aid for memorizing. Some students report reading better if they place a color transparency over a white page with black print. Also, placing a large sheet of colored paper under a book on a table or desk can help your mind focus on reading. Using colored notecards or different colored pens can help organize information. Color coding can also be an additional memory tool.

Lighting. Finding the right kind of light is important. Keeping your computer away from windows can eliminate glare and background lighting that can make the screen difficult to read. Some people find that fluorescent lights give them headaches or that the hum is distracting. Many students find that a strong, focused desk lamp best helps them focus on the materials they are studying.

Place. Students often concentrate better when visual distractions are kept to a minimum. A study carrel in the library can offer fewer distractions than a table by the window. Although the student union may be a good place to relax and socialize, it may be the worst place to study uninterrupted.

Mental Factors

Peak Energy Time. Most people's energy varies with the time of day. Being aware of your higher and lower energy times can help you decide when to study. Lower energy times are best spent on recreational activities or more routine study activities.

Relaxation. Most students store information more efficiently when they are relaxed. If you frequently feel stressed out, you may want to take a course in relaxation. One simple tip: Take three deep breaths before starting a learning task.

Physical Activity. Physical or motor activity can be an important part of an individual's learning style. Someone with a strong need to move around and be active might stifle learning by trying to study for hours at one time. A better strategy might be to study in small chunks of time, with short exercise breaks between study sessions. Some students take walks, ride an exercise bike, or use a stair-climber while reviewing exam questions. One student practices juggling before getting down to work or during study breaks. There are many motor techniques like these that help people learn and remember.

Focus. Some people need to organize their thoughts or slow them down. Some students are able to accomplish this by applying pressure to the tops of their heads. A simple technique is interlocking your fingers and pulling them downward over the head. Also, applying pressure to the shoulders can help to moderate your body and brain's speed. If this works for you, consider using these techniques during an exam. If breaks are allotted, walk up and down the hallway corridors carrying a heavy backpack. A more discreet manner of organizing your brain and keeping it on task is to press hard with your hands on the seat of your chair and lift your body slightly off your chair. All these techniques may help you slow your body and brain down when they seem to be overwhelmed, whether by stress or stimuli.

Alertness. Sometimes, the brain is a bit lethargic despite our best efforts, making information retrieval difficult. Discreetly playing with fidget toys (such as putty to squeeze or a small toy that moves or changes shape) can help to stimulate your brain. Chewing on ice, straws, hard candy, apples, or nuts can also aid some people. These strategies can help your brain move at a faster, more effective pace.

If you take medication for AD/HD or another condition, it will be important to know how it affects your alertness. With medications for AD/HD, there is frequently a window of time when you are at your most alert and attentive. With your doctor's guidance, you may need to adjust dosages or the times when you take these medications so that you are at your most alert when you need to be.

Finding the Best Way

Most of us have a feel for what makes us comfortable while we work, but we haven't given these idiosyncrasies any particular honor. If we do our best thinking lying down, or need to crunch apples and nuts while we read or write, we tend to shrug away such traits as weaknesses. But the truth is, these personal styles are assets. It can be a relief and a strength to know it's okay for each of us to find our best way.

Conclusion

There are many strategies that can help you learn new information. Likewise, there are many organizational planning, writing, and test-taking strategies that can help you show instructors what you have learned. All students, with and without disabilities, use strategies to successfully make it through school. The challenge is to find the strategies that are most effective and efficient for you and then to become an expert in using those strategies to your benefit.

Resources

BOOKS

Becoming a Master Student, 8th edition, 1997
Editor: Dave Ellis
Houghton Mifflin Company
1900 S. Batavia Ave
Geneva, IL 60134
Phone: (800) 733-2828
Fax: (800) 733-2098
E-mail: storemanager@hmco.com
http://www.schooldirect.com

Better Study Skills for Better Grades and Real Learning, 1996
ICPAC Information Series
Indiana Career and Postsecondary Advancement Center
2805 E. 10th Street
Bloomington, IN 47408
Phone: (800) 992-2076
http://icpac.indiana.edu

Essential Study Skills, 2nd edition, 1997
Author: Linda Wong
Houghton Mifflin Company
1900 S. Batavia Ave
Geneva, IL 60134
Phone: (800) 733-2828
Fax: (800) 733-2098
E-mail: storemanager@hmco.com
http://www.schooldirect.com

How to Study: And Other Skills for Success in College, 1993
Authors: James Deese and Ellen Deese
Glencoe/McGraw-Hill
P.O. Box 543
Blacklick, OH 43004-9902.
Phone: (800) 334-7344
Fax: (614) 860-1877
http://www.glencoe.com

How to Study: Suggestions for High School and College Students, 1993
Authors: Walter Kornhauser and Diane M. Emerson
University of Chicago Press
11030 South Langley Avenue
Chicago, IL 60628
Phone: (800) 621-2736
Fax: (800) 621-8476
E-mail: marketing@press.uchicago.edu
http://www.press.uchicago.edu

How to Study in College, 6th edition, 1996
Author: Walter Pauk
Houghton Mifflin Company
1900 S. Batavia Ave
Geneva, IL 60134
Phone: (800) 733-2828
Fax: (800) 733-2098
E-mail: storemanager@hmco.com
http://www.schooldirect.com

How to Study Mathematics: Effective Study Strategies for College and University Students, 1998
Author: Peter Schiavone
Prentice-Hall Trade/Simon and Schuster
P.O. Box 11071
Des Moines, IA 50336
Phone: (800) 223-2336
Http://www.prenhall.com

Reading, Writing and Reasoning: A Guide for Students, 2nd edition, 1996
Authors: Gavin J. Fairbairn and Christopher Winch
Open University Press/Taylor & Francis
47 Runway Road,
Levittown, PA 19057
Phone: (800) 821-8312
Fax: (215) 269-0363
E-mail: enquiries@openup.co.uk
http://www.taylorandfrancis.com/BOOKS

SOS, Strengthening of Skills Program, 1985
Author: Lynn O'Brien

Specific Diagnostic Studies
11600 Nebel Street
Suite 130
Rockville, MD 20852
Phone: (301) 468-6616

Speed Writing for Notetaking and Study Skills, 1991
Authors: Joe M. Pullis, Cheryl D. Pullis, and Irene Schindler
Glencoe/McGraw-Hill
P.O. Box 543
Blacklick, OH 43004-9902.
Phone: (800) 334-7344
Fax: (614) 860-1877
http://www.glencoe.com

Study and Critical Thinking Skills in College, 3rd edition, 1996
Author: Kathleen T. McWhorter
HarperCollins
10 East 53rd Street
New York, NY 10022
Phone: (800) 242-7737
Fax: (800) 822-4090
http://www.harpercollins.com

Study Skills
Author: Mary Margaret Hosler
Glencoe/McGraw-Hill
P.O. Box 543
Blacklick, OH 43004-9902.
Phone: (800) 334-7344
Fax: (614) 860-1877
http://www.glencoe.com

The Study Skills Handbook: More Than 75 Strategies for Better Learning, 1995
Author: Judith Dodge
Scholastic Trade
http://www.scholastic.com

Succeeding in College with Attention Deficit Disorders: Issues & Strategies for Students, Counselors, & Educators, 1996
Author: Jennifer Bramer

Specialty Press/ADD Warehouse
300 NW 70th Avenue, #102
Plantation, FL 33317
Phone: (800) 233-9273
Fax: (954) 792-8545
E-mail: sales@addwarehouse.com

Ten Steps to Building College Reading Skills, 2nd edition, 1998
Author: Bill Broderick
Townsend Press
Pavilions at Greentree 408
Marlton, NJ 08053
Phone: (800) 772-6410
Fax: (609) 753-0649
E-mail: TownsendNJ@aol.com
http://www.townsendpress.com

Ten Steps to Improving College Reading Skills, 1998
Author: John Langan
Townsend Press
See address above.

Webster's New World, Student's Writing Handbook, 1997
Author: Sharon Sorenson
Macmillan Publishing
135 South Mount Zion Road
Lebanon, IN 46052
Phone: (800) 428-5331
Fax: (800) 882-8583
http://www.mcp.com/online_catalog

Writing with a Point, 1986
Authors: Jeanne Stephens and Ann Harper
Educators Publishing Service, Inc.
31 Smith Place
Cambridge, MA 02138-1089
Phone: (800) 225-5750
Fax: (617) 547-0412
E-mail: epsbooks@epsbooks.com
http://www.epsbooks.com

FACT SHEET

Improving Quality of Student Notes, 1993
Author: Bonnie Potts
Eric Clearinghouse on Assessment and Evaluation,
College of Library and Information Services
University of Maryland
1129 Shriver Laboratory
College Park, MD 20742
Phone: (800) 464-3742
Fax: (301) 405-7449
http://www.ericae.net

WEBSITE

Study Skills Website
This is a site for students, created by students. It has helpful tips as well as helpful links. It is run by the New York State chapter of the International Dyslexic Association.
http://www.ldteens.org/Study%20Skills.html

CURRICULA

First Letter Mnemonic: A Learning Strategies Curriculum, 1998
Learning Plus/ETS
Phone: (800) 559-7587
Fax: (215) 321-4249

Paraphrasing (PASS): A Learning Strategies Curriculum
Authors: Charles Hughes, Jean Schumaker, Donald Deschler, and Cecil Mercer
Edge Enterprises, Inc.
P.O. Box 1304
Lawrence, KA 66044
Phone: (913) 749-1473
Fax: (913) 749-0207

The Test Taking Strategy, 1993
Authors: Charles A. Hughes, Jean B. Schumaker, Donald D. Deschler, and Cecil D. Mercer
Edge Enterprises, Inc.
See address above.

The Vocabulary Strategy, 1995
Author: Edwin S. Ellis

Edge Enterprises, Inc.
See address above.

ORGANIZATIONS

Contact information for the following useful organizations can be found beginning on page 347.

- American Coaching Association

- Association on Higher Education and Disability (AHEAD)

- Attention Deficit Information Network (Ad-IN)

- Children and Adults with Attention-Deficit/Hyperactivity Disorder (CHADD)

- Council on Learning Disabilities

- Educational Testing Service, Inc.

- The Federal Resource Center for Special Education

- Higher Education And The Handicapped (HEATH) Resource Center

- The International Dyslexia Association

- International Reading Association

- Internet Special Education Resources

- Learning Disabilities Association of America (LDA)

- National Association for Adults with Learning Difficulties (NAALD)

- National Attention Deficit Disorder Association (National ADDA)

- National Center for Learning Disabilities (NCLD)

- National Institute for Literacy Hotline

- NICHCY (National Information Center for Children and Youth with Disabilities)

- Roads To Learning/The Public Libraries' Learning Disabilities Initiative

AFTER SCHOOL, WHAT NEXT?

IN THIS CHAPTER:

- Overview
- Assessing Interests and Abilities
- Matching Job Opportunities with Personal Interest and Abilities
- Looking for a Position
- Preparing to Apply for a Job
- The Job Interview
- Job-Keeping Skills

Michelle Sarkees Wircenski,
Jerry Wircenski, & Lynda West

Overview

There are four basic options that you can pursue after completing high school. These options include:

1. attending a four-year college or university;

2. enrolling in a postsecondary training program or community college;

3. becoming an apprentice; or

4. entering the job market.

Whether you choose to go to work immediately after high school or go on to postsecondary education, eventually you will need to look for a job. This chapter provides a brief overview of factors to consider in choosing appropriate career fields and applying for a job.

Assessing Interests and Abilities

Before looking for employment, it is highly advisable to assess your individual interests and abilities. In fact, it is a good idea to do this well in advance of looking for a job. If you are in college, this is a step you may want to take before choosing a major. If you are planning to go to work right after high school, it is wise to assess your interests and abilities before graduation.

Methods of assessing job interests and abilities include:

- Filling out an interest inventory—a form that asks questions about your likes and dislikes that can tell you what career cluster or occupational area interests you.

- Taking ability or aptitude tests—paper-and-pencil or hands-on tests that assess your skills in certain areas and indicate what careers you probably would be very good at if you were provided with training.

- Seeking the advice of people you respect, such as parents, teachers, friends, and counselors, to help you identify a career that matches your interests and abilities.

- Reviewing any experiences you have had with internships, volunteering, or part-time jobs and evaluating what you did and did not enjoy about those experiences.

Getting Assistance with Assessment

If you are still in high school, the guidance counselor can probably arrange for you to take interest inventories or aptitude tests. If you are in college, this service will probably be available at the campus Career Center, as well as counseling about good career choices for you. At any stage of life, if you qualify for services from Vocational Rehabilitation, they can provide a variety of services to help you understand what kinds of careers fit your interests and abilities. See Chapter 5 for more information about Vocational Rehabilitation.

TABLE 12.1—Job Seeking Inventory

What kind of job environment do I prefer?

___ working primarily indoors
___ the same office space every day
___ a quiet office setting
___ a private working space
___ traveling frequently for work
___ working primarily outdoors

How do I work best with other people?

___ work alone with little interaction
___ work closely supervised and monitored
___ work independently with occasional supervision for guidance and feedback
___ work in a large organization with numerous people fulfilling various jobs
___ work in a small organization

What sort of work schedule and time responsibilities do I prefer?

___ a set work schedule
___ a flexible work schedule
___ a schedule with regular routines
___ a schedule with regular lunch hours
___ a schedule where overtime is not acceptable
___ night work
___ weekend work
___ a job where work often needs to be taken home
___ a schedule with occasional overtime when needed

What sort of compensation/benefits do I prefer?

___ a stable salary (weekly/monthly)
___ working for commission on sales or tips
___ working for bonuses depending upon my performance
___ medical insurance
___ tuition reimbursements
___ opportunities for career advancement
___ frequent salary reviews
___ retirement plan/401 K plan
___ paid vacation

Questions to Help You Identify Your Interests

First-time job seekers can explore what their interests are by using the following chart. Answering the questions can help you zero in on a job that will suit your needs, interests, and abilities.

Matching Job Opportunities with Personal Interests and Abilities

Once you have examined your list of preferences, they need to be matched with the results of your interest and ability tests. Now the question "What type of job am I best suited for?" can be answered.

Within each category of business, there are hundreds of different types of jobs. You might be interested in a job that deals primarily with people, information/data, or things. For example, within the broad category of financial services, typical employment opportunities might be a teller (working with people), a loan officer (working with information/data), and an ATM (Automated Teller Machine) technician (working with things). Some jobs involve working with a combination of all three—people, information/data, and things. Different jobs within broad categories often demand different types of schedules, are performed in different types of settings, offer different amounts of compensation, and have different potentials for advancement.

TABLE 12.2—Categories of Business

■ advertising	■ agriculture	■ automotive
■ banking	■ chemicals	■ computers
■ construction	■ education	■ electronics
■ fashion	■ food & beverage	■ forestry
■ health services	■ hospitality	■ insurance
■ manufacturing	■ metals and mining	■ paper & printing
■ public utilities	■ publishing	■ retailing
■ telecommunications	■ transportation	■ travel

To get assistance matching your interests and abilities with specific jobs, once again you can turn to your high school guidance counselor, college Career Center, or Vocational Rehabilitation office.

Another good way to match your interests and abilities with different types of jobs is to consult the *Occupational Outlook Handbook.* This book describes hundreds of types of jobs, and provides information about the nature of the work, working conditions, education and experience required, and whether the number of job openings is increasing or decreasing. The handbook is published every two years by the U.S. Department of Labor. Look for it in your public or university library, or order it from:

> Superintendent of Documents
> U.S. Government Printing Office
> Mail Stop: SOP
> Washington, DC 20402-9328
> http://www.espan.com/docs/oohand.html

As you begin to focus on a particular type of job, you may find that you need further education or training to be qualified for the job. For example, you may find that job announcements ask for experience with software that you have never used, or training in using specific types of equipment. If so, you might be able to take classes through an adult education program or a local community college to improve skills in this area. Vocational Rehabilitation might also be able to help you find training.

FACTS AND REALITIES ABOUT WORK

1. All individuals have their own interests, abilities, and preferences when it comes to employment.

2. There is no such thing as a perfect job.

3. Many full-time jobs are first obtained as part-time jobs.

4. Many jobs today require evening and/or weekend work.

5. A positive attitude and a willingness to learn often make up for temporary job deficiencies.

6. Many first-time job seekers place salary as a top priority as opposed to work environment.

7. Getting along with coworkers is important in any job.

8. The boss/supervisor may not always be right . . . but he/she is always the boss/supervisor.

Looking for a Position

You can use any number of methods to seek job openings in your chosen area of work. Employment opportunities can be located through:

- Want ads in newspapers or in newsletters or journals for your profession;

- Job tips and leads from family, friends, instructors;

- Internet sites that post available jobs or allow you to post information about yourself for interested employers;

- Networking—for example, at conventions for people in your field and at professional meetings;

- Vocational Rehabilitation Services;

- Placement services at your school or in your community;

- Professional and community organizations;

- Your state Bureau of Employment Services.

As you explore sources of job openings, make a list of positions or organizations that you are interested in exploring further. The next step is to research each job opening or company using the local library, online sources, and through networking. It is important to learn about the company, its products or services, specific support services available, and opportunities for advancement.

Preparing to Apply for a Job

Writing an Award-Winning Resume

A resume is a brief snapshot of your career objective, educational preparation, and related experiences. It is designed to give potential employers a clear picture of your experience and qualifications. You can send it in response to a job announcement or use it as a means of introducing yourself during an initial meeting with a prospective employer.

Once a job has been advertised, an employer may receive hundreds, if not thousands, of resumes and cover letters. Ideally, you should limit your resume to about one page, to increase the chances that it will be read. You still need to tailor it to the specific requirements of the job you are seeking, however.

Format

There is no "magic format" for a resume, yet all resumes consist of a number of specific components. These components are:

1. **Personal information:** This section of the resume includes your formal name, street address, city and state, phone number, and e-mail address.

2. **Career objective or goal:** The career objective or goal is a brief statement describing the type of position you are seeking. This information should be tailored to the position you are applying for. For example:

   - *sales associate in the men's clothing department at a major retail store*

   - *entry level record-keeping position in a physician's office*

   - *automotive specialist in hydraulics*

   - *middle school language arts teacher*

3. **Education:** In this section of the resume, you may want to include a listing of schools attended, including names, dates, and major/specialization. In addition, items such as grade point average, honors, extracurricular activities, membership in school and community clubs/organizations, and leadership positions might be included.

4. **Work experience:** In this section you should provide job titles, employer's name, address and phone number, and a brief description of the duties and responsibilities held at each place of employment.

5. **Accomplishment statements:** An accomplishment can be anything that you have done that has made a positive difference: a goal that has been achieved, a product that has been produced, a service that has been provided, or a problem that has been solved. Employers look at this section of the resume to identify unique and exemplary prospective employees. Accomplishment state-

Aaron Smith
1632 Morgan Street, Dallas, TX 76311
214/ 555-1212
ASmith@serviceprovider.com

Career Objective or Goal
A beginning position as a foreman in a construction related business.

Education
Dallas High School, Dallas, Texas, September, 1993-May 1997, Major: Vocational Education. Diploma Received - May 1997

Dallas County Community College, Dallas, Texas, September 1997 - Present, Major courses of study: Construction Technology, Graduation - A.A. Degree, June 2001

Work Experience
Newspaper carrier, <u>Dallas Star</u>, P.O. Box 12667, Dallas, Texas, 214/555-1212. Responsible for the home delivery of morning newspapers to 100 customers.

J.& L. Construction Company, 1610 S. Edmonds, St. Lewisville, Texas, 972/555-2211. Duties included general laborer work in housing industry.

Accomplishments
- Led a team of students that won the district and state prepared speech contest.

- Worked as a member of the school newspaper staff.

- Maintained a 3.3 grade point average throughout high school.

- Received the 1997 Mayor's Award for Outstanding Community Service.

References
Mr. Jack Pool, Supervisor, <u>Dallas Star</u>, P.O. Box 127, Dallas, Texas 76203 214/555-1212.

Mr. J.L. Johnson, President, J & L. Construction Company, 1601 S. Edmonds St., Lewisville, Texas 75067 972/555-2211.

Father John O'Malley, Pastor, St. Mary's Church, 123 Main St., Lewisville, Texas 75067 972/555-1122.

ments are usually one sentence in length and start with an action verb. For example:

- *served as student body president during my junior and senior years of high school*

- *organized and led a fund-raising drive to finance a state-of-the-art computer lab in my school*

- *won the John Philip Sousa Award for outstanding high school band students*

- *worked on a team that re-forested 5 acres of parkland devastated by fire*

6. **References:** References are individuals who can speak directly about your abilities, personality, and experience. References might be the school counselor, a teacher, current employer, a former employer, or a clergy member. Do not include parents, family members, or friends as references. All of the necessary information regarding references should be included in the resume, such as name, title, address, and phone number. It is always a good practice to alert an individual that his/her name has been placed as a reference in your resume.

A sample resume is provided on the left page.

Be certain that your resume looks professional. You can use a software template such as is available with Word to help you format your resume. It might also be worthwhile to employ a professional to lay out and word process your resume.

Your Cover Letter

When you send your resume in response to an ad, it should be accompanied by a brief cover letter. The cover letter is designed to open a dialogue with the prospective employer. An example is on page 328.

The Job Application

For some job openings, you may be required to fill out a job application instead of, or in addition to, providing a resume. For ease in completing job applications, you should have a copy of your resume at hand along with your driver's

Personnel Department
Acme Roofing Supply
1234 Business Park
Dallas, TX 76203-1331

To Whom It May Concern:

This letter is written in response to your advertisement in the July 12th issue of the *Dallas Star* for a yard foreman at Acme Roofing Supply. I am seeking a challenging opportunity to work my way up through the retail construction material distribution business and to some day own my own business.

I have one year of successful experience as a general laborer at J. and L. Construction Company and I am familiar with all types of building materials commonly found in the residential construction business.

Enclosed is a copy of my resume. You may reach me at 214/555-1212. I look forward to hearing from you soon.

Sincerely,

Aaron Smith
1632 Morgan St.
Dallas, TX 76311

license and social security number. Although you may be tempted to leave parts of the application form blank, this is never appropriate or acceptable. The only exception is if an application includes a question asking whether or not you have a disability. It is illegal for employers to ask this question, so you should leave it blank if they do.

Tips and Techniques for Completing a Job Application

- Read the application thoroughly. Each application is different. Be certain to pay particular attention to the information being requested.

- Complete the application honestly. Do not provide any false information, because this can be grounds for immediate dismissal. For example, if the application asks whether you currently hold a driver's license, do not mark it "yes" if you have not passed the state-licensed vehicle operators' test.

- Print clearly using blue or black ink. Do not use pencil.

- Be certain that handwriting is neat and legible. Use correct spelling. Do not misspell the names of previous employers, supervisors, schools, or references.

- Do not leave lines or sections of the application blank. If the question is not applicable, mark "N/A" (not applicable) in the space provided.

- Many applications will ask you the salary that you expect or anticipate. It is best to write "open" or "negotiable" in this section.

A sample job application is provided on pages 330-331.

The Job Interview

A job interview gives you a golden opportunity to show your best face to prospective employers. Up until this point, employers have formed a picture of you based only on your cover letter, resume, and job application. Now you will be meeting the prospective employer face-to-face. You should approach the interview as an opportunity to highlight the accomplishments, education, and work achievements outlined in your resume. In addition, the interview is your chance to find out more information about the employer and the specific position under consideration.

Before the Interview

It is critical to prepare for each and every interview individually. The following suggestions will assist you in getting ready:

1. Find out as much information about the employer and the company/business as possible. Review brochures, catalogs, or any printed material that is available. Perhaps a trip to the local library or a search on the Internet can help to serve this purpose.

2. **Practice interviewing skills.** Role play the interview process. Ask a teacher, counselor, parent, or friend to play the part of the interviewer to become comfortable with the process. Typical interview questions that the employer may ask are:

ACME ROOFING SUPPLY
Application for Employment

Personal Information

Name: Last	First	Middle	Social Security Number
Address Street	City	State Zip Code	Phone

Employment Sought

Position Sought	Date You Can Start	Salary Expectations
Are you currently employed?	If so, may we check with your present employer?	

Education

Name & Location of School	Years Attended	Date Graduated
Elementary School		
High School		
College		
Other		

General Information

Do you speak Spanish fluently?   Read?   Write?   What are your word processing/skills?
U.S. Military Service   Rank
Have you been convicted of a crime in the past 10 years? Yes___ No___ If yes, describe.
Are you willing to submit to a drug test?   Yes____ No____   If no, explain.

Physical History

| Do you have any physical conditions that prevent you from doing certain types of labor? |
| If Yes, explain. |

Have you every filed for workman's compensation? Yes___   No___
If Yes, give details

In Case of Emergency, Contact:
Name   Address   Phone Number

Employment History (List below the last four employers starting with last one first)

Date/Month/ Year	Employer Name and Address	Salary	Position	Reason for Leaving
From To				
Responsibilities				
From To				
Responsibilities				
From To				
Responsibilities				
From To				
Responsibilities				

References (Give below the names of three persons not related to you whom you have known at least one year)

Name	Address	Business	Years

I understand that misrepresentation or omission of facts is grounds for dismissal.

Signature _____   Date _____

- What are your career goals?

- Which subjects did you like best in school and why?

- Could you tell me a little bit about yourself? (Refer to your resume.)

- Why do you want to work here? (Show that you know something about the company.)

- Why did you leave your last employer?

- What are your greatest strengths and weaknesses?

- What would you like to know about this company/job? (Ask about future goals for the company, opportunities for advancement.)

- What experiences have you had that will help you with this job?

- What are your expectations for advancement?

- What type of salary are you seeking?

- Do you plan to continue your education?

- Do you have a car or access to public transportation?

- If you had a problem with one of your coworkers on the job, what would you do? (Ask a supervisor for advice or assistance.)

3. **Dress appropriately for the job interview.** This includes good hygiene (e.g., brushing teeth, washing and combing hair, taking a shower or bath, cleaning fingernails, and wearing deodorant). Be well groomed, always wear dress slacks or a skirt/dress (not too short), and a clean shirt/blouse. Do not wear jeans, shorts, sandals, or t-shirts. Do not chew gum or smoke during the interview.

4. **Anticipate the expected and the unexpected.** Before or during the interview, you may be expected to complete a standard application. Be certain to bring your driver's license, social security number, and resume. Don't forget to bring a pen or a pencil. You may be advised to be prepared to complete an employment screening test over basic skills (writing, mathematics). You should also be prepared to take a drug/alcohol screening test.

5. Arrive a few minutes early. Allow plenty of time to deal with traffic, weather conditions, or parking problems. Arrive early enough (10-15 minutes) to complete a job application before the interview. Be certain to greet the receptionist and announce your name and appointment time.

During the Interview

1. **Show enthusiasm.** Shake hands, make eye contact, and smile. Do not sit down until asked. When seated, do not slouch.

2. **Answer the interviewer's questions with more than a "yes" or "no" response.** For example, "Do you enjoy retail sales?" Instead of responding "yes," respond by saying something like "Yes, I enjoy meeting people and helping them in making their purchases."

3. **Show a positive attitude.** Demonstrate a willingness to learn new things and face new challenges. Never make a negative statement about any former coworkers or supervisors.

4. **Do not discuss salary or benefits until the job has been offered.**

5. **Finish strong.** Close the interview by standing up, maintaining eye contact, and thanking the interviewer for his or her time.

After the Interview

1. **Keep all information you were given during the interview.** This way it is available if the employer calls you back for a second interview or to offer you the job.

2. **Jot down any thoughts and feelings about the interview.** Write down your impressions of the company, the interviewer, and the job discussed. Make note of which questions or parts of the interview you found most difficult for future reference.

3. **Send a follow-up thank you note to the interviewer within 24 hours.** Thank the individual for giving you the opportunity to interview for the job. This is not frequently done by many applicants, and it might just be the action that convinces the employer that you are the right person for the job.

To Disclose or Not to Disclose

There is a long-standing debate on whether "to disclose or not to disclose" a disability when interviewing for a job. As Chapter 3 explains, the Americans with Disabilities Act (ADA) makes it illegal for a prospective employer to ask whether you have a disability. So, the decision to disclose is entirely up to you.

The ADA also makes it illegal for an employer to use a disability as the reason not to hire someone. This makes some applicants wonder what it could hurt to mention their disability during an interview. Still, employers usually turn away many qualified applicants for any given job. If an employer does reject you due to your disability, it can be difficult if not impossible to prove. For this reason, many job applicants with LD and/or AD/HD choose not to disclose their disability until after they are hired.

An alternative to disclosing a disability during the interview might be to talk in a general way about accommodations that can make you more successful. For example, you might choose to let the employer know that you may need more lead time in preparing written documents (but do a superb job when given the time!). You would not need to say that the reason for needing more lead time is that you have a specific written language learning disability.

Here are some things to consider when deciding whether to disclose or not to disclose information about yourself:

1. Are accommodations needed for you to be successful on the job? (But remember: you can always discuss these *after* you are hired.)

2. Will this disclosure help or hinder my goal?

3. What might the reactions be after the disclosure?

Job-Keeping Skills

Once you have been hired, the task becomes to keep the job that you have worked so hard to get. New employees must demonstrate good employability skills. These are often called job-keeping skills. The following are examples:

- maintaining a positive attitude,

- being on time,

- following directions,
- being productive,
- being dependable,
- working cooperatively with coworkers,
- providing good customer service,
- completing job assignments,
- taking initiative,
- solving problems,
- making decisions,
- managing work-related conflicts,
- being an honest employee,
- communicating effectively,
- following directions,
- accepting criticism.

If you have problems with any of these skills due to your disability, you will need to figure out what accommodations you need and then implement them. This does not necessarily mean disclosing your disability. In some instances, you may be able to self-accommodate. For example, if you have trouble following spoken directions, you might informally ask your supervisor to send you the instructions via internal e-mail, or ask if he or she minds jotting down the steps for you. Or if you read so slowly that you are falling behind your coworkers, you might come in to work earlier or stay later than others.

If you decide you need an accommodation that you cannot afford yourself or that you cannot use without questions being asked, you will probably need to disclose your disability. It is often best to discuss this with your immediate supervisor first. For example, you might think that installing voice output software on your computer would greatly increase your productivity. You might begin by explaining the current problems you are having with reading and explain why this software would help you. You would come prepared to explain how you would keep this from disturbing nearby coworkers (e.g., headphones), and your right to the accommodation, if necessary. See the Resource Guide for materials that can give you additional information about requesting and implementing accommodations on the job.

KEEPING A JOB IF YOU HAVE AD/HD

Any job can be boring, limiting, or even uninteresting at times. People with AD/HD, however, may have more difficulty than usual staying challenged in the workplace. Here are some tips to help you stay motivated and succeed:

- When you are on the job, remove distractions and look for ways to provide the structure and organization you need. For example, turn your desk so you cannot see other coworkers. Use calendars as described on page 278 to help you break down tasks and get them done in time.

- Learn to multitask. People with AD/HD often get bored with repetitive tasks. Having several projects going at one time can provide the stimulation and challenge necessary to be very successful. To multitask, you must be organized, creating personal deadlines on projects. Also consider breaking tasks into smaller, more manageable pieces.

- Consider the advantages of disclosing your AD/HD to the employer. This is especially important if accommodations are needed. Accommodations can provide added support when learning a new job.

Conclusion

Getting your first job can be an end in itself, or it can be a stepping stone to bigger and better things. You may find a job where you can focus on your strengths and interests, enabling you to feel fulfilled and useful. Or you may find a job that is not a good match for you—whether because you are not challenged, feel like you're in over your head, or just can't get along with coworkers or supervisors. If you do find yourself in a dead-end job or one you are simply not satisfied with, remember there are several ways out:

- You can start the job search process all over again, polish up your resume, and look for a better position.

- To get the qualifications needed for a more satisfying or challenging job, you can pursue further education, using the guidelines supplied in this book.

- You can request assistance from Vocational Rehabilitation during your job search.

In the past, many people with LD and/or AD/HD were underemployed or unemployed. Today, however, there is no reason you should not be able to succeed in the world of work. The ADA backs up your right to work and to get the accommodations you need to do the job. There are many organizations and agencies that can give you guidance, information, and support. And of course, you have increased rights to, and access to information about, attending the postsecondary programs that can help qualify you for a fulfilling job. With motivation and determination, you can get that job you want!

Resources

BOOKS

ADD in the Workplace, 1997
Author: Kathleen Nadeau
Taylor and Francis/Brunner-Mazel
47 Runway Road
Levittown, PA 19057
Phone: (800) 821-8312
Fax: (215) 785-5515
http://www.bmpub.com/fager/index.htm

A.D.D. on the Job: Making Your A.D.D. Work for You, 1996
Author: Lynn Weiss
Taylor Publishing Company
1550 Mockingbird Lane
Dallas, TX 75235
Phone: (800) 677-2800
Fax: (214) 819-8580
http://www.taylor.com

Adventures in Fast Forward: Life, Love, and Work for the ADD Adult, 1996
Author: Kathleen Nadeau
Taylor and Francis/Brunner-Mazel
47 Runway Road
Levittown, PA 19057
Phone: (800) 821-8312
Fax: (215) 785-5515
http://www.bmpub.com/fager/index.htm

The Career Discovery Project, 1993
Author: Gerald M. Sturman
Doubleday/Mainstreet Books
1540 Broadway
New York, NY 11036
Phone: (800) 223-5780
E-mail: webmaster@bdd.com
http://www.bdd.com

Career Focus: A Personal Job Search Guide, 1998
Author: Helene M. Lamarre
Prentice-Hall Publishers
P.O. Box 11071
Des Moines, IA 50336
Phone: (800) 947-7700
http://www.viacom.com

Designing the Perfect Resume, 1995
Author: Pat Criscito
Barron's/Protype Ltd.
P.O. Box 49552
Colorado Springs, CO 80949
Phone: (800) 369-2834
Fax: (609) 520-4731
E-mail: protype@compuserve

Federal Jobs: The Ultimate Guide, 2nd edition, 1997
Authors: Dana Morgan and Robert Goldenkoff
Simon & Schuster
200 Old Tappan Road
Old Tappan, NJ 07675
Phone: (800) 223-2336
Fax: (800) 445-6991
http://www.simonsays.com

First Job Survival Guide, 1997
Author: Andrea J. Sutcliffe
Henry Holt & Company
115 West 18th St.
New York, NY 10111
Phone: (800) 488-5233

How to Find the Work You Love, 1996
Author: Lawrence G. Boldt
Arkana Books/Penguin Books
Phone: (800) 363-2665

***How to Provide Accommodations for Students with Learning Disabilities:
Creating Employment Opportunities***, 1994
Author: Martha Wille Gregory
Creating Employment Opportunities Project
Center for Innovations in Special Education
Parkade Center, Suite 152
601 Business Loop 70 West
Columbia, MO 65211
Phone: (573) 884-7275
E-mail: mocise@muccmail.missouri.edu
http://www.coe.missouri.edu/~mocise

Interview Strategies That Will Get You the Job You Want, 1996
Author: Andrea Kay
Betterway Books/F & W Publishing
1507 Dana Avenue
Cincinnati, OH
Phone: (800) 289-0963

Job Hunting Tips for the So-Called Handicapped or People Who Have Disabilities: A Supplement to What Color is Your Parachute?, 1992
Author: Richard Nelson Bolles
Ten Speed Press
P.O. Box 7123
Berkeley, CA 94707
Phone: (800) 841-2665
Fax: (510) 559-1629
E-mail: order@tenspeed.com
http://www.tenspeedpress.com

***Learning a Living: A Guide to Planning Your Career and Finding a Job for
People with LD, ADD, and Dyslexia***, 2000
Author: Dale S. Brown
Woodbine House
6510 Bells Mill Road
Bethesda, MD 20817

Phone: (800) 843-7323
Fax: (301) 897-5838
E-mail: info@woodbinehouse.com
http://www.woodbinehouse.com

Learning Disabilities and Employment, 1997
Editors: Paul Gerber and Dale Brown
Pro-Ed
8700 Shoal Creek Blvd.
Austin, TX 78757-6897
Phone: (800) 897-3202
Fax: (800) 397-7633
http://www.proedinc.com

Learning Disabilities and the Workplace, 1993
Author: E.S. Reisman
Learning Disabilities Association
4156 Library Road
Pittsburgh, PA 15234-1349
Phone: (412) 341-1515
Fax: (412) 344-0224
E-mail: ldanatl@usaor.net
http://www.ldanatl.org

The O*Net Dictionary of Occupational Titles
Department of Labor
Employment and Training Administration Superintendent of Documents
Government Printing Office
Washington, DC 20402
Phone: (202) 512-1800
Fax: (202) 512-2250
E-mail: wwwadmin@www.access.gpo.gov
http://www.access.gpo.gov

Resumes in Cyberspace: A Complete Guide to a Computerized Job Search, 1997
Author: Pat Criscito
Barron's/Protype Ltd.
P.O. Box 49552
Colorado Springs, CO 80949
E-mail: protype@compuserve.com

Revised Handbook for Analyzing Jobs, 1991
Materials Development Center
Stout Vocational Rehabilitation Institute University of Wisconsin-Stout
Menomonie, WI 54751
Phone: (715) 232-1342
E-mail: botterbuschd@uwstout.edu

Succeeding in the Workplace: A Guide for Success (ADD and LD), 1994
Authors: Patricia and Peter Latham
Learning Disabilities Association
4156 Library Road
Pittsburgh, PA 15234-1349
Phone: (412) 341-1515
Fax: (412) 344-0224
E-mail: ldanatl@usaor.net
http://www.ldanatl.org

Successful Job Search Strategies for the Disabled: Understanding the ADA, 1994
Author: Jeffrey Allen
John Wiley & Sons
605 Third Avenue
New York, NY 10158-0012
Phone: (212) 850-6000
Fax: (212) 850-6088
E-mail: info@wiley.com
http://www.wiley.com

Summer Jobs: Test Driving Life While Smoothing the Road to College, 1998
Author: Charlotte Thomas
Peterson's Guides
P.O. Box 2123
Princeton, NJ 08543-2123
Phone: (800) 225-0261
Fax: (609) 243-9150
E-mail: custsvc@pgi.petersons.com
http://www.petersons.com

Transition to Employment, 1998
Author: Craig Michaels
Pro-Ed
8700 Shoal Creek Blvd.

Austin, TX 78757-6897

Phone: (800) 897-3202

Fax: (800) 397-7633

http://www.proedinc.com

What Color Is Your Parachute? A Practical Manual for Job Hunting and Career Changes, annual

Author: Richard Nelson Bolles

Ten Speed Press

P.O. Box 7123

Berkeley, CA 94707

Phone: (800) 841-2665

Fax: (510) 559-1629

E-mail: order@tenspeed.com

http://www.tenspeedpress.com

Work and Disability: Issues and Strategies in Career Development and Job Placement, 1996

Authors: Edna Szymanski and Randall Parker

Pro-Ed

8700 Shoal Creek Blvd.

Austin, TX 78757-6897

Phone: (800) 897-3202

Fax: (800) 397-7633

http://www.proedinc.com

Working Together: Workplace Culture, Supported Employment, and Persons with Disabilities, 1993

Author: David Hagner and Dale Dileo

Brookline Books/Lumen Editions

P.O. Box 1047

Cambridge, MA 02238

Phone: (800) 666-2665

Fax: (617) 868-1772

E-mail: BROOKLINEBKS@delphi.com

http://people.delphi.com/brooklinebks/brooklin.htm

VIDEOS

The Employment Interview and Disclosure: Tips for Job Seekers with Learning Disabilities, 1997

Learning Disabilities Association

4156 Library Road
Pittsburgh, PA 15234-1349
Phone: (412) 341-1515
Fax: (412) 344-0224
E-mail: ldanatl@usaor.net
http://www.ldanatl.org

Interviewing Skills for Job Candidates with Learning or Other Hidden Disabilities
Program Development Associates
P.O. Box 2038
Syracuse, NY 13220
Phone: (800) 543-2119
Fax: (315) 452-0710
http://www.pdassoc.com

PAMPHLETS
The Americans with Disabilities Act (ADA) and Working
Office of Public Information
Employment and Training Administration
See address above.

The Bottom Line: Basic Skills in the Workplace
Office of Public Information
Employment and Training Administration
U.S. Department of Labor
200 Constitution Ave., NW
Room 52307
Washington, DC 20210
Phone: (202) 219-6871

Linkages — Workplace Literacy: Employment Issues for the Adult Learner with Learning Disabilities
National Adult Literacy and Learning Disabilities Center (ALLD)
1875 Connecticut Ave., NW
Washington, DC 20009-1202
Phone: (800) 953-2553
Fax: (202) 884-8422
E-mail: info@nalldc.aed.org
http://www.ld-read.org
(go to publications)

Working! A Guide for Young Adults
Author: Brynda Shore Fraser, 1992
National Institute for Work and Learning
Academy for Educational Development
1825 Connecticut Avenue, NW
Washington, DC 20009-5721
Phone: (202) 884-8186
Fax: (202) 884-8422
E-mail: NIWL@aed.org
http://www.niwl.org

SOFTWARE

Program for Assessing Your Employability
Educational Testing Services
Rosedale Road
Princeton, NJ 08541
Phone: (609) 921-9000
Fax: (609) 734-5413
E-mail: etsinfo@ets.org
http://www.ets.org

WEBSITES

America's Job Bank
For job seekers and employers, this site offers job announcements, talent banks, and information about getting a job.
http://www.ajb.dni.us

Career Connections
In addition to job announcements and an online application, this site also has "cyber-job fairs."
http://www.career.com

Finding Your Career: The Holland Interest Inventory
This is a very comprehensive site, including information on self-assessment of skills and matching them to a career.
http://icpac.indiana.edu/infoseries/is-50.html

On-line Career Resources
This site has numerous resources for successfully getting a job: assessment tools, helpful information, tutorials, labor market information, links, etc.
http://www.jobhunt.org/career.html

O*Net: The Department of Labor's Occupational Information Network

This site has useful information as well as numerous links to government resources. Great for job hunters, employers, and teachers.

http://www.doleta.gov/programs/onet

Peterson's Education & Career Center

This site has helpful articles and helpful links. There are postings for full- and part-time jobs, as well as summer job opportunities.

http://www.petersons.com

Yellow Pages

This site is helpful for gathering contact information while researching possible job paths.

http://www.switchboard.com

ORGANIZATIONS

Contact information for the following useful organizations can be found beginning on page 347.

- American Congress of Community Supports & Employment Services

- American Guidance Services (AGS)

- Americans with Disabilities Act (ADA) Technical Assistance Information Line

- Association for Career and Technical Education (ACTE), *formerly American Vocational Association (AVA)*

- Attention Deficit Information Network (Ad-IN)

- Center on Education for Training and Employment

- Center on Education and Work

- Children and Adults with Attention-Deficit/Hyperactivity Disorder (CHADD)

- Clearinghouse on Disability Information

- Council for Adult and Experiential Learning (CAEL)

- Employment and Training Administration

- General Education Development (GED)

- Internet Special Education Resources

- JIST Works, Inc.

- Job Accommodation Network

- National Alliance of Business (NAB)

- National Association of Vocation and Education Special Needs Personnel (NAVESNP)

- National Attention Deficit Disorder Association (National ADDA)

- National Center for the Study of Postsecondary Educational Supports, Rehabilitation Research & Training Center (RRTC)

- National Institute for Work and Learning

- Office for Civil Rights National Office

- Office on the Americans with Disabilities Act

- President's Committee on Employing People with Disabilities

- Presidential Task Force on Employment of Adults with Disabilities

- Regional Disability and Business Accommodation Centers

- Social Security Administration

RESOURCES

Businesses, Organizations, and Government Offices

Academy for Educational Development
1875 Connecticut Ave., NW
Washington, DC 20009-1202
Phone: (800) 953-2553
Fax: (202) 884-8400
E-mail: admin@aed.org
http://www.aed.org

ACT, Inc.
(American College Testing)
P.O. Box 168
2201 North Dodge Street
Iowa City, IA 52243-0168
Phone: (319) 337-1000
http://www.act.org

Alexander Graham Bell Association for the Deaf and Hard of Hearing
3417 Volta Place, NW
Washington, DC 20007-2778
Phone: (202) 337-5220
http://www.agbell.org

American Association for Adult and Continuing Education (AAACE)
1200 19th Street, NW, Suite 300
Washington, DC 20036-2422
Phone: (202) 429-5131
Fax: (202) 223-4579
http://www.albany.edu/aaace

American Association of State Colleges and Universities
1307 New York Ave, NW
Suite 500
Washington, DC 20005
Phone: (202) 293-7070
Fax: (202) 296-5819
http://www.aascu.org

American Association of the Deaf-Blind
814 Thayer Ave., #302
Silver Spring, MD 20910,
Phone: (800) 735-2258
Fax: (301) 588-8705
http://www.tr.wosc.osshe.edu/DBLINK/aadb.htm

American Association of University Affiliated Programs for Persons with Developmental Disabilities
8630 Fenton St., #410
Silver Spring, MD 20910
Phone: (301) 588-8252
http://www.aauap.org

American Coaching Association
P.O. Box 353
Lafayette Hill, PA 19444
Phone: (610) 825-4505
Fax: (610) 825-4505
E-mail: 75471.3101@compuserve.com
http://www.americoach.com

American Congress of Community Supports & Employment Services
1875 Eye Street, NW - Twelfth Floor
Washington, D.C. 20006
Phone: (888) 285-4742
http://accses.firminc.com

American Council of the Blind
1155 15th St. NW, Suite 720
Washington, DC 20005
Phone: (800) 424-8666
Fax: (202) 467-5085
http://www.acb.org

American Council on Education (ACE)
1 Dupont Circle, NW
Suite 800
Washington, DC 20036
Phone: (202) 939-9300

E-mail: web@ace.nche.edu
http://www.acenet.edu

American Foundation for the Blind
11 Penn Plaza, Suite 300
New York, NY 10001
Phone: (800) 232-5463
Fax: (212) 502-7662
E-mail: afbinfo@afb.org
http://www.afb.org/afb

American Guidance Services (AGS)
4201 Woodland Road
P.O. Box 99
Circle Pines, MN 55014-1796
Phone: (800) 328-2560
Fax: (800) 471-8457
E-mail: agsmail@agsnet.com
http://www.agsnet.com

American Printing House for the Blind
P.O. Box 6085
Louisville, KY 40206
Phone: (800) 223-1839
Fax: (502) 899-2284
E-mail: sales@aph.org
E-mail: info@aph.org
http://www.aph.org

American Psychiatric Association
1400 K. St., NW
11th Floor
Washington, DC 20005
Phone: (800) 368-5777
Fax: (202) 682-6850
E-mail: apa@psych.org
http://www.psych.org/main.html

American Speech, Language, Hearing Association
10801 Rockville Pike
Rockville, MD 20852
Phone: (800) 498-2071
Fax: (301) 571-0457
E-mail: actioncenter@asha.org
http://www.asha.org

Americans with Disabilities Act (ADA)
Technical Assistance Information Line

Phone: (800) 949-4232
Spanish translation available
E-mail: adainfo@transcen.org

Apple Computer, Inc.
Worldwide Disability Solutions Group
One Infinite Loop, M-S 38-DS
Cupertino, CA 95014
Phone: (800) 800-2775 (APPL)
http://www.apple.com/disability/default.htm

The Arc
500 E. Border St., Suite 300
P.O. Box 1047
Arlington, TX 76010
Phone: (800) 433-5255
Fax: (817) 277-3491
E-mail: thearc@metronet.com
http://www.TheArc.org/welcome.html

Association for Career and Technical Education (ACTE),
formerly American Vocational Association (AVA)
1410 King Street
Alexandria, VA 22314
Phone: (800) 826-9972
E-mail: avahq@acteonline.org
http://www.acteonline.org

Association for Childhood Education International (ACEI)
17904 Georgia Ave., Suite 215
Olney, MD 20832
Phone: (800) 423-3563
E-mail: aceihq@aol.com
http://www.udel.edu/bateman/acei

Association for the Advancement of Rehabilitation Technology (RESNA)
1700 North Moore Street, #1540
Arlington, VA 22209
Phone: (703) 524-6686
Fax: (703) 524-6630
E-mail: nationaloffice@resna.org
http://www.resna.org

Association for Persons with Severe Handicaps (TASH)
29 W. Susquehanna Ave., #210
Baltimore, MD 21204
Phone: (410) 828-1306
Fax: (410) 828-6706

E-mail: info@tash.org
http://www.tash.org

Association on Higher Education and Disability (AHEAD)
P.O. Box 21192
Columbus, OH 43221-0192
Phone: (614) 488-4972
Fax: (614) 488-1174
E-mail: ahead@postbox.acs.ohio-state.edu
http://www.ahead.org

Association of Specialized and Cooperative Library Agencies (ASCLA)
American Library Association (ALA)
50 Huron Street
Chicago, IL 60611
Phone: (800) 545-2433
Fax: (312) 440-9374
http://www.ala.org

American Vocational Association (AVA)
See Association for Career and Technical Education (ACTE)

ATP Services for Handicapped Students
CN6400
Princeton, NJ 08541-6400
Phone: (609) 734-5350

Attention Deficit Information Network (Ad-IN)
475 Hillside Avenue
Needham, MA 02194
Phone: (617) 455-9895

Auditory-Verbal International
2121 Eisenhower Ave.,
Suite 402
Alexandria, VA 22314
Phone: (703) 739-1049
Fax: (703) 739-0395
E-mail: avi@auditory-verbal.org
http://www.auditory-verbal.org

Beach Center on Families and Disability
3111 Haworth Hall
University of Kansas
Lawrence, KA 66045
Phone: (785) 864-7600
Fax: (785) 864-7605
E-mail: beach@dole.lsi.ukans.edu
http://www.lsi.ukans.edu/beach/beachhp.htm

Braille Institute of America
741 N. Vermont Ave.
Los Angeles, CA 90029
Phone: (213) 663-1111
http://www.brailleinstitute.org

Bytes of Learning
Phone: (800) 465-6428
E-mail: custservice@bytesoflearning.com
http://www.bytesoflearning.com

CCWAVES: Commission on Certification of Work Adjustment and Vocational Evaluation Specialists
1444 I St., NW, Suite 700
Washington, DC 20005-2210
Phone: (202) 712-9044
Fax: (202) 216-9646
E-mail: info@ccwaves.org
http://www.ccwaves.org

Center for Applied Special Technology (CAST)
39 Cross Street
Peabody, MA 01960
Phone: (978) 531-8555
Fax: (978) 531-0192
E-mail: cast@cast.org
http://www.cast.org

Center for Innovations in Special Education
University of Missouri-Columbia
Parkade Center, Suite 152
601 Business Loop 70 West
Columbia, MO 65211-8020
Phone: (573) 884-7275

Center for Mental Health Services
Office of Consumer, Family, and Public Information
5600 Fishers Lane, Room 15-105
Rockville, MD 20857
Phone: (800) 789-2647
E-mail: ken@mentalhealth.org
http://www.mentalhealth.org

Center on Education and Work
University of Wisconsin-Madison
321 Educational Science Building
1025 West Johnson Street
Madison, WI, 53706
Phone: (608) 263-3415

Center on Education for Training and Employment
Ohio State University
1960 Kenny Road
Columbus, OH 43210
Phone: (800) 848-4815
http://www.osu.edu/units/ucomm/points/edutrain.html

Children and Adults with Attention-Deficit/Hyperactivity Disorder (CHADD)
8181 Professional Place, Suite 201
Landover, MD 20785
Phone: (800) 233-4050
Fax: (301) 306-7090
E-mail: national@chadd.org
http://www.chadd.org

Clearinghouse on Adult Education
Division of Adult Education
Office of Vocational and Adult Education
U.S. Department of Education
Switzer Building
330 C St., SW
Washington, DC 20202
Phone: (800) 227-0216

Clearinghouse on Disability Information
Office of Special Education and Rehabilitative Services (OSERS)
U.S. Department of Education
Switzer Building
330 C. St., SW
Washington, DC 20202-2524
Phone: (202) 205-8241
http://www.ed.gov/OFFICES/OSERS

Closing the Gap
526 Main St.
Henderson, MN 56044
Phone: (507) 248-3294
Fax: (507) 248-3810
E-mail: info@closingthegap.com
http://www.closingthegap.com

Council for Adult and Experiential Learning (CAEL)
10840 Little Patuxent Parkway
Suite 203
Columbia, Maryland 21044

Council for Exceptional Children
1920 Association Drive

Reston, VA 22091
Phone: (800) CEC-SPED
Fax: (703) 620-3660
http://www.cec.sped.org

Council of Administrators of Special Education
615 16th St., NW
Albuquerque, NM 87104
Phone: (505) 243-7622

Council on Learning Disabilities
P.O. Box 40303
Overland Park, KS 66204
Phone: (913) 492-8775
Fax: (913) 492-2546
http://www1.winthrop.edu/cld

Disability Rights Education and Defense Fund (DREDF)
2212 6th St.
Berkeley, CA 94710
Phone: (800) 466-4232
Fax: (510) 841-8645
E-mail:dredf@dredf.org
http://www.dredf.org

Disabilities Studies and Resource Center
1825 Connecticut Avenue, NW
Washington, DC 20009
Phone: (202) 884-8200
http://www.dssc.org

Dragon Systems, Inc.
320 Nevada Street
Newton, MA 02160
Phone: (800) 437-2466
E-mail: info@dragonsys.com
http://www.dragonsys.com

Education Development Center, Inc.
55 Chapel Street
Newton, Massachusetts 02158-1060
Phone: (617) 969-7100
http://www.edc.org

Educational Testing Service, Inc.
Rosedale Road
Princeton, NJ 08541
Phone: (609) 921-9000

Fax: (609) 734-5413
E-mail: etsinfo@ets.org
http://www.ets.org

Employment and Training Administration
Office of Public Affairs
U.S. Department of Labor
200 Constitution Ave., NW
Room S4206
Washington, DC 20210
Phone: (202) 219-6871

ERIC Clearinghouse on Assessment & Evaluation
College of Library and Information Services
University of Maryland-College Park
1129 Shriver Laboratory
College Park, MD 20742
Phone: (800) 464-3742
Fax: (301) 405-7449
http://ericae.net

ERIC Clearinghouse on Disability & Gifted Education
1920 Association Drive
Reston, VA 22091
Phone: (703) 620-3660
Fax: (703) 264-9494
http://www.cec.sped.org/ericec.htm

The Federal Resource Center for Special Education
Academy for Educational Development
1875 Connecticut Avenue NW, Suite 900
Washington, DC 20009
Phone: (202) 884-8215
Fax: (202) 884-8443
E-mail: frc@aed.org
http://www.dssc.org/frc

Federal Student Aid Information Center
P.O. Box 84
Washington, DC 20044
Phone: (800) 433-3243
http://www.ed.gov/finaid.html

General Education Development (GED)
GED Fulfillment Service
P.O. Box 261
Annapolis Junction, MD 20701
Phone: (800) 626-9433

E-mail: ged@ace.nche.edu
http://www.acenet.edu/calec/ged/home.html

Higher Education And The Handicapped (HEATH) Resource Center
One Dupont Circle, Suite 800
Washington, DC 20036-1193
Phone: (800) 544-3284
Fax: (202) 833-4760
E-mail: heath@ace.nche.edu
http://www.acenet.edu/About/programs/Acess&Equity/HEATH

IBM
Dept. YES98
P.O. Box 2690
Atlanta, GA 30301
Phone: (888) 411-1932
Fax: (800) 242-6329
E-mail: E-mailibm_direct@vnet.ibm.com
http://www.software.ibm.com

Independent Living Research Utilization Program (ILRUP)
2323 South Shepherd, #1000
Houston, TX 77019
Phone: (713) 797-0200
Fax: (713) 520-5785
E-mail: ilru@ilru.org
http://www.ilru.org

The International Dyslexia Association
8600 LaSalle Road
Chester Building, Suite 382
Baltimore, MD 21286-2044
Phone: (800) 222-3123
Fax: (410) 321-5069
http://www.interdys.org

International Reading Association
800 Barksdale Road
P.O. Box 8139
Newark, DE 19714-8139
Phone: (302) 731-1600
Fax: (302) 731-1057
E-mail: pubinfo@reading.org
http://www.reading.org

International Society for Technology in Education (ISTE)
1787 Agate St.
Eugene, OR 97403-1923

Phone: (800) 336-5191
Fax: (541) 302-3778
http://www.iste.org

Internet Special Education Resources
1723 Marshall Court
Los Altos, CA 94024
Phone: (800) 657-9833
http://www.iser.com

JIST Works, Inc.
720 North Park Avenue
Indianapolis, IN 46202-3490
Phone: (800) 648-5478
E-mail: Jistmktg@aol.com
http://www.jist.com

Job Accommodation Network
West Virginia University
P.O. Box 6080
Morgantown, WV 26506-6080
Phone: (800) 526-7234
E-mail: jan@jan.icdi.wvu.edu
http://janweb.icdi.wvu.edu

Kurzweil Educational Systems Group
Lernout & Hauspie Speech Products
52 Third Avenue
Burlington, MA 01803
Phone: (781) 203-5000
Fax: (781) 238-0986
E-mail: education.info@lhsl.com
http://www.lhsl.com/education

Learning Disabilities Association of America (LDA)
4156 Library Road
Pittsburgh, PA 15234-1349
Phone: (412) 341-1515
Fax: (412) 344-0224
E-mail: ldanatl@usaor.net
http://www.ldanatl.org

National Alliance for the Mentally Ill (NAMI)
200 North Glebe Road, #1015
Arlington, VA 22203-3754
Phone: (800) 950-6264
Fax: (703) 524-9094
http://www.nami.org

National Association for Adults with Learning Difficulties (NAALD)
P.O. Box 716
Bryn Mawr, PA 19010
Phone: (610) 525-8336
Fax: (610) 525-8337

National Alliance of Business (NAB)
1201 New York Avenue, NW
Suite 700
Washington, DC 20005-6143
Phone: (202) 289-2888
E-mail: info@nab.com
http://www.nab.com

National Association of Private Schools for Exceptional Children (NAPSEC)
1522 K Street, NW, Suite 1032
Washington, DC 20005
Phone: (202) 408-3338
E-mail: napsec@aol.com
http://www.napsec.com

National Association of School Psychologists
4340 East-West Highway, #402
Bethesda, MD 20814
Phone: (301) 657-0270
Fax: (301) 657-0275
http://www.naspweb.org

National Association of Vocation and Education Special Needs Personnel (NAVESNP)
Special Needs Division
Association for Career and Technical Education (ACTE)
1410 King Street
Alexandria, VA 22314
Phone: (800) 826-9972
Fax: (703) 683-7424
E-mail: avahq@avaonline.org
http://www.avaonline.org

National Attention Deficit Disorder Association (National ADDA)
P.O. Box 1303
Northbrook, IL 60065-1303
Phone: (800) 487-2282
E-mail: mail@add.org
http://www.add.org

National Braille Press
88 St. Stephen Street

Boston, MA 02115
Phone: (800) 548-7323
Fax: (617) 437-0456
E-mail: orders@ngp.org
http://www.npb.org

National Center for Learning Disabilities (NCLD)
381 Park Avenue South, #1401
New York, NY 10016
Phone: (888) 575-7373
Fax: (212) 545-9665
http://www.ncld.org

National Center for Research in Vocational Education
University of Illinois
Education Building, Room 345
1310 S. Sixth Street
Champaign, IL 61820,
Phone: (800) 762-4093
Fax: (217) 244-5632

National Center for the Study of Postsecondary Educational Supports, Rehabilitation Research & Training Center (RRTC)
University of Hawaii at Manoa
1776 University Avenue, UA 4-6
Honolulu, HI 96822
E-mail: CDs@hawaii.edu
http://www.rrtc.hawaii.edu

National Clearinghouse of Rehabilitation Training Materials (NCHRTM)
Oklahoma State University
5205 N. Richmond Hill Drive
Stillwater, OK 74078-4080
Phone: (800) 223-5219
Fax: (405) 624-0695
http://www.nchrtm.okstate.edu

National Council on Disability
800 Independence Ave., SW, #814
Washington, DC 20591
Phone: (202) 267-3846
http://www.ncd.gov

National Information Center for Children and Youth with Disabilities
See NICHCY

National Institute for Literacy Hotline
800 Connecticut Avenue, NW

Suite 200
Washington, DC 20006
Phone: (800) 228-8813
http://novel.nifl.gov

The National Institute on Disability and Rehabilitation Research (NIDRR)
Office of Special Education and Rehabilitation Services
U.S. Department of Education
Switzer Building
330 C St., SW
Washington, DC 20202-2524
Phone: (800) 872-5327
http://www.ed.gov/offices/OSERS/NIDRR

National Institute for Work and Learning
Academy for Educational Development
1825 Connecticut Avenue, NW
Washington, DC 20009-5721
Phone: (202) 884-8186
Fax: (202) 884-8422
E-mail: NIWL@aed.org
http://www.niwl.org

National Joint Committee on Learning Disabilities
c/o Stan Dublinske
10801 Rockville Pike
Rockville, MD 20852
http://www.ldonline.org/njcld

National Library Service for the Blind and Physically Handicapped (NLS)
Library of Congress
Washington, DC 20542
Phone: (800) 424-8567
E-mail: nls@loc.gov
http://www.loc.gov/nls

National Mental Health Association
1021 Prince Street
Alexandria, VA 22314-2971
Phone: (800) 969-6642
E-mail: namiofc@aol.com
http://www.cais.com/vikings/nami/index

National Occupational Information Coordinating Committee (NOICC)
2100 M St., NW, #156
Washington, DC 20037
Phone: (202) 653-5665
E-mail: noicc@dol.gov
http://www.noicc.gov

National Office Technology Access Center
2175 E. Francisco Blvd.
Suite L
San Rafael, CA 94901
Phone: (415) 455-4575
Fax: (415) 455-0654
E-mail: ATAinfo@ATAccess.org
http://www.ATAccess.org

National Organization on Disability
910 16th Street, NW, #600
Washington, DC 20006
Phone: (202) 293-5960
Fax: (202) 293-7999
E-mail: ability@nod.org
http://www.nod.org

National Parent Network on Disabilities
1730 17th Street, NW
Suite 400
Washington, DC 20036
Phone: (202) 463-2299
Fax: (202) 638-0509
E-mail: npnd@cs.com
http://www.npnd.org

National Parent to Parent Support
and Information Service (NPPSIS)
P.O. Box 907
Blue Ridge, GA 30513
Phone: (800) 651-1151
E-mail: nppsis@ellijay.com
http://www.nppsis.org

National Rehabilitation Information Center (NARIC)
8455 Colesville Road., Suite 935
Silver Spring, MD 20910-3319
Phone: (800) 346-2742
Fax: (301) 587-1967
E-mail: naric@capacess.org
http://www.naric.com/naric

National School-to-Work Learning & Information Center
400 Virginia Avenue, SW
Room 210
Washington, DC 20024
Phone: (800) 251-7236
E-mail: stw-lc@ed.gov
http://www.stw.ed.gov

National Transition Alliance for Youth with Disabilities
Transition Research Institute
University of Illinois
113 Children's Research Center
51 Gerty Drive
Champaign, IL 61820
Phone: (217) 333-2325
E-mail: nta@aed.org
http://www.dssc.org/nta/html/index_2.htm

NICHCY (National Information Center for Children and Youth with Disabilities)
P.O. Box 1492
Washington, DC 20013
Phone: (800) 695-0285
Fax: (202) 884-8441
E-mail: nichcy@aed.org
http://www.nichcy.org

NIMH Public Inquiries
5600 Fishers Lane
Room 7C-02, MSC 8030
Bethesda, MD 20892-8030
E-mail: nimhinfo@nih.gov
http://www.nimh.nih.gov/home.htm

Office for Civil Rights - National Office
U.S. Department of Education, Room # 5000
400 Maryland Avenue, SW
Washington, DC 20202
Phone: (800) 421-3481
Fax: (202) 205-9862
E-mail: OCR@ED.Gov
http://www.ed.gov/offices/OCR

Office of Special Education & Rehabilitative Services (OSERS)
U.S. Department of Education
400 Maryland Avenue, SW
Washington, DC 20202
Phone: (800) 872-5327
E-mail: CustomerService@inet.ed.gov
http://www.ed.gov/offices/OSERS

Office of Special Education Programs (OSEP)
Office of Special Education and Rehabilitative Services (OSERS)
U.S. Department of Education
400 Maryland Avenue, SW
Washington, DC 20202
Phone: (800) 872-5327

E-mail: CustomerService@inet.ed.gov
http://www.ed.gov/offices/OSERS/OSEP

Office on the Americans with Disabilities Act
Civil Rights Division
U.S. Department of Justice
P.O. Box 66118
Washington, DC 20035-6118
Phone: (202) 514-0301

PACER Center
4826 Chicago Avenue, South
Minneapolis, MN 55417-1098
Phone: (888) 248-0822
Fax: (612) 827-3065
E-mail: webster@pacer.org
http://www.pacer.org

People First International
P.O. Box 12642
Salem, OR 97309
Phone: (503) 362-0336
Fax: (503)585-0287
E-mail: people1@open.org
http://www.open.org/~people1

President's Committee on Employment of People with Disabilities
1331 F Street, NW, 3rd floor
Washington, DC 20004
Phone: (202) 376-6200
E-mail: info@pcepd.gov
http://www.pcepd.gov

Presidential Task Force on Employment of Adults with Disabilities
U.S. Department of Labor
200 Constitution Avenue, NW, #S-2220D
Washington, DC 20210
Phone: (202) 693-4939
E-mail: ptfead@dol.gov.
http://www.dol.gov/dol/_sec/public/
programs/ptfead/main.htm

Recording for the Blind and Dyslexic (RFB&D)
20 Roszel Road
Princeton, NJ 08540
Phone: (800) 221-4792
E-mail: custserv@rfbd.org
http://www.rfbd.org

Regional Disability and Business Accommodation Centers
Phone: (800) 949-4232
This automatically connects you to your regional office.

Rehabilitation and Disability Services/ABLEDATA
8401 Colesville Road, #200
Silver Spring, MD 20910
Phone: (800) 227-0216
Fax: (301) 608-8958
http://www.abledata.com

The Rehabilitation Resource Center
Stout Vocational Rehabilitation Institute
University of Wisconsin-Stout
Menomonie, WI 54751-0790
Phone: (715) 232-1342

Rehabilitation Services Administration
U.S. Department of Education
400 Maryland Avenue, SW
Washington, DC 20202
Phone: (800) 872-5327
E-mail: CustomerService@inet.ed.gov
http://www.ed.gov/offices/OSERS/OSEP

RESNA. *See* Association for the Advancement of Rehabilitation Technology (RESNA)

Roads To Learning
The Public Libraries' Learning Disabilities Initiative
50 East Huron Street
Chicago, Illinois 60611
Phone: (800) 545-2433, ex. 4027
Fax: (312) 944-8085
http://www.ala.org/roads/basics.html

Roger Wagner Publishers
Phone: (800) 497-3778

SHHH: Self Help for Hard of Hearing People
7910 Woodmont Ave., #1200
Bethesda, MD 20814
Phone: (301) 657-2248
Fax: (301) 913-9413
E-mail: National@shhh.org
http://www.shhh.org

Social Security Administration
Office of Public Inquiries

6401 Security Blvd.
Room 4-C-5 Annex
Baltimore, MD 21235-6401
Phone: (800) 772-1213
http://www.ssa.gov

TASH - Disability Advocacy Worldwide
29 West Susquehanna Avenue, #210
Baltimore, MD 21204
Phone: (800) 482-TASH
Fax: (410) 828-6706
http://www.tash.org

Technical Assistance Alliance for Parent Programs
PACER Center
4826 Chicago Avenue, South
Minneapolis, MN 55417-1098
Phone: (888) 248-0822
Fax: (612) 827-3065
E-mail: alliance@taalliance.org

Technical Assistance on Training about the Rehabilitation Act (TATRA),
PACER Center
4826 Chicago Avenue South
Minneapolis, MN 55417-1098
Phone: (612) 827-2966
Fax: (612) 827-3065
http://www.pacer.org/tatra/tatra.htm

U.S. Department of Education
400 Maryland Avenue, SW
Washington, DC 20202-0498
Phone: (800) USA-LEARN
E-mail: CustomerService@inet.ed.gov
http://www.ed.gov
To order publications:
ED Pubs
P.O. Box 1398
Jessup, MD 20794-1398
Phone: (877) 4-ED-PUBS
Fax: (301) 470-1244
http://www.ed.gov/pubs/edpubs.htm

Vocational Evaluation and Work Adjustment Association (VEWAA)
202 E. Cheyenne Mountain Blvd.
Suite N
Colorado Springs, CO 80906
Phone: (719) 527-1800

Fax: (719) 576-1818
http://www.vewaa.org

YMCA of the USA
101 North Wacker Drive
Chicago, IL 60606
Phone: (312) 977-0031
Fax: (312) 977-9063
http://www.ymca.net/findy/findyoury.htm

CONTRIBUTORS

Denise Bello, M.A., Projector Director, Department of Teacher Preparation and Special Education, George Washington University, Washington, DC

Arden Boyer-Stephens, Student Services Coordinator, Colombia Area Career Center, Colombia, Missouri

Joanne Cashman, Ed.D., Director, The Policymaker Partnership, National Association of State Directors of Special Education, Alexandria, VA

Stephanie Corbey, Special Education Director, Burnsville/Eagan/Savage School District, Eagan, MN

Jeanne Embich. Ed.D., Projector Director, Department of Teacher Preparation and Special Education, George Washington University, Washington, DC

Arline Halper, Ed.D., University of California, Los Angeles, Learning Disabilities Program Coordinator, Office for Students with Disabilities, Los Angeles, CA

Jordan Knab, Ed. S., Project Director, Disabilities Studies and Services Center, Academy for Educational Development, Washington, DC

Carol Kochhar-Bryant, Ed.D., Professor of Special Education, Department of Teacher Preparation and Special Education, George Washington University, Washington, DC

Pamela Leconte, Ed.D., Professor of Special Education, Department of Teacher Preparation and Special Education, George Washington University, Washington, DC

David Malouf, Ph.D., Senior Research Analyst, U.S. Department of Education, Office of Special Education and Rehabilitation Services, Washington, DC

Robert Rahamin, Ed.D., Associate Professor of Special Education, Delaware State University, Dover, DE

Ginny Salus, Ed.D., Assistant Professor, College of Education, Lynn University, Boca Raton, FL

Michelle Sarkees-Wircenski, Ph.D., Professor, Department of Applied Technology, Training and Development, University of North Texas, Denton, Texas

Stefanie Coale Silvers, Ed.S., Special Education Teacher, Arlington County Public Schools, Arlington, VA

John Staba, M. A., K - 12 Special Educator, Secondary School Life Skills Teacher & Coordinator, Minneapolis Public School District, Minneapolis, MN

Madeline Sullivan, M.A, K-12 Special Educator, Washington

Susan Sussman, M.Ed., Director, American Coaching Association, Lafayette Hill, PA

Juliana Taymans, Ph.D., Professor of Special Education, Department of Teacher Preparation and Special Education, George Washington University, Washington, DC

Mary Beth Turanchik, special education teacher, Fairfax (VA) County Public Schools

Michael Ward, Ph.D., Director, National Center on Self-Determination and 21st Century Leadership, Oregon Health Sciences University, Portland, OR

Lynda West, Ph.D., Professor of Special Education, Department of Teacher Preparation and Special Education, George Washington University, Washington, DC

Jerry Wircenski, Professor, Department of Applied Technology, Training and Development, University of North Texas, Denton, TX

**I**NDEX